The typographic experiments found in the front and back matter of this book are by Kristin Hughes. About this work she states: "During the summer of 1997, the streets of Chicago became my studio. Used tickets, glass shards, colored bits of paper, and other discards spoke to me significantly, and I appropriated these elements for explorations of type and image. The computer was used to scan and manipulate these images, and to synthesize them into abstract visual sequences. My hope is that viewers will form their own stories, impressions, and interpretations. I gave myself only one hour to pick and choose from among the found elements. This rather severe limitation led to a more spontaneous and playful result."

Don't shoot.
Please bandage me.
Please carry me.
Don't touch me.
I wish the doctor.
Take me to the hospital.
I am cold.
Yes.
No.
I cannot remember.
I have forgotten.
I know nothing about that.

Working

with

Computer

Type

# Experimental Typography

Typography

A RotoVision Book
Published and Distributed by RotoVision SA
Rue du Bugnon 7
CH - 1299 Crans - Pres - Celigny
Switzerland

RotoVision SA Sales & Editorial Office
Sheridan House
112–116a Western Road
Hove, East Sussex
BN3 1DD. England

Tel. +44 (0)1273 72 72 68
Fax. +44 (0)1273 72 72 69
e-mail sales@RotoVision.com

Distributed to the trade in the United States by

Watson Guptill Publications
1515 Broadway
New York, New York 10036



ISBN 2-88046-279-7

Cover design by John Malinoski
Book design by Rob Carter

Production and separations in Singapore by

ProVision Pte. Ltd.
Tel +65 334 7720
Fax +65 334 7721



This book is dedicated
to my brother
Scott Averett Carter
1955-1996

king

**Rob Carter**

# Computer Type

# Experimental Typography

RotoVision

contents

# Introduction

With the advent of desktop publishing, two seemingly incompatible approaches to typographic practice have emerged. The first holds faithfully to typographic tradition. The second rebels from tradition, sometimes appearing to cajole and harass the typographic establishment by seeking alternative means for typographic expression. Inevitably, we come to the conclusion that both approaches are valid, for typographic design is always contextual in nature: different problems require different solutions. A look at today's typography reveals tremendous diversity from traditional books to the effusive pages of subculture magazines.

Typographic standards have endured for centuries because they are thought to make type more legible, and thus more readable. But legibility has become a relative concept. The immediacy of television and electronic media, and new trends in printed communication have in recent years raised the level of typographic literacy among the general public. What was considered unreadable yesterday is readable today. The public is more visually sophisticated and typographically savvy than ever before.

The personal computer has become as much a toy as a tool, inspiring designers to playfully stretch typographic boundaries. "Rules" from past generations are ceremoniously bent, twisted, skewed, and ignored. The pixel has freed designers from the restraints of metal and film, enabling them to freely explore the language of type. If there is a loss of tradition, there is most certainly a gain in creative invention and discovery.

Typographic experimentation is not new. Art and design movements from the dawn of the 20th century – Futurism, de Stijl, Dada, Constructivism, and Post-Modernism – responded to new technologies, challenged the status quo, and made significant advances in the field of typography. But of all technologies, none (save the invention of moveable type) has rocked the typographic establishment's boat as vigorously as computer desktop technology.

Ultimately, this book is a call to action. It challenges you to extend your understanding of typography and its visual potential by using the computer to engage in risk-taking experimentation. This can occur in the process of working on actual projects, or as an end in itself by playing with type during moments of free time. Squeeze in the time whenever possible. Exploring type is fun, and ultimately, it changes the way you think about type and work with it.

Before throwing yourself into experimentation, it is essential to have a firm grasp of traditional typography. Walking precedes running. You will find this book enthusiastically supporting this premise.

Chapter 1 provides a review of long-established typographic guidelines. These "rules" provide a meaningful departure point for typographic experimentation. Chapter 2 offers a systematic way of breaking the rules and freely and effectively exploring the visual and expressive nature of typography. Chapter 3 takes you on a journey of typographic exploration and presents a portfolio of experimental compositions by typography students. Chapter 4 reveals the results of an experimental typographic workshop by a group of Dutch and American students. Chapter 5 profiles four international typographic designers. Included are portfolios of each designer's work, and typographic experiments made specifically for this book.

# O

# 1

# Obeying the rules

The division pages located at the beginning of each chapter constitute a typographic experiment by Erik Brandt. He comments: "Letterforms are the architectural elements of our being-toward-reality. As such, they can be treated as both syntactic and semantic vehicles. These pages are simple attempts to isolate and experiment. They are intended as quiet moments to consider: How much experimentation is actually necessary? I urge that simplicity achieves both maximum clarity and maximum entropy."

# Obeying the rules

Over the centuries, typographic guidelines have been developed to provide consistency and competency within the profession, to preserve the beauty and legibility of typographic form, and to ensure that typography functions as often mandated: to clearly represent the thoughts of the author.

The guidelines presented in this chapter are not absolute or definitive, but they are representatives of a sturdy, time-tested collection of typographic "rules." They are presented here to provide a context for informed typographic exploration. In other words, rules must first be understood before they can be broken. Once it is known how to obey the rules, one can freely journey into unconventional terrain. For some readers, these guidelines offer a welcome review. For those new to the fascinating but often confusing world of typography, they provide a critical foundation for informed and responsible practice.

## Rule 1:
## For optimum legibility, choose classical, time-tested typefaces with a proven track record.

Well-seasoned typographic designers can usually count their favorite typefaces on one hand. Most often, they are those typefaces that are drawn and crafted with consistency among characters, and those that exhibit highly legible proportions.

1
**The book, *Typographic Specimens: The Great Typefaces,* co-authored by Philip Meggs and Rob Carter, presents 38 typefaces regarded as classical and timeless. The selection of these typefaces was based on the results of a survey sent to more than 100 prominent typographic designers. Admirable representatives of these classics are found here, and include both serif and sans serif faces. All of these typefaces are available for use on the electronic desktop.**

Baskerville
Bembo
Bodoni
Caslon
Centaur
Franklin Gothic
Frutiger
Futura
Garamond
Gill Sans
Goudy Old Style
Helvetica
News Gothic
Palatino
Perpetua
Sabon
Times New Roman
Univers

1

## Rule 2:
# Be mindful not to use too many different typefaces at any one time.

The primary purpose for using more than one typeface is to create emphasis or to separate one part of the text from another. When too many different typefaces are used, the page becomes a three-ring circus, and the reader is unable to determine what is and what is not important.

The role of typographic experimentation is to extend the boundaries of language by freely probing visual and verbal syntax and the relationships between **WORD** and image. Syntactic exploration enables designers to discover among typographic **media** an enor-

2

The role of typographic experimentation is to extend the boundaries of language by freely probing visual and verbal syntax and the relationships between **word and image**. Syntactic exploration enables designers to discover among typographic media an enormous

**The role of typographic experimentation is to extend the boundaries of language by freely probing visual and verbal syntax and the relationships between** word and image. **Syntactic exploration enables designers to discover among typographic media an**

3

## Rule 3:
# Avoid combining typefaces that are too similar in appearance.

If the reason for combining typefaces is to create emphasis, it is important to avoid the ambiguity caused by combining types that are too similar in appearance. When this occurs, it usually looks like a mistake, because not enough contrast exists between the typefaces.

The role of typographic experimentation is to extend the boundaries of language by freely probing visual and verbal syntax and the relationships between word and image. Syntactic exploration enables designers to discover among typographic media an enormous poten-

The role of typographic experimentation is to extend the boundaries of language by freely probing visual and verbal syntax and the relationships between word and image. Syntactic exploration enables designers to discover among typographic media an enormous potential to

4

The role of typographic experimentation is to extend the boundaries of language by freely probing visual and verbal syntax and the relationships between *word and image.* Syntactic exploration enables designers to discover among typographic media an enormous

The role of typographic experimentation is to extend the boundaries of language by freely probing visual and verbal syntax and the relationships between ***word and image.*** Syntactic exploration enables designers to discover among typographic media an enormous

5

2
**Using too many different typefaces on a page or within text is very distracting, and the reader's ability to discern what is and what is not important is compromised. Excellent results may be obtained by combining two or three different typefaces, as long as the role of each is carefully considered.**

3
**When mixing different typefaces, a good rule of thumb is to use typefaces that appear very different from one another. A serif typeface combined with a sans serif typeface can be effective (top), as can a lightweight typeface combined with a heavy-weight face (bottom).**

4
**Combining Helvetica with Univers (top), or Caslon with Goudy Old Style (bottom) makes absolutely no sense because the typeface pairings are too similar in appearance.**

5
**Why not use just one typeface and create emphasis by changing weight, width, or slant, or combine typefaces having more obvious contrasts.**

## Rule 4:
## Text set in all capital letters severely retards reading. Use upper- and lower-case letters for optimum readability.

Lower-case letters provide the necessary visual cues to make text most readable. This is due to the presence of ascenders, descenders, and the varied internal patterns of lower-case letters. Using both upper- and lower-case letters is the most normative means for setting text type, and a convention to which readers are most accustomed. Upper-case letters can success-fully be used for display type, however.

type TYPE

6

THE ROLE OF TYPOGRAPHIC EXPERIMEN-TATION IS TO EXTEND THE BOUNDARIES OF LANGUAGE BY FREELY PROBING VISUAL AND VERBAL SYNTAX AND THE RELATIONSHIPS BETWEEN WORD AND IMAGE. SYNTACTIC EXPLORATION

the role of typographic experimentation is to extend the boundaries of language by freely probing visual and verbal syntax and the rela-tionships between word and image. syntactic exploration enables designers to discover among typographic media an enormous poten-

7

The role of typographic experimentation is to extend the boundaries of language by freely probing visual and verbal syntax and the rela-tionships between word and image. Syntactic exploration enables designers to discover among typographic media an enormous poten-

8

## Rule 5:
## For text type, use sizes that according to legibility studies prove most readable.

These sizes generally range from 8 to 12 points (and all sizes in between) for text that is read from an average distance of 12 to 14 inches. However, it is important to be aware of the fact that typefaces of the same size may actually appear different in size depending upon the x-height of the letters (the distance between the baseline and meanline).

**8 point**
The role of typographic experimentation is to extend

**9 point**
The role of typographic experimentation is to

**10 point**
The role of typographic experimentation is

**11 point**
The role of typographic experimenta-

**12 point**
The role of typographic experimen-

9

The role of typographic experimentation is to extend the boundaries of language by freely probing visual and verbal syntax and the relationships between word and image. Syntactic exploration enables designers to discover among typographic media an enormous potential to edify, entertain, and surprise. As in other

The role of typographic experimentation is to extend the boundaries of language by freely probing visual and verbal syntax and the rela-tionships between word and image. Syntactic exploration enables designers to discover among typographic media an enormous

The role of typographic experimentation is to extend the boundaries of language by freely probing visual and verbal syntax and the relationships between word and image. Syntactic exploration enables designers to discover among typographic media an enormous potential to

10

6
**Lower-case letters have ascenders and descenders that give words distinct, memorable shapes. Words set entirely in upper-case letters form monotonous, rectangular shapes.**

7
**Text set entirely in upper-case letters lacks rhythmic variety and is therefore diffi-cult to read (top). Text set entirely in lower-case letters is easier to read due to distinct visual patterns (bottom).**

8
**The most familiar means for setting text is to employ both upper- and lower-case letters. Capitals clearly mark the beginnings of sentences.**

9
**The most readable sizes of text type range from 8 to 12 points. These specimens are set in Minion Regular.**

10
**Compare the perceived sizes of Bodoni (top), Helvetica (middle), and Frutiger (bottom), each of which is set to 8 points in size.**

## Rule 6: Avoid using too many different type sizes and weights at the same time.

You only need to use as many different sizes and weights as needed to establish a clear hierarchy among parts of information. Josef Müller-Brockmann advocates using no more than two sizes, one for display titles and one for text type. Restraint in the number of sizes used leads to functional and attractive pages.

Type and experiment

The role of typographic experimentation is to extend the boundaries of language by freely probing visual and verbal syntax and the relationships between word and image. Syntactic exploration enables designers to

11

**Type and experiment**

The role of typographic experimentation is to extend the boundaries of language by freely probing visual and verbal syntax and the relationships between word and image. Syntactic exploration enables designers to discover

12

Type **and** experiment

The role of typographic experimentation is to **extend** the boundaries of language by freely probing visual and verbal syntax and the relationships between word and image. Syntactic exploration enables designers to discover

13

## Rule 7: Use text types of book weight. Avoid typefaces appearing too heavy or too light.

The weight of typefaces is determined by the thicknesses of the letter strokes. Text typefaces that are too light cannot easily be distinguished from their backgrounds. In typefaces that are too heavy, counterforms diminish in size, making them less legible. Book weights strike a happy medium, and are ideal for text.

**The role of typographic experimentation is to extend the boundaries of language by freely probing visual and verbal syntax and the relationships between word and image. Syntactic exploration enables designers to**

**The role of typographic experimentation is to extend the boundaries of language by freely probing visual and verbal syntax and the relationships between word and image. Syntactic exploration enables designers to**

14

The role of typographic experimentation is to extend the boundaries of language by freely probing visual and verbal syntax and the relationships between word and image. Syntactic exploration enables designers to discover among typographic media an enormous potential to edify, entertain, and surprise.

15

The role of typographic experimentation is to extend the boundaries of language by freely probing visual and verbal syntax and the relationships between word and image. Syntactic exploration enables designers to discover among typographic media an enormous

16

11
**Using the same type size and weight for titles and text works fine, as long as the two elements are separated by an interval of space.**

12
**Using two sizes and weights of type for titles and text establishes a clear and simple hierarchy. It is important to create plenty of contrast. If elements are too close in size or weight, they lack contrast and their relationship is ambiguous.**

13
**Too many different sizes and weights give the page a haphazard look.**

14
**Two typefaces of extremely heavy weight are difficult to read due to an imbalance between the letter strokes and counterforms. These faces are best reserved for display type or small amounts of text. Note the extreme contrast in the strokes of the bottom example, a quality that also impedes readability.**

15
**This very thin typeface appears to almost fade into its background.**

16
**A typeface of book weight provides excellent readability.**

## Rule 8:
# Use typefaces of medium width. Avoid typefaces that appear extremely wide or narrow in width.

Distorting text to make letters wider or narrower by stretching or squeezing them with a computer impedes the reading process. The proportions of such letters are no longer familiar to us. Well designed type families include condensed and extended faces that fall within accepted proportional norms.

The role of typographic experimentation is to extend the boundaries of language by freely probing visual and verbal syntax and the relationships between word and image. Syntactic exploration enables designers to discover among typographic media an enormous poten-

The role of typographic experimentation is to extend the boundaries of language by freely probing visual and verbal syntax and the relationships between word and image. Syntactic exploration enables designers to discover among typographic media an enormous potential to edify, entertain, and surprise. As in other forms of language typography is

The role of typographic experimentation is to extend the boundaries of language by freely probing visual and verbal syntax and the relationships between word and image. Syntactic exploration enables designers to dis-

17

The role of typographic experimentation is to extend the boundaries of language by freely probing visual and verbal syntax and the relationships between word and image. Syntactic exploration enables designers to discover among typographic media an enormous potential to edify, entertain, and surprise. As in other forms of language typography is capable of infinite expression. The only limits to typographic discovery are those imposed by the designer herself.

The role of typographic experimentation is to extend the boundaries of language by freely probing visual and

18

## Rule 9:
# For text type, use consistent letter and word spacing to produce an even, uninterrupted texture.

Letters should flow gracefully and naturally into words, and words into lines. This means that word spacing should increase proportionally as letter spacing increases.

The role of typographic experimentation is to extend the boundaries of language by freely probing visual and verbal syntax and the relationships between word and image. Syntactic exploration enables designers to discover among typographic media an enormous poten-

The role of typographic experimentation is to extend the boundaries of language by freely probing visual and verbal syntax and the relationships between word and image. Syntactic exploration enables designers to discover among typographic media an enormous potential to

The role of typographic experimentation is to extend the boundaries of language by freely probing visual and verbal syntax and the relationships between word and image. Syntactic exploration enables designers to

The role of typographic experimentation is to extend the boundaries of language by freely probing visual and verbal syntax and the relationships between word and image. Syntactic exploration enables designers to discover among typographic media an

The role of typographic experimentation is to extend the boundaries of language by freely probing visual and verbal syntax and the relationships between word and image. Syntactic exploration enables designers to discover among typographic media an enormous potential to edify, entertain,

19

17
**The typeface Trade Gothic Regular (top) can be compared with condensed (middle) and extended (bottom) versions. While the condensed and extended variations are useful and carefully designed additions to the Trade Gothic family, large amounts of text set in them prove difficult to read.**

18
**As you can see in this example, extreme stretching and squeezing of roman letterforms via computer renders text nearly illegible.**

19
**Excellent letter and word spacing. From top to bottom: letter and word spacing appearing too tight; letter spacing appearing too loose; letter spacing appearing too tight and word spacing too loose; letter and word spacing appearing too tight.**

**Letters abhor crowding, but they also wish not to lose sight of their neighbors.**

**Another important consideration is that lighter typefaces look best with more generous letter spacing, while the reverse is true of heavier faces.**

## Rule 10:

# Use appropriate line lengths. Lines that are too short or too long disrupt the reading process.

When lines of type are either too long or too short, the reading process becomes tedious and wearisome. As the eye travels along overly long lines, negotiating the next line becomes difficult. Reading overly short lines creates choppy eye movements that tire and annoy the reader.

---

The role of typographic experimentation is to extend the boundaries of language by freely probing visual and verbal syntax and the relationships between word and image. Syntactic exploration enables designers to discover among typographic media an enormous potential to edify, entertain, and surprise. As in other forms of language typography is capable of infinite expression. The only limits to typographic discovery are those imposed by the designer herself.

The role of typographic experimentation is to extend the boundaries of language by freely probing visual and verbal syntax and the relationships between word and image. Syntactic exploration enables designers to discover among typographic media an enormous potential to edify, entertain, and surprise. As in other forms of language typography is capable of infinite expression. The only limits to typographic discovery are those imposed by the designer herself.

20

---

The role of typographic experimentation is to extend the boundaries of language by freely probing visual and verbal syntax and the relationships between word and image. Syntactic exploration enables designers to discover among typographic media an enormous potential to edify, entertain, and surprise. As in other forms of language typography is capable of infinite expression. The only limits to typographic discovery are those imposed by the

The role of typographic experimentation is to extend the boundaries of language by freely probing visual and verbal syntax and the relationships between word and image. Syntactic exploration enables designers to discover among typographic media an enormous potential to edify, entertain, and surprise. As in other forms of language typography is capable of infinite expression. The only limits to typographic discovery are those imposed by

The role of typographic experimentation is to extend the boundaries of language by freely probing visual and verbal syntax and the relationships between word and image. Syntactic exploration enables designers to discover among typographic media an enormous potential to edify,

21

20
**When working with text type, a maximum of about 70 characters (ten to twelve words) per line is thought to be most acceptable. The top example far exceeds this recommendation. Though the measure is the same in the bottom example, an increase in the size of the type lessens the number of characters per line.**

21
**Text set into short lines produces rather choppy reading (left). Line length is of particular importance when setting justified type because space is distributed evenly among words. This results in awkward and irregular spaces between words (middle). While using longer lines lessens this problem, it does not eliminate it completely (right).**

## Rule 11:
# For text type, use line spacing that easily carries the eye from one line to the next.

Lines of type with too little space between them slow the reading process; the eye is forced to take in several lines at once. By adding one to four points of space between lines of type – depending on the specific nature of the typeface – readability can be improved.

**1.5 points line spacing**

The role of typographic experimentation is to extend the boundaries of language by freely probing visual and verbal syntax and the relationships between word and image. Syntactic exploration enables designers to discover among typographic media an enormous poten-

**2 points line spacing**

The role of typographic experimentation is to extend the boundaries of language by freely probing visual and verbal syntax and the relationships between word and image. Syntactic exploration enables designers to discover

**3 points line spacing**

The role of typographic experimentation is to extend the boundaries of language by freely probing visual and verbal syntax and the relationships between word and image. Syntactic exploration enables designers to discover

22

**set solid**

The role of typographic experimentation is to extend the boundaries of language by freely probing visual and verbal syntax and the relationships between word and image. Syntactic exploration enables designers to discover among typographic media an enormous poten-

**set solid**

The role of typographic experimentation is to extend the boundaries of language by freely probing visual and verbal syntax and the relationships between word and image. Syntactic exploration enables designers to discover among typographic media an enormous potential to edify, entertain, and

23

**negative line spacing**

The role of typographic experimentation is to extend the boundaries of language by freely probing visual and verbal syntax and the relationships between word and image. Syntactic exploration enables designers to discover among typographic media an enormous potential to edify, entertain, and surprise. As in other

24

22
**Text blocks containing acceptable amounts of line spacing. As more space is introduced, lines appear more separate and the text block calmer.**

23
**Though the two text blocks in this example are technically identical in size and line spacing, the top block, due to a larger x-height, appears tighter in line spacing than the bottom block. Lines of text with large x-heights should be spaced appropriately to compensate for their larger appearance. Lines with no additional space between them are said to be set "solid."**

24
**With a computer, it is possible to establish negative line spacing. However, for optimum readability, this practice should be avoided. Note the overlapping ascenders and descenders.**

25
**The four primary methods for aligning text type.**

## Rule 12:
# For optimum readability, use a flush left, ragged right type alignment.

Although in special situations, other methods of type alignment (flush right, ragged left; centered, and justified) are acceptable, the tradeoff is always a loss – however slight – in readability.

**flush left, ragged right**

The role of typographic experimentation is to extend the boundaries of language by freely probing visual and verbal syntax and the relationships between word and image. Syntactic exploration enables designers to discover among typographic media an enormous poten-

**flush right, ragged left**

The role of typographic experimentation is to extend the boundaries of language by freely probing visual and verbal syntax and the relationships between word and image. Syntactic exploration enables designers to discover among typographic media an enormous

**justified**

The role of typographic experimentation is to extend the boundaries of language by freely probing visual and verbal syntax and the relationships between word and image. Syntactic exploration enables designers to discover among typographic media an enormous poten-

**centered**

The role of typographic experimentation is to extend the boundaries of language by freely probing visual and verbal syntax and the relationships between word and image. Syntactic exploration enables designers to discover among typographic media an

25

## Rule 13:
## Strive for consistent, rhythmic rags.

Avoid rags in which strange and awkward shapes are formed as a result of line terminations. Also avoid rags that produce a repetitious and predictable pattern of line endings.

## Rule 14:
## Clearly indicate paragraphs, but be careful not to upset the integrity and visual consistency of the text.

The two most common means of indicating paragraphs are by indenting and inserting additional space between paragraphs. It is not necessary to indent the first paragraph in a column of text.

The role of typographic experimentation is to extend the boundaries of language by freely probing visual and verbal syntax and the relationships between word and image. Syntactic exploration enables designers to discover among typographic media an enormous

26

The role of typographic experimentation is to extend the boundaries of language by freely probing visual and verbal syntax and the relationships between word and image. Syntactic exploration enables designers to discover in typographic media an enormous potential to

The role of typographic experimentation is to extend the boundaries of language by freely probing visual and verbal syntax and the relationships between word and image. Syntactic exploration enables designers to discover among typographic media an enor-

The role of typographic experimentation is to extend the boundaries of language by freely probing visual and verbal syntax and the relationships between word and image. Syntactic exploration enables designers to discover among typographic media an

27

The role of typographic experimentation is to extend the boundaries of language by freely probing visual and verbal syntax and the relationships between word and image. Syntactic exploration enables designers to discover among typographic media an enormous poten-

The role of typographic experimentation is to extend the boundaries of language by freely probing visual and verbal syntax and the relationships between word and image. Syntactic exploration enables designers to discover among typographic media an

The role of typographic experimentation is to extend the boundaries of language by freely probing visual and verbal syntax and the relationships between word and image.

Syntactic exploration enables designers to discover among typographic media an enormous potential to edify, entertain, and surprise. As in other forms of language typography is capable of infinite expression.

28

**The purpose of effective rags is not only to achieve aesthetic beauty. When rags consist of line endings that are carefully articulated, rhythmic and consistent, they enable readers to move gently and effortlessly down a text column. Rags provide logical points of departure from one line to the next.**

26
**Effective rags consist of lines establishing an informal but consistent pattern of line endings. The rag edge should appear to fade off gradually.**

27
**Rags are less effective when line endings are not distinct enough from one another (top), when weird shapes and contours emerge (middle), or when long and short lines are so similar that they create a repetitive and predictable pattern (bottom).**

28
**Common paragraph indication by means of indenting (top), and intervals of space separating paragraphs (bottom).**

# Rule 15: Avoid widows and orphans whenever possible.

A widow is a word or very short line at either the beginning or the end of a paragraph. An orphan is a single syllable at the end of a paragraph. Both of these lonely conditions should be avoided whenever possible, for they destroy the continuity of text blocks, create spotty pages, and interfere with concentration in reading.

29
**Other methods of paragraph indication are plentiful; these, however, should be used with caution. In these examples, paragraphs are indicated (top to bottom) by the following means: bold type for the first letter, small squares, reverse indenting, small caps for the first word, and a large first letter placed into the margin.**

30
**When encountering widows and orphans, rework text as necessary to avoid them. This may require changing the spacing, altering the rag, or rewriting copy.**

**T**he role of typographic experimentation is to extend the boundaries of language by freely probing visual and verbal syntax and the relationships between word and image. **S**yntactic exploration enables designers to discover among typographic media an enormous potential to edify, entertain, and surprise. As in other forms of language typog-

■The role of typographic experimentation is to extend the boundaries of language by freely probing visual and verbal syntax and the relationships between word and image.
■Syntactic exploration enables designers to discover among typographic media an enormous potential to edify, entertain, and

The role of typographic experimentation is to extend the boundaries of language by freely probing visual and verbal syntax and the relationships between word and image.
Syntactic exploration enables designers to discover among typographic media an enormous potential to edify, entertain, and

THE role of typographic experimentation is to extend the boundaries of language by freely probing visual and verbal syntax and the relationships between word and image. SYNTACTIC exploration enables designers to discover among typographic media an enormous poten-

The role of typographic experimentation is to extend the boundaries of language by freely probing visual and verbal syntax and the relationships between word and image.
Syntactic exploration enables designers to discover among typographic media an

29

The role of typographic experimentation is to extend the boundaries of language by freely probing visual and verbal syntax and the relationships between word and image. Syntactic exploration enables designers to discover among typographic media an enormous potential to edify, entertain, and surprise. As in other forms of language typography is capable of infinite expression. The only limits to typographic discovery are those imposed by the designer herself.

herself.

The role of typographic experimentation is to extend the boundaries of language by freely probing visual and verbal syntax and the relationships between word and image. Syntactic exploration enables designers to discover among typographic media an enormous potential to edify, entertain, and surprise. As in other

The role of typographic experimentation is to extend the boundaries of language by freely probing visual and verbal syntax and the relationships between word and image. Syntactic exploration enables designers to discover among typographic media an enormous potential.

30

## Rule 16:

# Emphasize elements within text with discretion and without disturbing the flow of reading.

Never overdo it. Use minimum means for maximum results. The ultimate purposes for emphasizing elements within text are to clarify content and distinguish parts of information.

The role of typographic experimentation is to extend the boundaries of language by freely probing visual and verbal syntax and the relationships between *word and image.* Syntactic exploration enables designers to discover among typographic media an enormous poten-

The role of typographic experimentation is to extend the boundaries of language by freely probing visual and verbal syntax and the relationships between word and image. Syntactic exploration enables designers to discover among typographic media an enormous poten-

The role of typographic experimentation is to extend the boundaries of language by freely probing visual and verbal syntax and the relationships between word and image. Syntactic exploration enables designers to discover among typographic media an enormous poten-

The role of typographic experimentation is to extend the boundaries of language by freely probing visual and verbal syntax and the relationships between word and image. Syntactic exploration enables designers to discover among typographic media an enormous poten-

The role of typographic experimentation is to extend the boundaries of language by freely probing visual and verbal syntax and the relationships between WORD AND IMAGE. Syntactic exploration enables designers to discover among typographic media an enormous poten-

The role of typographic experimentation is to extend the boundaries of language by freely probing visual and verbal syntax and the relationships between WORD AND IMAGE. Syntactic exploration enables designers to discover among typographic media an

The role of typographic experimentation is to extend the boundaries of language by freely probing visual and verbal syntax and the relationships between **word and image.** Syntactic exploration enables designers to discover among typographic media an

**The role of typographic experimentation is to extend the boundaries of language by freely probing visual and verbal syntax and the relationships between** word and image. **Syntactic exploration enables designers to discover among**

The role of typographic experimentation is to extend the boundaries of language by freely probing visual and verbal syntax and the relationships between word and image. Syntactic exploration enables designers to discover among typographic media an enor-

The role of typographic experimentation is to extend the boundaries of language by freely probing visual and verbal syntax and the relationships between word and image. Syntactic exploration enables designers to discover among typographic media an enormous poten-

31

**Several methods for emphasizing units of information within text are shown. These include using italics, underlined type, color type, different typeface, small capitals, capitals, bold type within light type, light type within bold type, larger type, and outline type (left to right, top to bottom). While none of these possibilities are invasive to the text, some are obviously more pronounced than others.**

## Rule 17: Always maintain the integrity of type. Avoid arbitrarily stretching letters.

Well designed typefaces exhibit visual qualities that make them readable. Letters are painstakingly designed with specific proportional attributes in mind. Arbitrarily distorting them compromises their integrity.

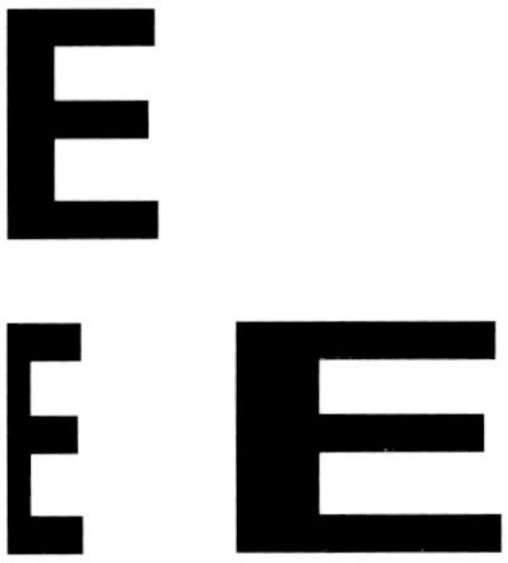

32

32
A Univers 65 *E* appears normal (top). The deliberate and refined proportions of this letter are entirely compromised in the two bottom examples. Here, letterforms have been vertically and horizontally scaled by the computer, resulting in an arbitrary and awkward proportional relationship between the thick and thin strokes of the letters.

33

33
If a more condensed or extended version of a typeface is desired, use a version designed specifically for that particular type family. In this example, Univers 67 Condensed and Univers Ultra Condensed letters are shown. Notice how the thick and thin relationships of the letter strokes correspond in intent to those of the Univers 65 letter.

## Rule 18: Always align letters and words on the baseline.

Letters are designed to coexist side-by-side on an invisible baseline. When they stray from this orientation, they appear to be out of control, their readability greatly compromised.

The role of typographic experimentation is to

The role of typographic experimentation

e
x
p
e
r
i
m
e
n
t
a
t
i
o
n

34

34
Because letters are specifically designed to align side-by-side on a baseline for optimum readability, any deviation from this norm is highly questionable. Consider the three anomalies shown in this example. Never stack letters.

## Rule 19:
## When working with type and color, ensure that sufficient contrast exists between type and its background.

Too little contrast in hue, value, or saturation, or a combination of these factors, can result in type that is difficult, if not impossible, to read.

| | |
|---|---|
| The role of typographic experimentation is to extend the boundaries of language by freely probing visual and verbal syntax and the relationships between word and image. Syntactic | The role of typographic experimentation is to extend the boundaries of language by freely probing visual and verbal syntax and the relationships between word and image. Syntactic |

35

| | |
|---|---|
| The role of typographic experimentation is to extend the boundaries of language by freely probing visual and verbal syntax and the relationships between word and image. Syntactic | The role of typographic experimentation is to extend the boundaries of language by freely probing visual and verbal syntax and the relationships between word and image. Syntactic |
| The role of typographic experimentation is to extend the boundaries of language by freely probing visual and verbal syntax and the relationships between word and image. Syntactic | The role of typographic experimentation is to extend the boundaries of language by freely probing visual and verbal syntax and the relationships between word and image. Syntactic |
| The role of typographic experimentation is to extend the boundaries of language by freely probing visual and verbal syntax and the relationships between word and image. Syntactic | The role of typographic experimentation is to extend the boundaries of language by freely probing visual and verbal syntax and the relationships between word and image. Syntactic |

36

35
**Black type on a white background is the most legible of color combinations, and this is what we are most accustomed to in reading. Any deviation from this norm compromises readability to a degree. White type on a black background reverses this color relationship, and is harder to read.**

36
**By considering the color contrast relationships between type and its background, type can be rendered more readable. The type and background color relationships in the left-hand column are problematic due to inadequate color contrasts. Compare these with the examples in the right-hand column where color adjustments are made in hue, value, saturation, or in a combination of these factors. These adjustments improve legibility.**

# B

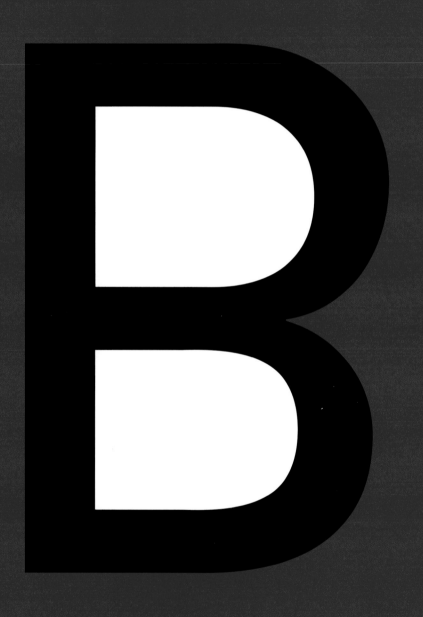

# Breaking the rules

# 2

# Breaking the rules

Typography can function to dutifully deliver a message, just as a postman delivers a letter, but it can also provide the elements and inspiration for uninhibited play. Through play we experience the pure joy of typographic expression, and our eyes and minds are open to new ways of solving typographic problems. Old habits and formulas are replaced by a more active and vigorous way of working with type.

To effectively and freely explore typography, it is essential to eliminate all biases, preconceptions, and expectations regarding results. For the beginner, this is not such a problem. But for the experienced typographic designer, changing old habits can be a formidable challenge. Typographic experimentation can ultimately lend fresh insight to the designer, help break formulaic chains, and move projects into more challenging directions.

Putting the first marks on a piece of virgin paper when beginning a drawing is often very intimidating. Likewise, the initial stages of typographic experimentation can leave you scratching your head. This chapter is devoted to helping you overcome any fears associated with launching into the world of typographic experimentation.

Because type is viewed as well as read, it is governed by the principles of visual syntax. Whether you are consciously aware of it or not, you regularly use these principles when working with type. The first step in exploring type is to have an understanding of these factors and the ability to consciously apply them.

A morphology is a collection of factors that help us work with type. It can be used by designers as an effective tool to explore typographic possibilities and seek new alternatives. Often used in graphic design education, morphologies visibly and methodically provide students with a usable typographic vocabulary. Several precedents exist for the use of morphologies in design and typography, and they take many forms. The designer Karl Gerstner pioneered a logical morphology based on the formal language of type. Wolfgang Weingart's Morphological Typecase, consisting of categories such as sunshine, religious, typewriter, and stair typography, reflects his broad point of view. For Weingart, everything can potentially relate to and inspire typographic practice.

This chapter presents a morphology that can be used to usher you into a shameless flurry of typographic experimentation. Presented on the facing page, this morphology includes 25 typographic factors or variables in four categories. These categories are 1) typographic, 2) form, 3) space, and 4) typographic support. *Typographic* factors relate specifically to the manipulation of letters and words. *Form* factors involve the alteration of existing typographic forms. *Space* factors address how elements are physically related to one another on a page. *Support* factors include nontypographic elements that augment typographic forms. The 25 factors are further subdivided into more specific factors. For example, distortion, which is a form factor, is subdivided into specific kinds of distortion, including fragmentation, skewing, bending, stretching, etc. In addition, each main factor includes a "combination" factor that serves to describe combinations of factors. Elements of the morphology are numbered and keyed for reference to examples and experiments found throughout the book.

In the pages that follow, the morphological factors are examined as they relate first to display type and second to text type. Be mindful that a morphology can provide nearly infinite possibilities for typographic experimentation. The examples shown in this chapter are intended to describe factors in most basic terms. They offer merely a departure point for your own typographic explorations.

**Note:** The boxes in this morphology filled with black represent other possibilities that may be added as needed.

| | | | | | | | | | |
|---|---|---|---|---|---|---|---|---|---|
| **Typographic factors** | | | | | | | | | |
| **1.1** case | **1.1.1** upper | **1.1.2** lower | **1.1.3** combination | | | | | | |
| **1.2** face | **1.2.1** serif | **1.2.2** sans serif | **1.2.3** script | **1.2.4** eccentric | **1.2.5** combination | | | | |
| **1.3** size | **1.3.1** small | **1.3.2** medium | **1.3.3** large | **1.3.4** combination | | | | | |
| **1.4** slant | **1.4.1** slight | **1.4.2** medium | **1.4.3** extreme | **1.4.4** combination | | | | | |
| **1.5** weight | **1.5.1** light | **1.5.2** medium | **1.5.3** heavy | **1.5.4** combination | | | | | |
| **1.6** width | **1.6.1** narrow | **1.6.2** medium | **1.6.3** wide | **1.6.4** combination | | | | | |
| **Form factors** | | | | | | | | | |
| **2.1** blending | **2.1.1** linear | **2.1.2** radial | **2.1.3** combination | | | | | | |
| **2.2** distortion | **2.2.1** fragmenting | **2.2.2** skewing | **2.2.3** bending | **2.2.4** stretching | **2.2.5** blurring | **2.2.6** inverting | **2.2.7** mutilating | **2.2.8** combination | |
| **2.3** elaboration | **2.3.1** addition | **2.3.2** subtraction | **2.3.3** extension | **2.3.4** combination | | | | | |
| **2.4** outline | **2.4.1** thin | **2.4.2** medium | **2.4.3** thick | **2.4.4** broken | **2.4.5** combination | | | | |
| **2.5** texture | **2.5.1** fine | **2.5.2** coarse | **2.5.3** regular | **2.5.4** irregular | **2.5.5** combination | | | | |
| **2.6** dimensionality | **2.6.1** volumetric | **2.6.2** shadowing | **2.6.3** combination | | | | | | |
| **2.7** tonality | **2.7.1** light | **2.7.2** medium | **2.7.3** dark | **2.7.4** combination | | | | | |
| **Space factors** | | | | | | | | | |
| **3.1** balance | **3.1.1** symmetrical | **3.1.2** asymmetrical | **3.1.3** combination | | | | | | |
| **3.2** direction | **3.2.1** horizontal | **3.2.2** vertical | **3.2.3** diagonal | **3.2.4** circular | **3.2.5** combination | | | | |
| **3.3** ground | **3.3.1** advancing | **3.3.2** receding | **3.3.3** combination | | | | | | |
| **3.4** grouping | **3.4.1** consonant | **3.4.2** dissonant | **3.4.3** combination | | | | | | |
| **3.5** proximity | **3.5.1** overlapping | **3.5.2** touching | **3.5.3** separating | **3.5.4** combination | | | | | |
| **3.6** repetition | **3.6.1** few | **3.6.2** many | **3.6.3** random | **3.6.4** pattern | **3.6.5** combination | | | | |
| **3.7** rhythm | **3.7.1** regular | **3.7.2** irregular | **3.7.3** alternating | **3.7.4** progressive | **3.7.5** combination | | | | |
| **3.8** rotation | **3.8.1** slight | **3.8.2** moderate | **3.8.3** extreme | **3.8.4** combination | | | | | |
| **Support factors** | | | | | | | | | |
| **4.1** ruled lines | **4.1.1** horizontal | **4.1.2** vertical | **4.1.3** diagonal | **4.1.4** curved | **4.1.5** stair-stepped | **4.1.6** thin | **4.1.7** medium | **4.1.8** thick | **4.1.9** combination |
| **4.2** shapes | **4.2.1** geometric | **4.2.2** organic | **4.2.3** background | **4.2.4** adjacent | **4.2.5** combination | | | | |
| **4.3** symbols | **4.3.1** normal | **4.3.2** manipulated | **4.3.3** combination | | | | | | |
| **4.4** images | **4.4.1** background | **4.4.2** adjacent | **4.4.3** contained | **4.4.4** manipulated | **4.4.5** combination | | | | |

## 1.1 Case

Most typefaces are designed to include both upper- and lower-case letters. Upper-case letters (figs. **1, 2**) stand straight and tall. They are more formal than lower-case letters (figs. **3, 4**), which appear more informal in posture. Traditionally, upper- and lower-case letters are used together in titles and text. The upper-case letters visually mark the beginnings of sentences (figs. **5,6**), and this is the norm. But many possibilities exist for playful (and odd) combinations of upper- and lower-case letters in display and text settings (figs. **7, 8**).

---

**TYPE**

1 **1.1.1** upper

THE ROLE OF TYPOGRAPHIC EXPERI-
MENTATION IS TO EXTEND THE
BOUNDARIES OF LANGUAGE BY
FREELY PROBING VISUAL AND VERBAL
SYNTAX AND THE RELATIONSHIPS

2 **1.1.1** upper

**type**

3 **1.1.2** lower

the role of typographic experimentation is to extend the boundaries of
language by freely probing visual and
verbal syntax and the relationships
between word and image. syntactic

4 **1.1.2** lower

**Type**

5 **1.1.3** combination

The role of typographic experimentation is to extend the boundaries of
language by freely probing visual and
verbal syntax and the relationships
between word and image. Syntactic

6 **1.1.3** combination

**tYpE**

7 **1.1.3** combination

The role of typographic experimentation
IS TO EXTEND THE BOUNDARIES OF
language by freely probing visual and
VERBAL SYNTAX AND THE RELATION-
ships between word and image. Syntac-

8 **1.1.3** combination

When experimenting with type, one of the most important considerations is typeface selection. With many thousands of type designs available today, the task of selecting just the right typeface can be overwhelming. When experimenting, try sampling many different typefaces. Try some that you have never before used. Try them in different and obscure combinations, and try them without any preconceptions or expectations of outcome. While typefaces are generally lumped into two broad categories, serif (figs. **9-12**) and sans serif (figs. **13-16**), permutations exist in astounding variety. Every typeface possesses a unique visual texture when set into text. Compare the textures of the text settings below.

---

type

9 **1.2.1** serif, Matrix

The role of typographic experimentation is to extend the boundaries of language by freely probing visual and verbal syntax and the relationships between word and image. Syn-tactic exploration enables designers to

10 **1.2.1** serif, Matrix

type

11 **1.2.1** serif, Glypha

The role of typographic experimentation is to extend the boundaries of language by freely probing visual and verbal syntax and the relationships between word and image. Syntactic exploration enables

12 **1.2.1** serif, Glypha

type

13 **1.2.2** sans serif, Officina Sans

The role of typographic experimentation is to extend the boundaries of language by freely probing visual and verbal syntax and the relationships between word and image. Syn-tactic exploration enables designers to

14 **1.2.2** sans serif, Officina Sans

type

15 **1.2.2** sans serif, Gill Sans

The role of typographic experimentation is to extend the boundaries of language by freely probing visual and verbal syntax and the relationships between word and image. Syntactic exploration enables designers to

16 **1.2.2** sans serif, Gill Sans

Scripts and faces that simulate handwriting can be informal or formal, casual or snooty (figs. **17, 18**). As a result of desktop publishing, an entire generation of new typefaces (also incorrectly referred to as fonts) has surfaced. Having jumped on the bandwagon of eccentric faces are the established type foundries, as well as small, one-person shops that peddle their exotic type designs on the Internet. In peculiarity, the new eccentric typefaces far exceed their grandparents, the wood types of the 19th century. Eccentric faces, these grungy and disrespectful upstarts, defy and challenge the honored traditions of typeface design. They express emotions, attitudes, and opinions; they confront and challenge the reader (figs. **19-22**). These typefaces do not quietly and objectively represent the thoughts of the author; they deliberately emit their own messages by virtue of their visual characteristics. When experimenting with different typefaces, try to identify how their shapes and textures might relate to content and message. Used in combination, eccentric typefaces produce unexpected and surprising results (figs. **23, 24**).

---

*type*

17 | **1.2.3** script, Brush Script

*The role of typographic experimentation is to extend the boundaries of language by freely probing visual and verbal syntax and the relationships between word and image. Syntactic exploration enables designers to discover*

18 | **1.2.3** script, Brush Script

type

19 | **1.2.4** eccentric, Template Gothic

The role of typographic experimentation is to extend the boundaries of language by freely probing visual and verbal syntax and the relationships between word and image. Syntactic exploration enables designers to

20 | **1.2.4** eccentric, Template Gothic

**type**

21 | **1.2.4** eccentric, Amplifier

**The role of typographic experimentation is to extend the boundaries of language by freely probing visual and verbal syntax and the relationships between word and image. Syntactic**

22 | **1.2.4** eccentric, Amplifier

type

23 | **1.2.5** combination; Democratica, Reporter Two

The role of typographic experimentation ***is to extend the boundaries of language by freely*** probing visual and verbal syntax and ***the relationships between word and image. Syntactic*** exploration enables designers to discover

24 | **1.2.5** combination, Democratica, Reporter Two

Scale relationships greatly influence the way in which type is perceived, for they provide a means to either emphasize or de-emphasize elements. Relative to larger elements, small type whispers, is timid and shy (fig. **25, 26**); relative to smaller elements, large type screams, is forceful and adamant (fig. **29, 30**). Scale is always a relative condition; large is large only in relationship to small, and vice versa (figs. **31, 32**). The illusion of spatial depth can also be achieved by means of scale adjustments. Larger type appears to advance in space, while smaller type recedes.

---

**type**

25 **1.3.1** small

The role of typographic experimentation is to extend the boundaries of language by freely probing visual and verbal syntax and the relationships between word and image. Syntactic exploration enables designers to discover among typographic media an enormous potential to edify, entertain, and surprise. As in other forms of language typography is capable of infinite expression. The only limits to typographic discovery are those imposed by the

26 **1.3.1** small

**type**

27 **1.3.2** medium

The role of typographic experimentation is to extend the boundaries of language by freely probing visual and verbal syntax and the relationships between word and image. Syntactic exploration enables designers to discover

28 **1.3.2** medium

**type**

29 **1.3.3** large

The role of typographic experimentation is to extend the boundaries of language by freely probing visual and

30 **1.3.3** large

**t y pe**

31 **1.3.4** combination

The role of typographic experimentation is to extend the boundaries of language by freely probing visual and verbal syntax and the relationships between word and image. Syntactic exploration enables designers to discover among typographic media an enormous potential to edify, entertain, and surprise. As in other forms of language typography is capable of infinite expression. The only limits to typographic discovery are those imposed by the designer herself.

32 **1.3.4** combination

## **1.4** Slant

When type is slanted, it assumes an active posture, is characteristically energetic and forceful, and appears to move forward in space. The more extreme the slant of type, the more kinetic and aggressive its appearance. Traditional italic type is usually slanted by approximately 13 to 16 degrees (figs. **33, 34**), but with the aid of the computer, roman letters can be slanted at any angle (figs. **37-40**). It is important to keep in mind that extremely slanted type is more difficult to read than moderately slanted type. But this concern is negligible when a dynamic effect is desired and the audience is not fussy about readability.

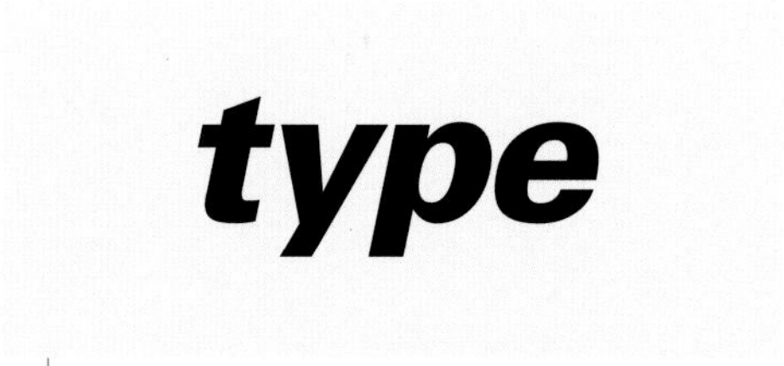
type

33 | **1.4.1** slight

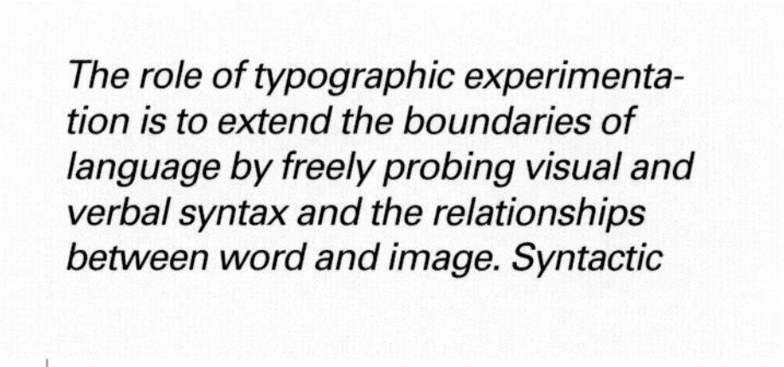
The role of typographic experimenta-
tion is to extend the boundaries of
language by freely probing visual and
verbal syntax and the relationships
between word and image. Syntactic

34 | **1.4.1** slight

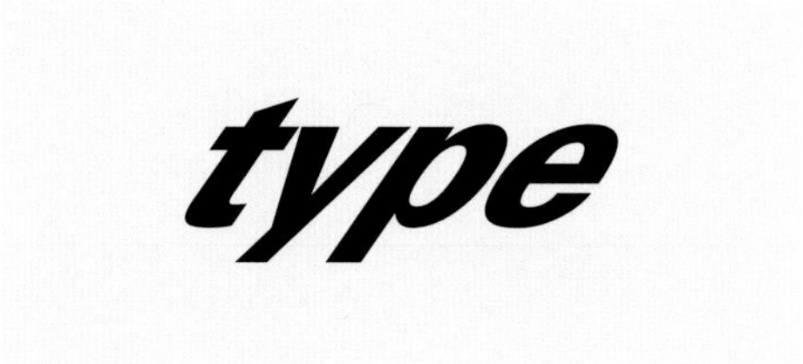
type

35 | **1.4.2** medium

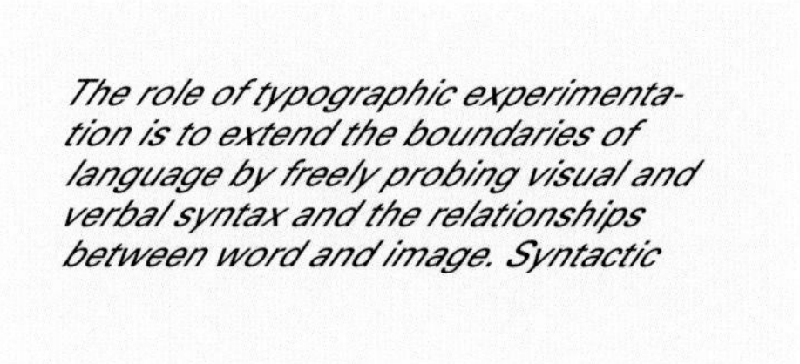
The role of typographic experimenta-
tion is to extend the boundaries of
language by freely probing visual and
verbal syntax and the relationships
between word and image. Syntactic

36 | **1.4.2** medium

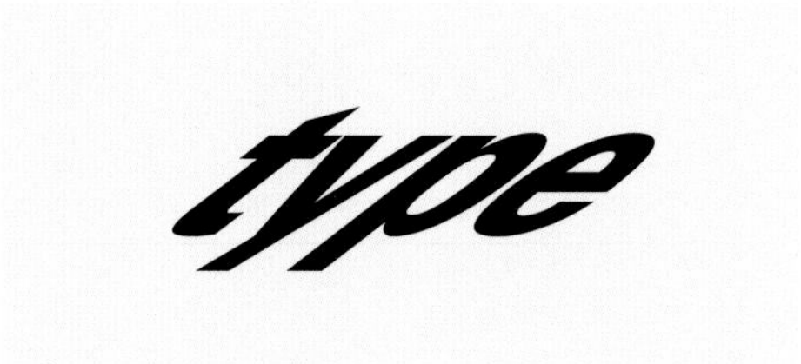
type

37 | **1.4.3** extreme

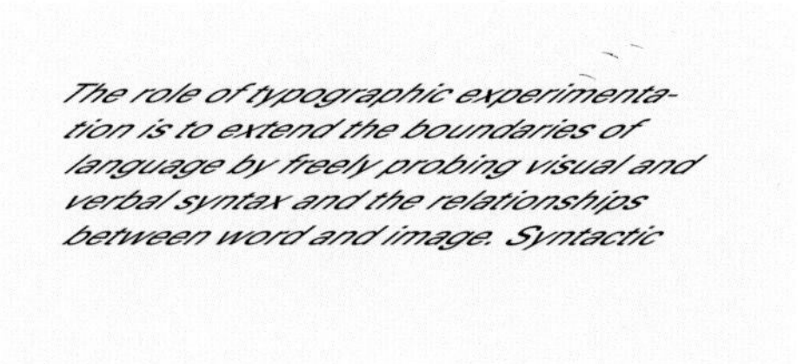
The role of typographic experimenta-
tion is to extend the boundaries of
language by freely probing visual and
verbal syntax and the relationships
between word and image. Syntactic

38 | **1.4.3** extreme

type

39 | **1.4.4** combination

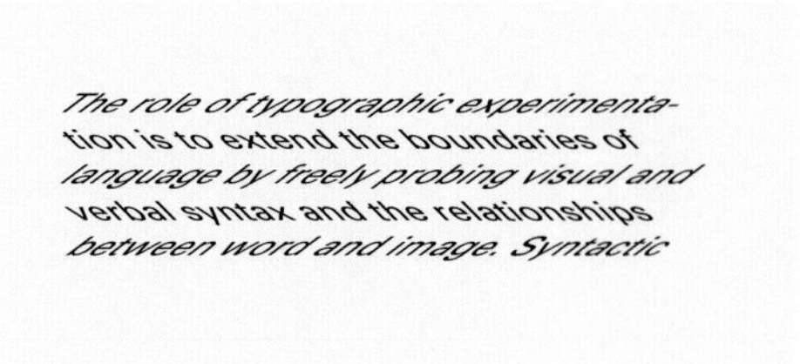
The role of typographic experimenta-
tion is to extend the boundaries of
language by freely probing visual and
verbal syntax and the relationships
between word and image. Syntactic

40 | **1.4.4** combination

## **1.5** Weight

All letterforms possess the property of weight, a factor determined by the thickness of letter strokes. Type with slight strokes appears thin and frail, while type with thick strokes appears robust and confident. Letters with thin strokes possess open and airy counterforms, which are the shapes within and surrounding letters (fig. **41**), while the opposite is true for heavy letters (fig. **45**). In fact, the counters of extremely heavy letters decrease significantly in size. Compare the varying weights of the letterforms shown below. In the course of typographic experimentation, consider which typographic elements should be emphasized and assign weights accordingly. Remember that extreme weight contrasts among typographic elements is almost always effective.

---

type

41 | **1.5.1** light

The role of typographic experimentation is to extend the boundaries of language by freely probing visual and verbal syntax and the relationships between word and image. Syntactic exploration enables

42 | **1.5.1** light

type

43 | **1.5.2** medium

The role of typographic experimenta-tion is to extend the boundaries of language by freely probing visual and verbal syntax and the relationships between word and image. Syntactic

44 | **1.5.2** medium

**type**

45 | **1.5.3** heavy

**The role of typographic experimenta-tion is to extend the boundaries of language by freely probing visual and verbal syntax and the relation-ships between word and image. Syn-**

46 | **1.5.3** heavy

**ty**y**p**e

47 | **1.5.4** combination

**The role of typographic experimen-**tation is to extend the boundaries of **language by freely probing visual** and verbal syntax and the relationships **between word and image. Syntactic**

48 | **1.5.4** combination

## **1.6** Width

Computer software enables the horizontal or vertical scaling of type, an effect that distorts the proportions of letterforms. When type is scaled vertically, horizontal strokes appear thicker (fig. **49**). When type is scaled horizontally, vertical strokes appear thicker (fig. **53**). Scaling type in this manner is abhorred by many type purists, for it detroys the integrity of the original type designs. While this is indeed a valid concern, violating letters in this way can also provide expressive and visually curious results.



---

type

49 **1.6.1** narrow

The role of typographic experimentation is to extend the boundaries of language by freely probing visual and verbal syntax and the relationships between word and image. Syntactic exploration enables designers to discover among typographic media an enormous potential to edify, entertain, and surprise. As in other forms of language typography is capable of infinite expression. The only

50 **1.6.1** narrow

type

51 **1.6.2** medium

The role of typographic experimentation is to extend the boundaries of language by freely probing visual and verbal syntax and the relationships between word and image. Syntactic

52 **1.6.2** medium

type

53 **1.6.3** wide

The role of typographic experimentation is to extend the boundaries of language by freely probing visual

54 **1.6.3** wide

type

55 **1.6.4** combination

The role of typographic experimentation is to extend the boundaries of language by freely probing visual and verbal syntax and the relationships between word and image. Syntactic exploration enables designers to discover among typographic media an enormous

56 **1.6.4** combination

## .1 Blending

Creating gradient transitions in color and tone modulates the surface of type and provides an illusion of dimensionality. Many blending possibilities exist, the two most common being linear and radial blends. Linear blends progress from one side of a letter or group of letters to another, and may be horizontal, vertical, or diagonal (figs. **57-60, 64**). Radial blends progress inwardly or outwardly, depending on tones and colors and their assigned positions in the blend (figs. **61, 62**). Blends are most vivid when the contrasts between color and tone are distinct, and most subtle when these contrasts are minimal.

57 **2.1.1** linear

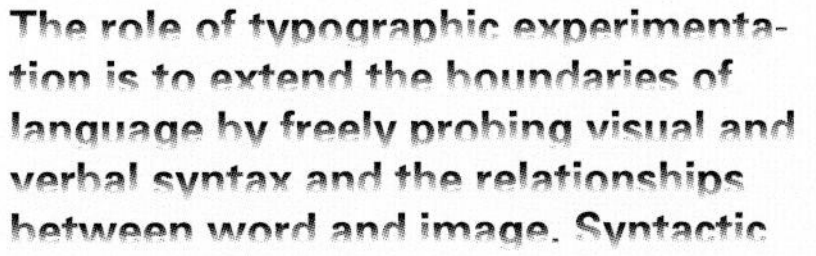


58 **2.1.1** linear

59 **2.1.1** linear

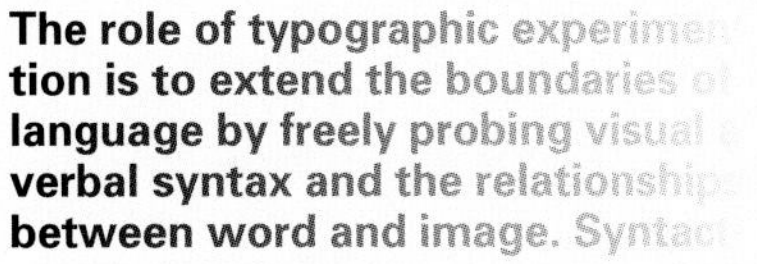


60 **2.1.1** linear

61 **2.1.2** radial

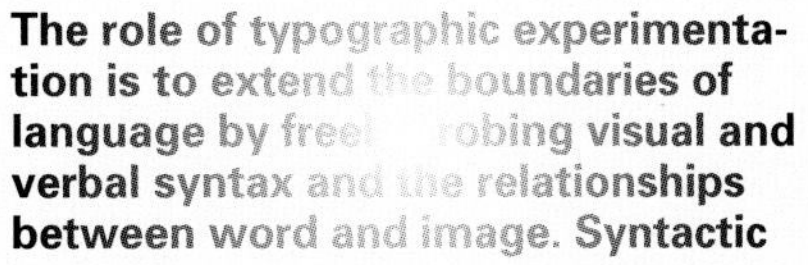


62 **2.1.2** radial

63 **2.1.3** combination

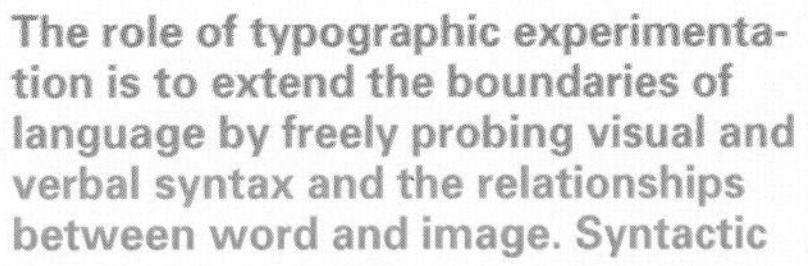


64 **2.1.1** linear

## 2.2 Distortion

Distorting type provocatively transports it into the visual realm, for letters and words that function normally as symbols for spoken sound are transformed into expressive images. When type is distorted, it acquires strange and unfamiliar visual characteristics. Depending upon how and why it is distorted, there exists a potential for new and extended meaning. Fragmented type, for example, may allude to disjointed conversation or chaos (fig. **65**), while blurred type may exude calm as it floats softly and atmospherically (figs. **73, 74**). Skewed and stretched type can represent movement or direction (figs. **67, 68, 71, 72**). Used in combination, the specific factors guiding type distortion can lend nearly infinite possibilities. All that is required is a sense of play, some ingenuity, and a bit of software knowledge. Text can appear to blister (fig. **70**), or blow in the wind like a flag (fig. **72**). Computer software provides typographic experimenters with a dazzling array of tools for distorting type.

65 | **2.2.1** fragmenting

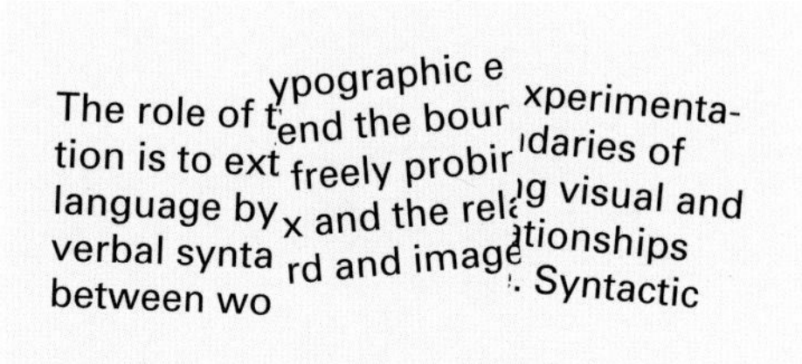


66 | **2.2.1** fragmenting

67 | **2.2.2** skewing

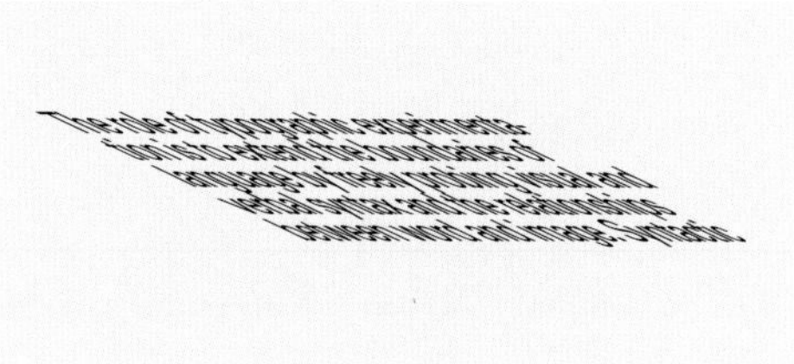

68 | **2.2.2** skewing

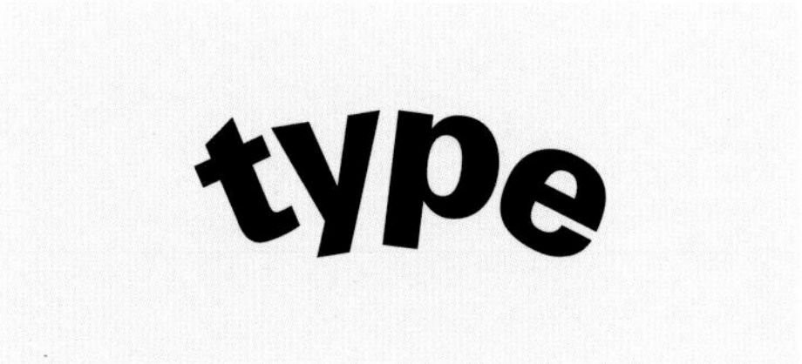


69 | **2.2.3** bending

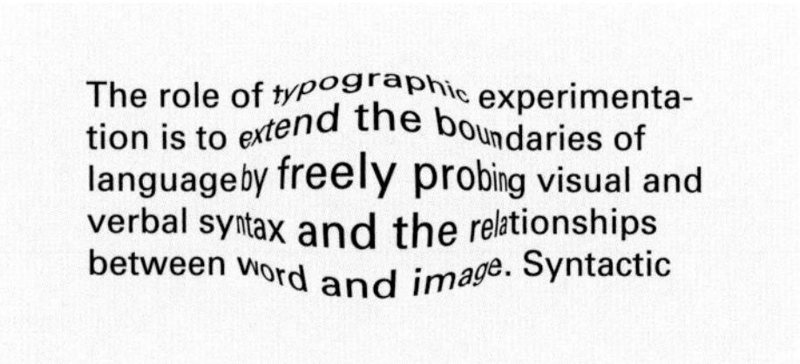


70 | **2.2.3** bending

71 | **2.2.4** stretching

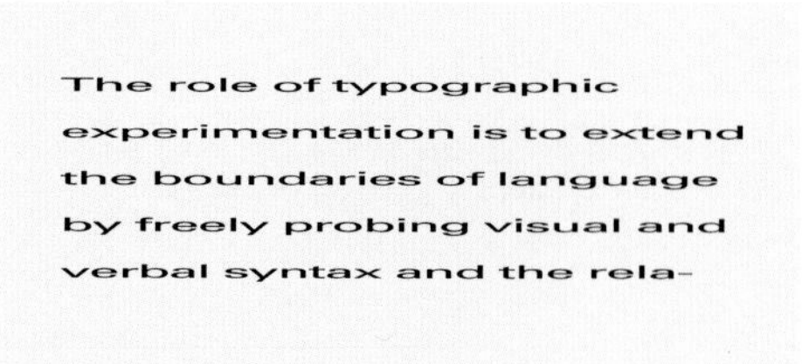


72 | **2.2.4** stretching

73 **2.2.5** blurring

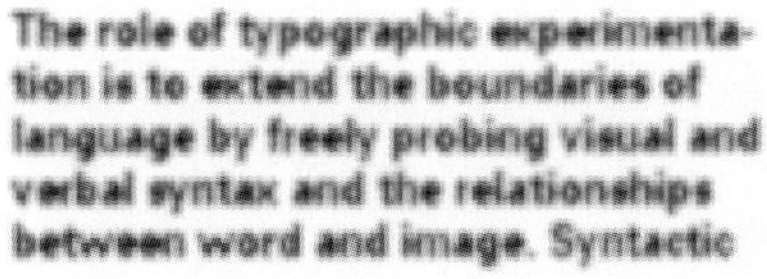


74 **2.2.5** blurring

75 **2.2.6** inverting

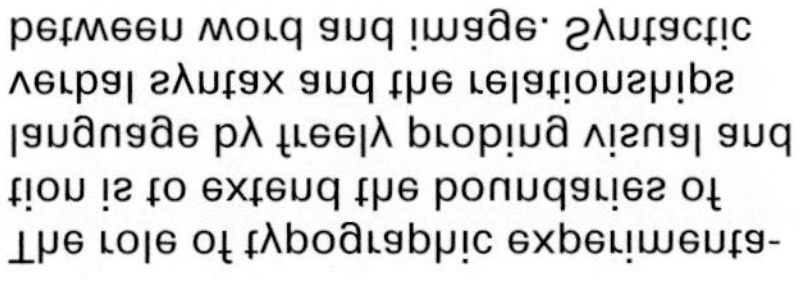


76 **2.2.6** inverting

77 **2.2.7** mutilating

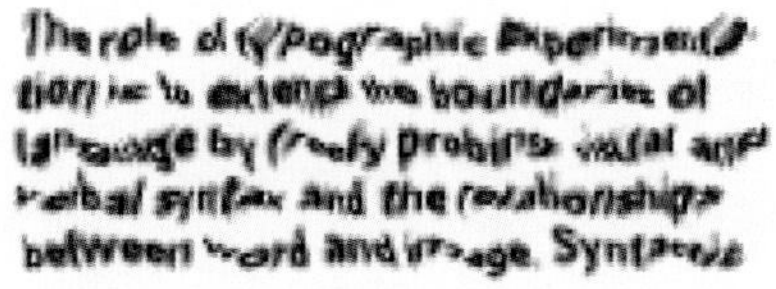

78 **2.2.7** mutilating

79 **2.2.8** combination

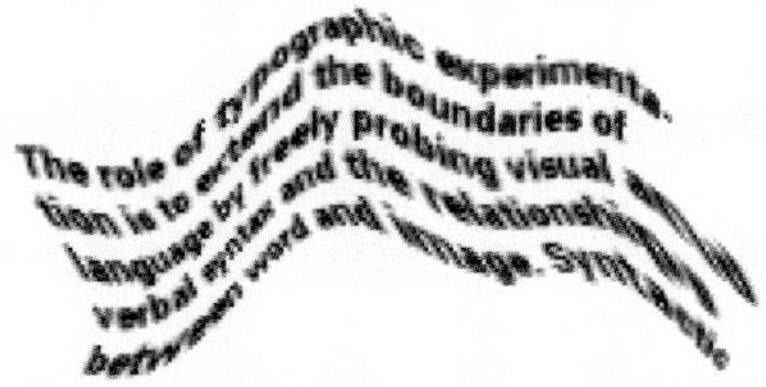

80 **2.2.8** combination

## **2.3** Elaboration

To elaborate upon type is to add or subtract from its complexity, or augment it with detail or ornamentation. The result of elaboration is a heightened emphasis of typographic elements. Enclosing letters or words within a shape (figs. **81, 87**), isolating letters by means of color (fig. **82**), and extending letter strokes (fig. **85**) are all tangible examples of elaboration. Removing letters or words from text (figs. **83-84**) emphasizes these elements by means of their conspicuous absence.

81 **2.3.1** addition

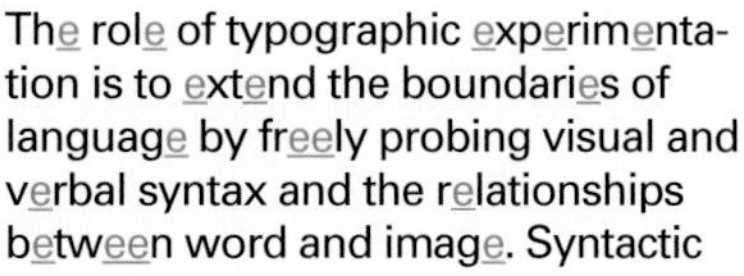


82 **2.3.1** addition

83 **2.3.2** subtraction

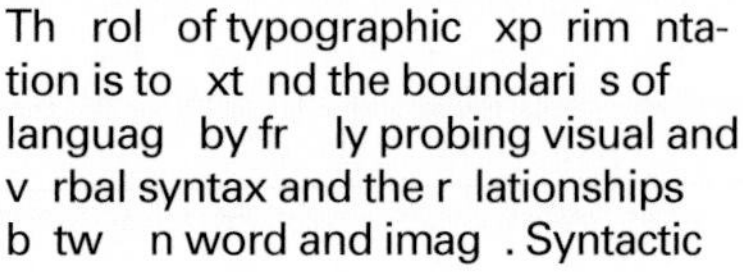

Th rol of typographic xp rim nta-
tion is to xt nd the boundari s of
languag by fr ly probing visual and
v rbal syntax and the r lationships
b tw n word and imag . Syntactic


84 **2.3.2** subtraction

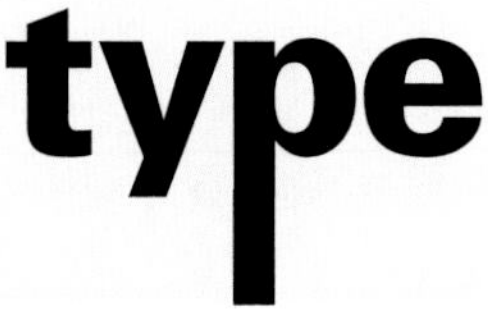


85 **2.3.3** extension

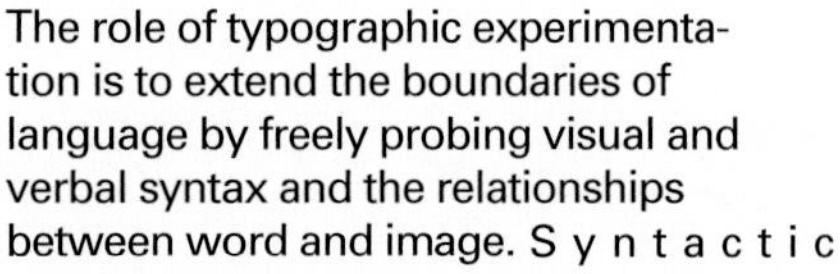


86 **2.3.3** extension

87 **2.3.4** combination

88 **2.3.4** combination

## .4 Outline

Letterforms can exist as solid shapes or as outlines. Outlines trace the contoured edges of letter shapes, and they appear in their most basic form as unbroken lines (fig. **89**). When text is outlined, its normal texture is transformed into a complex pattern, a transparent field of tiny windows (fig. **90**). More elaborate manifestations of outlined letters are those expressed with broken lines that are dotted, dashed, and intermittent (figs. **95, 97**). These letters suffer significantly in terms of legibility, but at the same time they achieve intriguing visual qualities. Letters expressed with just a few broken elements vaguely resemble the original form. These ambiguous letterforms provide a visual riddle for the reader's eye (fig. **99**). Outlines can also be expressed in various patterns and shapes (figs. **101-102**), and in many thought-provoking combinations (figs. **103, 104**). Text set in broken outlines sacrifices readability for visual tactility (figs. **98, 100**).

---

type

89 | **2.4.1** thin

The role of typographic experimentation is to extend the boundaries of language by freely probing visual and verbal syntax and the relationships between word and image. Syntactic

90 | **2.4.1** thin

type

91 | **2.4.2** medium

The role of typographic experimentation is to extend the boundaries of language by freely probing visual and verbal syntax and the relationships between word and image. Syntactic

92 | **2.4.2** medium

type

93 | **2.4.3** thick

The role of typographic experimentation is to extend the boundaries of language by freely probing visual and verbal syntax and the relationships between word and image. Syntactic

94 | **2.4.3** thick

type

95 | **2.4.4** broken

The role of typographic experimentation is to extend the boundaries of language by freely probing visual and verbal syntax and the relationships between word and image. Syntactic

96 | **2.4.4** broken

97 | **2.4.4** broken

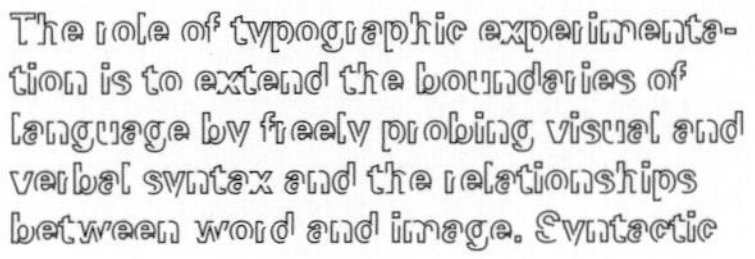


98 | **2.4.4** broken

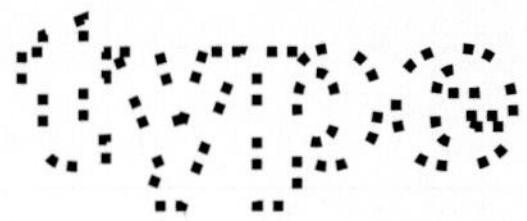


99 | **2.4.4** broken

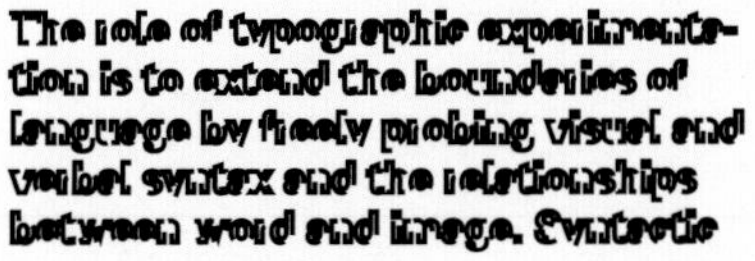


100 | **2.4.4** broken

101 | **2.4.4** broken

102 | **2.4.4** broken

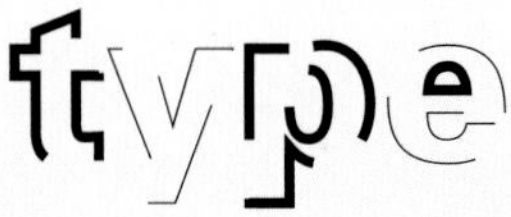


103 | **2.4.5** combination

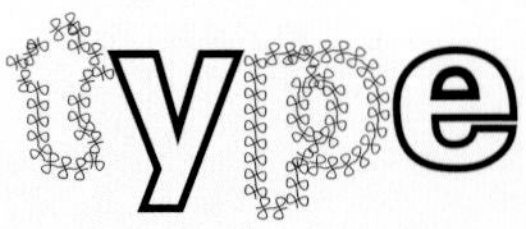


104 | **2.4.5** combination

# 2.5 Texture

When type is expressed as visual texture, it evokes tactile sensations. A reader's individual response to texture depends on a number of factors, among which are the fineness or coarseness of a texture, and the regularity or irregularity of its pattern.

In typography, texture can be observed in two ways. The first is naturally found in the tactile appearance of text, an effect established by individual letters in repetition. Differences in typeface design and in spacing of letters, words, and lines within text provide different textural qualities (figs. **106, 108**). A second means of achieving textural effects is by applying various textures directly to letter surfaces. As textures increase in coarseness, letterforms – depending upon their design and size – decrease in legibility (compare figs. **105, 107**). Infinitely varied textures may appear in

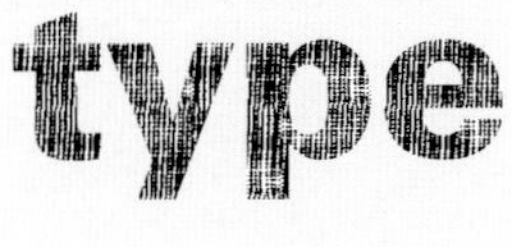


105 | **2.5.1** fine

The role of typographic experimentation is to extend the boundaries of
language by freely probing visual and
verbal syntax and the relationships
between word and image. Syntactic

106 | **2.5.1** fine

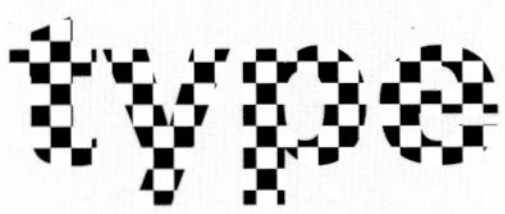


107 | **2.5.2** coarse

**The role of typographic experimen-
tation is to extend the boundaries
of language by freely probing
visual and verbal syntax and the
relationships between word and**

108 | **2.5.2** coarse

109 | **2.5.3** regular

THE ROLE OF TYPOGRAPHIC EXPERIMENTATION IS
TO EXTEND THE BOUNDARIES OF LANGUAGE BY
FREELY PROBING VISUAL AND VERBAL SYNTAX AND
THE RELATIONSHIPS BETWEEN WORD AND IMAGE.
SYNTACTIC EXPLORATION ENABLES DESIGNERS TO

110 | **2.5.3** regular

111 | **2.5.3** regular

**The role of typographic experimen-
tation is to extend the boundaries of
language by freely probing visual
and verbal syntax and the relationships between word and image.**

112 | **2.5.3** regular

regular patterns of dot, line, and other geometric parts (figs. **109, 111**), or in irregular patterns of organic shapes (figs. **113, 115**).

Letterform size also plays a significant role in the expression of texture. Used in combination, large and small letters provide a wide variety of dynamic textural effects (fig. **116**).

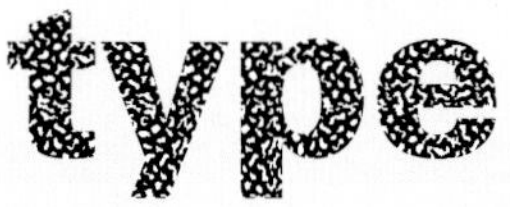

113 **2.5.4** irregular

The role of typographic experimentation is to extend the boundaries of language by freely probing visual and verbal syntax and the relationships between word and image.

114 **2.5.4** irregular

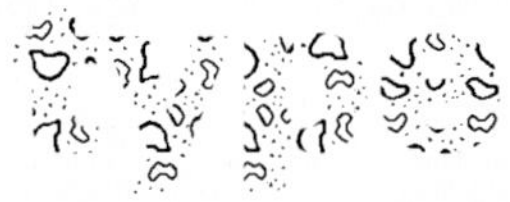

115 **2.5.4** irregular

The role of typographic experimentation is to extend the boundaries of language by freely probing visual and verbal syntax and the relationships between

116 **2.5.4** irregular

117 **2.5.5** combination

The role of typographic experimentation is to extend the boundaries of language by freely probing visual and verbal syntax and the relationships between word and image. Syntactic exploration enables

118 **2.5.5** combination

119 **2.5.5** combination

The role of typographic experimentation is to extend the boundaries of language by freely probing visual and verbal syntax and the relationships between word and image. Syntactic exploration enables designers to discover among typograph-

120 **2.5.5** combination

## .6 Dimensionality

The most basic means of achieving illusory space is to juxtapose letters of one size to those of another. Smaller letters appear to recede, while larger forms appear to advance in space. This effect is heightened with the use of color or tone: light and cool colors recede; dark and warm colors advance.

The illusion of spatial dimension is further intensified when letters appear to zoom forward or backward in space (figs. **121, 122**), bend and warp (figs. **123, 124**), or cast shadows (figs. **125-128**). The reason these effects are so intriguing to the viewer is because they do not exist in reality; they merely tease the eye through a suggestion of reality. With a visual sleight-of-hand, the designer-magician creates an illusion that surprises and woos the audience when effectively performed.

121 **2.6.1** volumetric

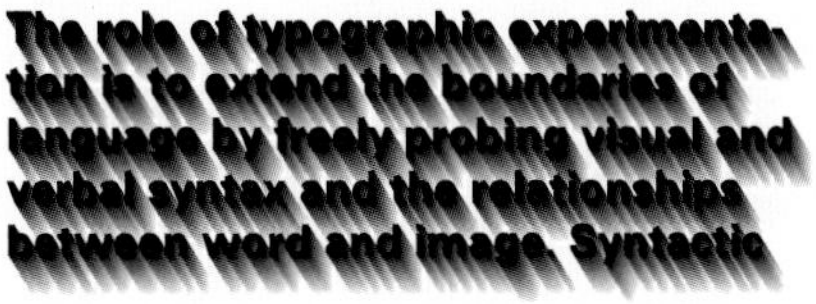


122 **2.6.1** volumetric

123 **2.6.1** volumetric

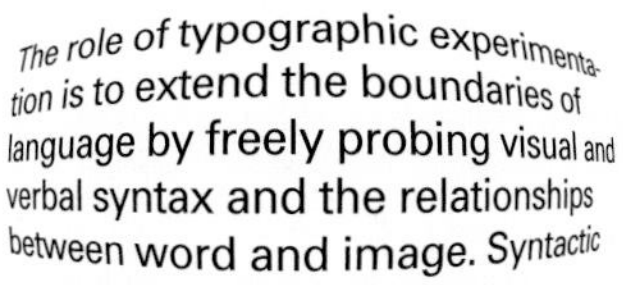


124 **2.6.1** volumetric

125 **2.6.2** shadowing

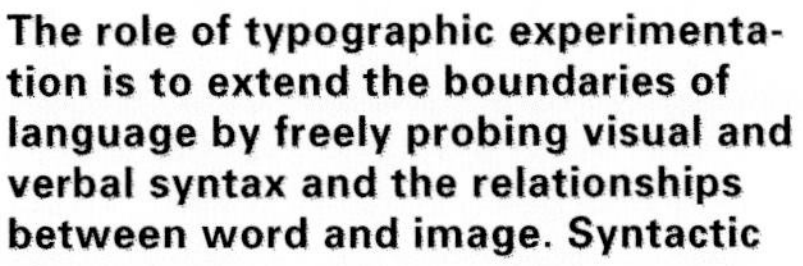


126 **2.6.2** shadowing

127 **2.6.2** shadowing

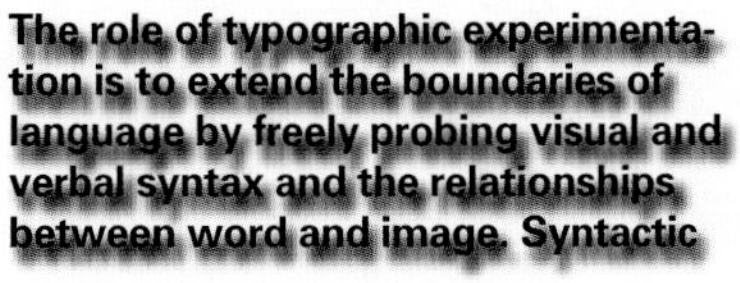


128 **2.6.2** shadowing

## **2.7** Tonality

Tonality refers to type that is a screen or a tint of black or a pure color (hue). It should not be confused with typographic "color," the relative lightness or darkness of text, which is inherently linked to the stroke weight of letters. Adjusting the tone of type provides a way to control emphasis: the lighter the type, and the closer it approximates the tone or value of its background, the more it appears to recede in space (figs. **129, 130**). Type assigned lighter tones is de-emphasized in relationship to darker type, providing a means to control the visual strength of elements within a given space (figs. **135, 136**).

129 | **2.7.1** light

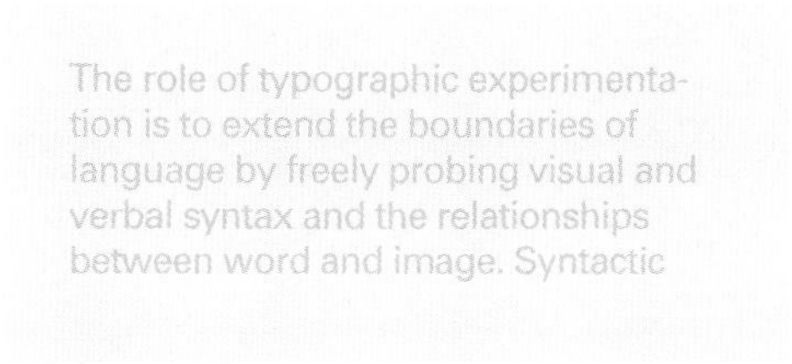


130 | **2.7.1** light

131 | **2.7.2** medium

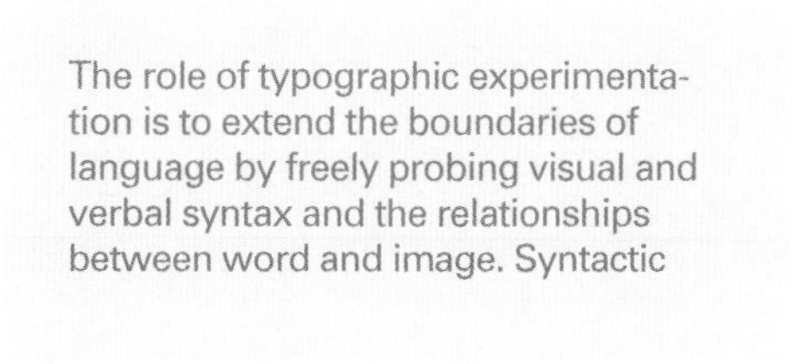


132 | **2.7.2** medium

133 | **2.7.3** dark

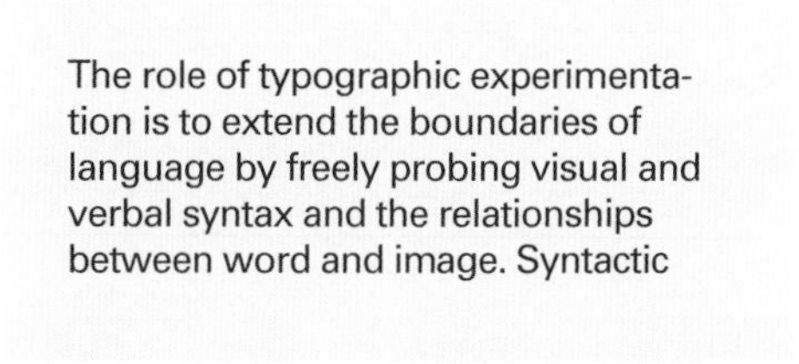


134 | **2.7.3** dark

135 | **2.7.4** combination

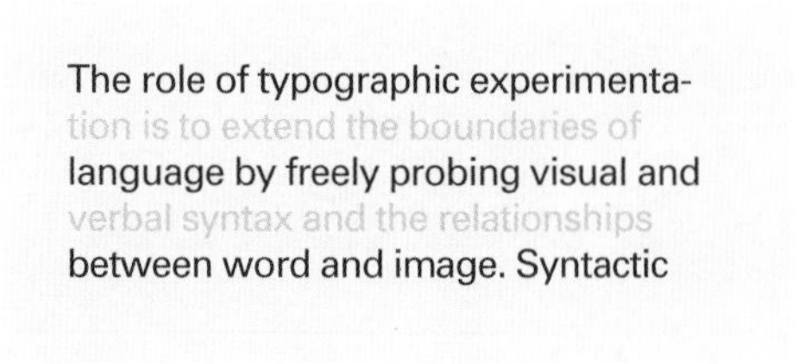


136 | **2.7.4** combination

## 3.1 Balance

Two basic models exist for structuring typographic elements in space: symmetry and asymmetry. Symmetrical organization produces a quiet, complacent, and formal setting, while asymmetrical organization creates a dynamic visual tension. Symmetry often consists of type elements placed bi-laterally along a centered axis. In other words, elements mirror each other and are distributed equally on either side of a central axis (figs. **137-140**). Asymmetry derives its energy from an interaction between positive and negative spaces. In other words, spatial harmony is achieved through a dialogue between typographic elements and the space surrounding them (figs. **141, 142**).

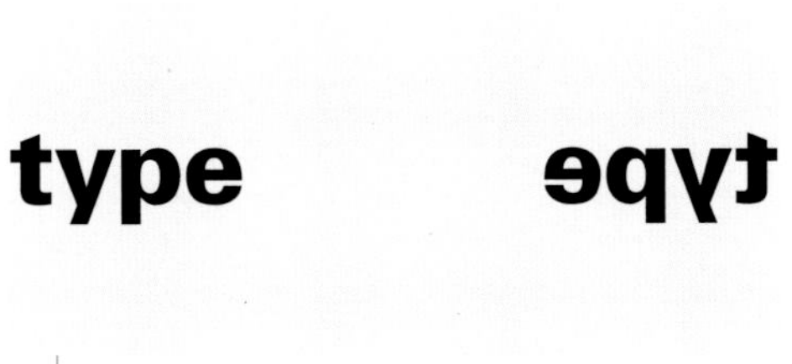

137 | **3.1.1** symmetrical

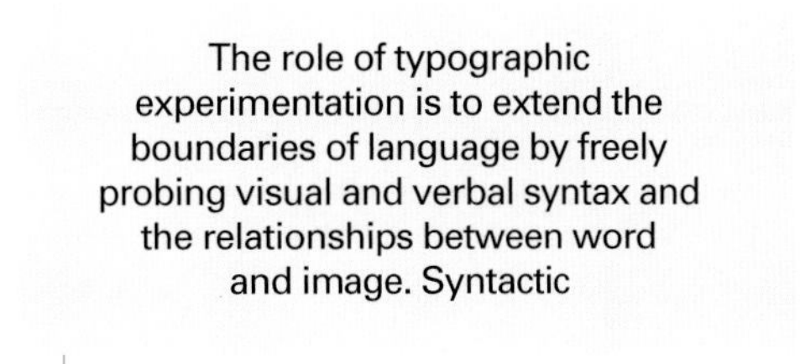
The role of typographic
experimentation is to extend the
boundaries of language by freely
probing visual and verbal syntax and
the relationships between word
and image. Syntactic
138 | **3.1.1** symmetrical

139 | **3.1.1** symmetrical

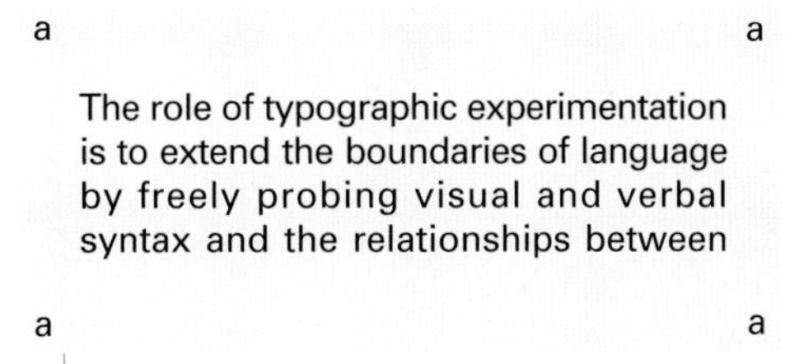

140 | **3.1.1** symmetrical

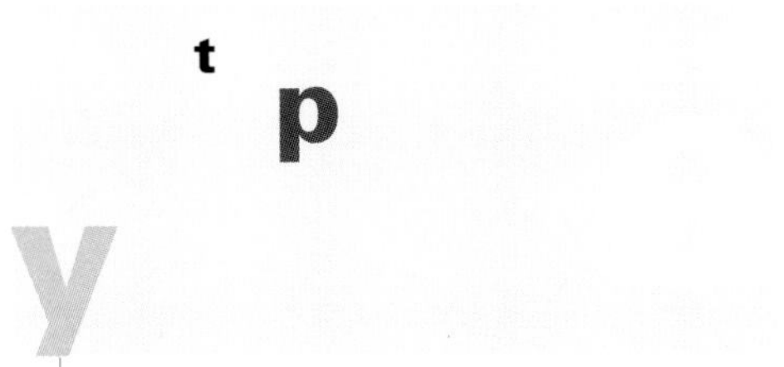

141 | **3.1.2** asymmetrical

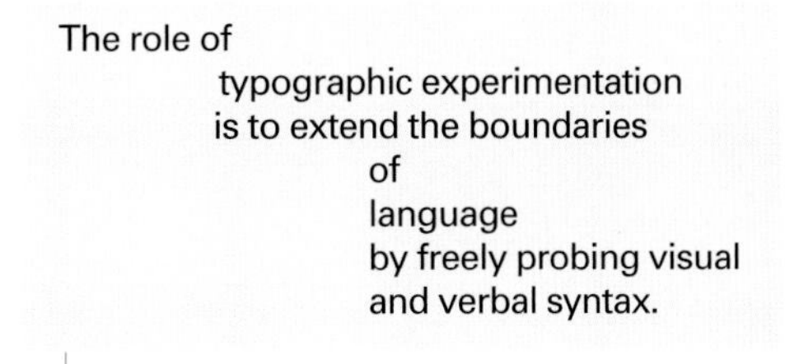

142 | **3.1.2** asymmetrical

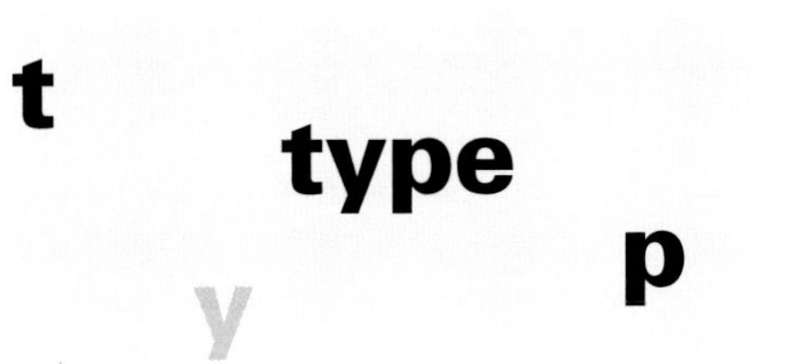

143 | **3.1.3** combination

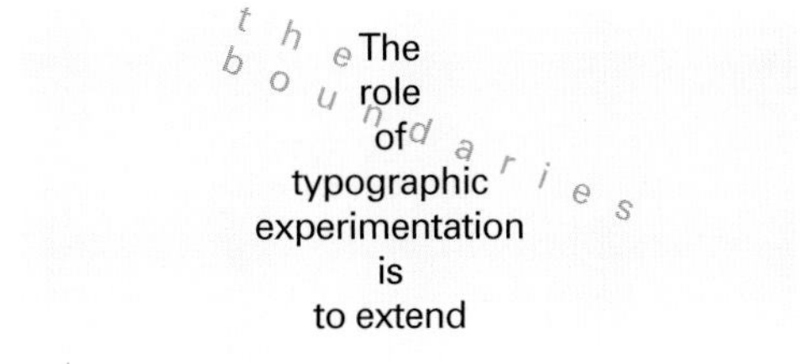

144 | **3.1.3** combination

## 3.2 Direction

Typographic elements exert directional energy by virtue of their intrinsic shapes and the positions they occupy on the page. Type is conventionally viewed horizontally and resting upon an imaginary baseline (figs. **145, 146**). Rotated at other angles, it is charged with varying degrees of energy (figs. **147-150**). Type moving in circular directions acquires a whimsical presence (figs. **151-152**).

type

145 **3.2.1** horizontal

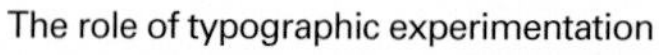
The role of typographic experimentation

146 **3.2.1** horizontal

type

147 **3.2.2** vertical

The role of typographic

148 **3.2.2** vertical

type

149 **3.2.3** diagonal

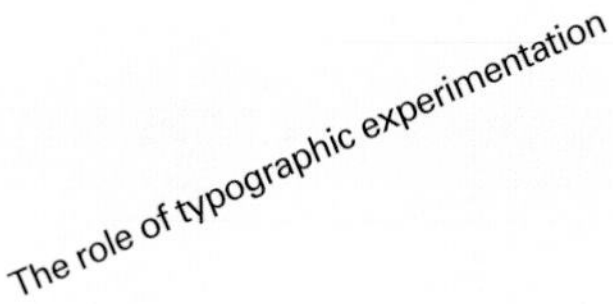
The role of typographic experimentation

150 **3.2.3** diagonal

type

151 **3.2.4** circular

The role of typographic experimentation is to extend the boundaries of language.

152 **3.2.4** circular

## .3 Ground

"Ground" refers to the background stage upon which type performs its many roles. It appears to advance or recede depending upon the proximity of its hue and value to the type. Basically, less contrast between the ground and type encourages the ground to advance (figs. **153-154**), while more contrast between the ground and type causes the ground to recede (figs. **155-156**).

153 | **3.3.1** advancing

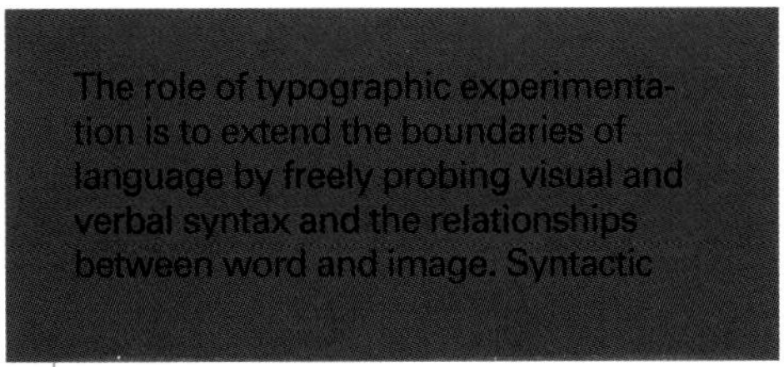
The role of typographic experimenta-
tion is to extend the boundaries of
language by freely probing visual and
verbal syntax and the relationships
between word and image. Syntactic

154 | **3.3.1** advancing

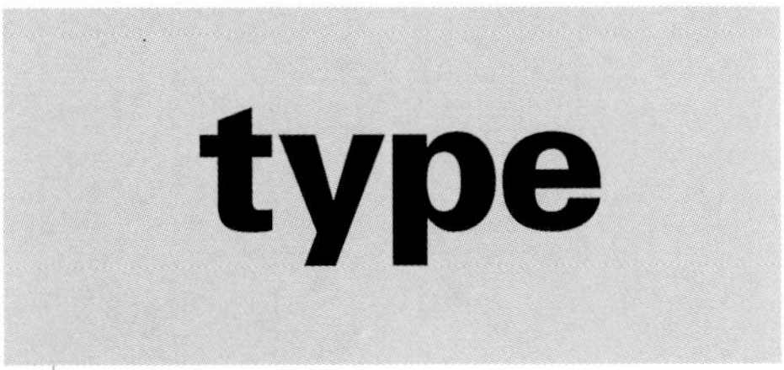


155 | **3.3.2** receding

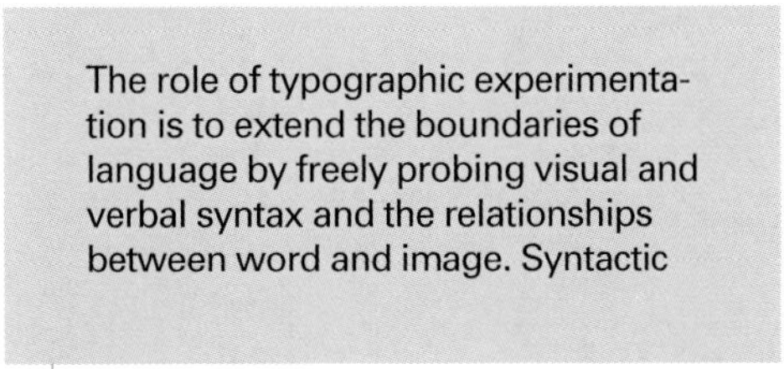
The role of typographic experimenta-
tion is to extend the boundaries of
language by freely probing visual and
verbal syntax and the relationships
between word and image. Syntactic

156 | **3.3.2** receding

157 | **3.3.3** combination

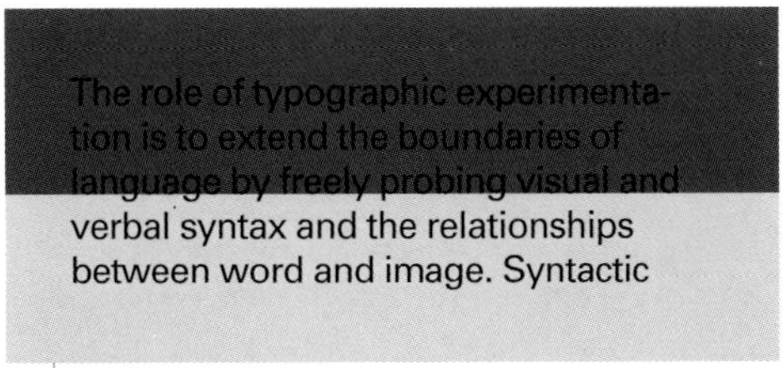
The role of typographic experimenta-
tion is to extend the boundaries of
language by freely probing visual and
verbal syntax and the relationships
between word and image. Syntactic

158 | **3.3.3** combination

159 | **3.3.3** combination

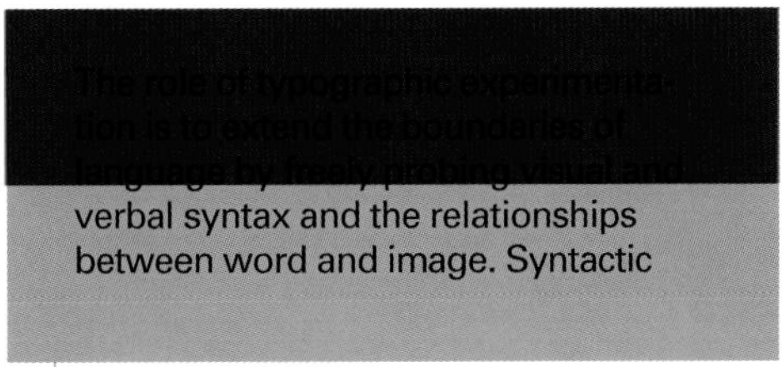


160 | **3.3.3** combination

## 3.4 Grouping

Two important principles should be kept in mind when grouping typographic elements. *Consonance* is a harmonious and unified relationship between elements, while *dissonance* is a discordant and chaotic relationship between elements. Letters may be carefully aligned and grouped into a tight community (fig. **161**). Figures **163** and **164** establish consonance as a result of a deliberate square structure. In contrast, figures **165** and **166** contain groupings of elements expanding outwardly and seemingly out of control. The visual effects achieved by the careful grouping of typographic elements can support and intensify a message's intended meaning.

161 | **3.4.1** consonant

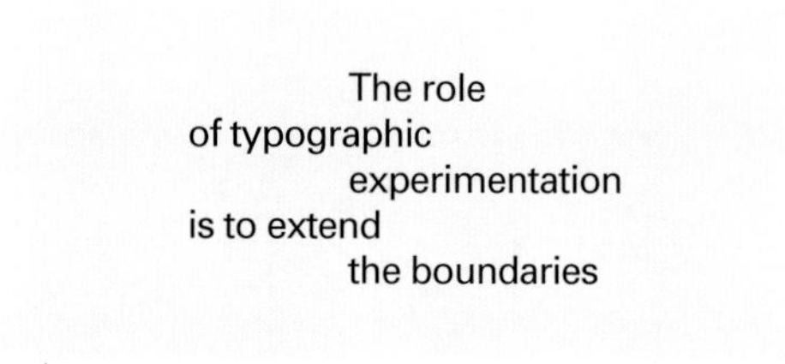
The role
of typographic
experimentation
is to extend
the boundaries

162 | **3.4.1** consonant

t y
p e

163 | **3.4.1** consonant

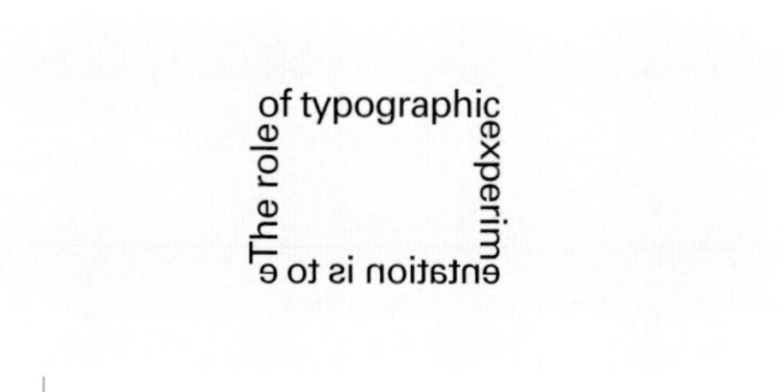
The role
of typographic
experim

164 | **3.4.1** consonant

165 | **3.4.2** dissonant

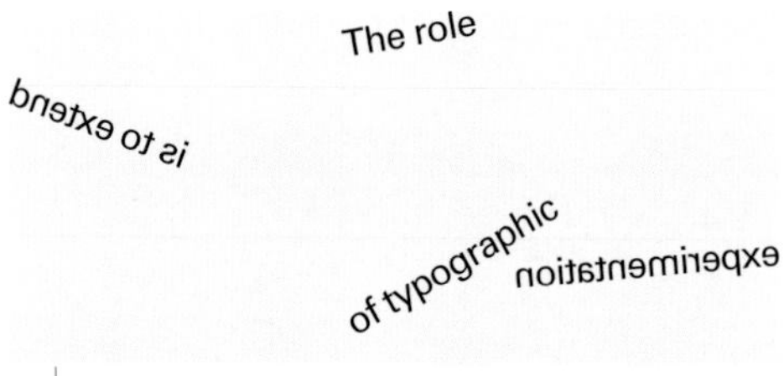
The role
of typographic

166 | **3.4.2** dissonant

167 | **3.4.3** combination

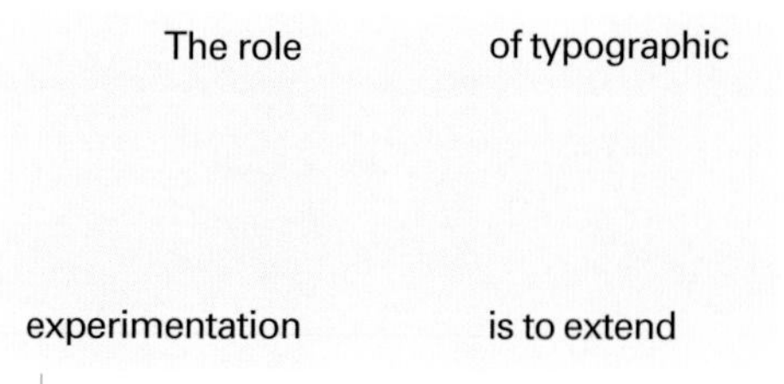
The role
of typographic
experimentation
is to extend

168 | **3.4.3** combination

## .5 Proximity

Related to the factor of typographic grouping, proximity offers another important variable for exploration. Letters, words, lines, and blocks of text may range from severely overlapping to generously spaced. When typographic elements overlap, legibility is severely reduced or eliminated. What is often gained from this compromise are intriguing typographic shapes created by overlapping letters (fig. **169**), or anxious textures established by overlapping lines of type (fig. **170**). The examples shown here merely scratch the surface of possibilities. Personal exploration will undoubtedly produce surprising and rewarding results.

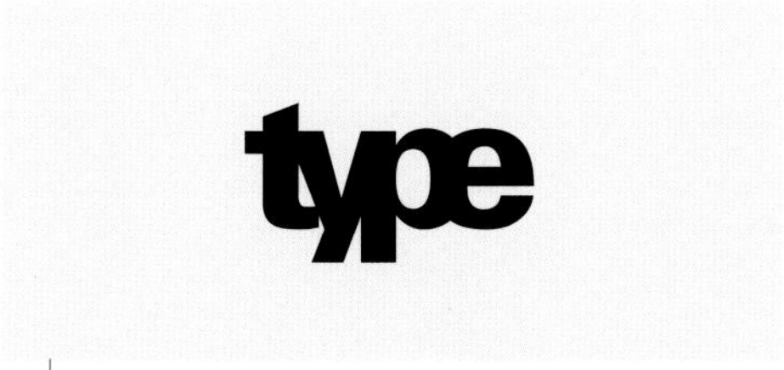


169 **3.5.1** overlapping

170 **3.5.1** overlapping

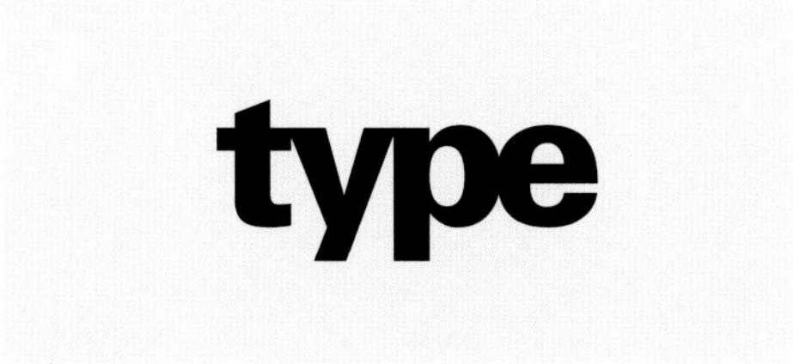


171 **3.5.2** touching

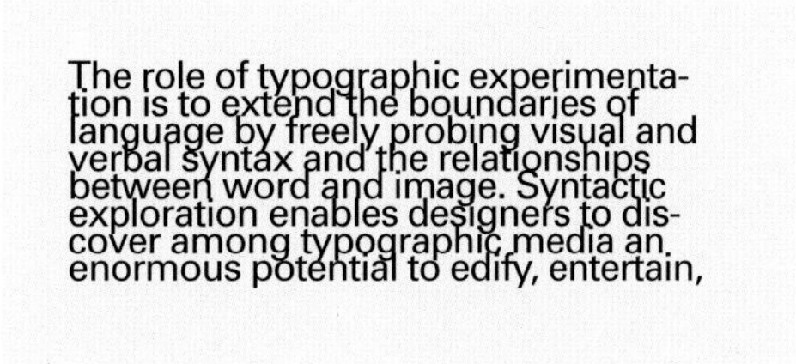


172 **3.5.2** touching

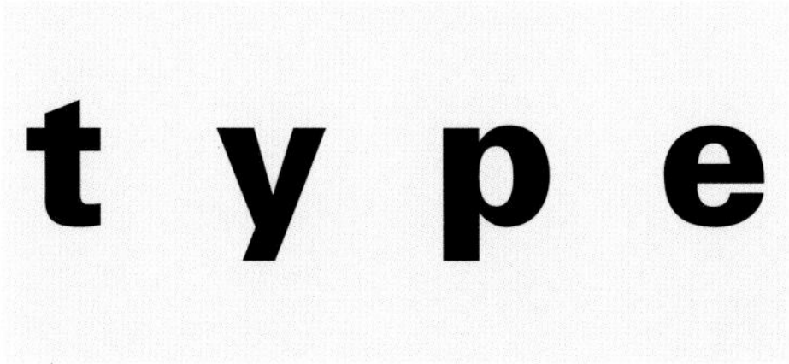


173 **3.5.3** separating

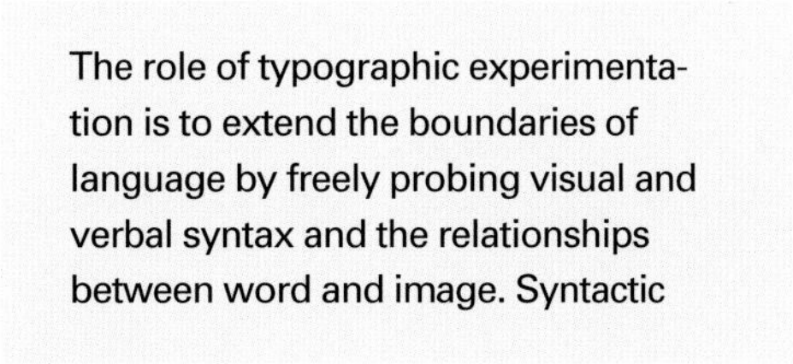


174 **3.5.3** separating

175 **3.5.4** combination

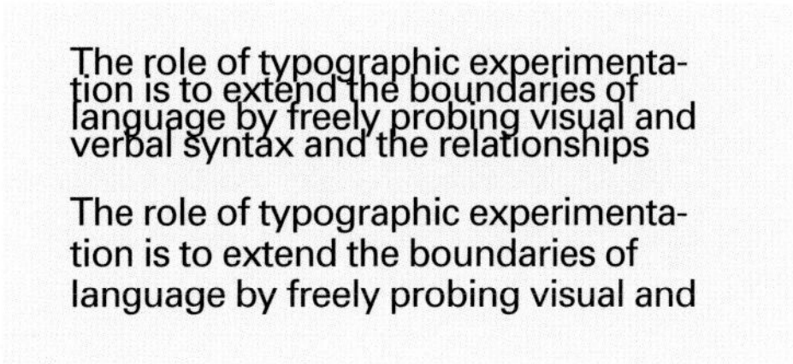


176 **3.5.4** combination

## 3.6 Repetition

Beyond the obvious but functional task of letters and words repeating one another to deliver written messages, repetition is an important factor in the process of typographic exploration. As typographic elements are repeated, thoughts and ideas are not only heightened through redundancy and exaggeration, but also a distinct visual resonance occurs. Often, dynamic visual patterns result from letters, words, and lines of type that are repeated (figs. **183, 184**). While exploring typographic repetition, keep in mind the degree of repetition (few or many), and whether the repetition calls for random or pattern.



**type**
**type**
**type**

177 | **3.6.1** few

The role of typographic experimentation
The role of typographic experimentation
The role of typographic experimentation

178 | **3.6.1** few

**type type type type type**
**type type type type type**
**type type type type type**
**type type type type type**

179 | **3.6.2** many

The role of typographic experimentation The role of typographic experimentation
The role of typographic experimentation The role of typographic experimentation
The role of typographic experimentation The role of typographic experimentation
The role of typographic experimentation The role of typographic experimentation
The role of typographic experimentation The role of typographic experimentation
The role of typographic experimentation The role of typographic experimentation
The role of typographic experimentation The role of typographic experimentation
The role of typographic experimentation The role of typographic experimentation
The role of typographic experimentation The role of typographic experimentation
The role of typographic experimentation The role of typographic experimentation
The role of typographic experimentation The role of typographic experimentation

180 | **3.6.2** many

**type type type type type type type type type type type type type type type**

181 | **3.6.3** random

The role of typographic experimentation
The role of typographic experimentation
The role of typographic experimentation
The role of typographic experimentation
The role of typographic experimentation
The role of typographic experimentation
The role of typographic experimentation
The role of typographic experimentation
The role of typographic experimentation
The role of typographic experimentation
The role of typographic experimentation

182 | **3.6.3** random

**type type type**
**type type type type**
**type type type type type**
**type type type type type**
**type type type type**
**type type type**

183 | **3.6.4** pattern

The role of typographic experimentation
The role of typographic experimentation
The role of typographic experimentation
The role of typographic experimentation
The role of typographic experimentation
The role of typographic experimentation
The role of typographic experimentation
The role of typographic experimentation
The role of typographic experimentation
The role of typographic experimentation
The role of typographic experimentation
The role of typographic experimentation
The role of typographic experimentation
The role of typographic experimentation
The role of typographic experimentation
The role of typographic experimentation

184 | **3.6.4** pattern

## 7 Rhythm

Because it is linear in structure, typography is analogous to music; it may be thought of as the visual equivalent of music. The principles of repetition and rhythm are tied closely together. But unlike repetition, wherein identical elements are repeated, rhythm occurs through the repetition of contrasting elements. In other words, for rhythm to be born, typographic parts must not only be repeated, they must also oppose one another in a distinct rhythmic sequence. Contrast in typography may be established by juxtaposing different type sizes, faces, weights, widths, colors, and the intervals of space separating typographic elements. Demonstrated in the examples below are four distinct rhythmic variations that can be instituted while exploring typography. Regular rhythm repeats similar typographic parts separated by equal intervals of space (figs. **185, 186**). This is typography's most common rhythmic quality. Irregular rhythm is characterized by elements – identical or contrasted – separated

---

**t y p e**

185 | **3.7.1** regular

The role of typographic experimentation is to extend the boundaries of
language by freely probing visual and
verbal syntax and the relationships
between word and image. Syntactic

186 | **3.7.1** regular

**t yp e**

187 | **3.7.2** irregular

The role of typographic experimentation is to extend the boundaries of

language by freely probing visual and

verbal syntax and the relationships

between word and image. Syntactic

188 | **3.7.2** irregular

**t y p e**

189 | **3.7.3** alternating

The role of typographic experimentation is to extend the boundaries of
language by freely probing visual and
verbal syntax and the relationships
between word and image. Syntactic

190 | **3.7.3** alternating

**t** y **p** e

191 | **3.7.3** alternating

The role of typographic experimenta-
**tion is to extend the boundaries of**
language by freely probing visual and
**verbal syntax and the relationships**
between word and image. Syntactic

192 | **3.7.3** alternating

by unequal intervals of space (figs. **187, 188**). In alternating rhythm, the typographic parts alternate between two contrasting attributes (size, weight, tone, etc.). Spatial intervals remain constant between the parts (figs. **189-192**). Progressive rhythm occurs when element attributes and/or the intervals of space separating the elements increase or decrease gradationally (figs. **193-196**). The rhythmic variations discussed here may be combined and expanded into nearly infinite possibilities.

---

**ty p e**

193 | **3.7.4** progressive

The role of typographic experimentation is to extend the boundaries of language by freely probing visual and verbal syntax and the relationships between word and image. Syntactic

194 | **3.7.4** progressive

t y **p e**

195 | **3.7.4** progressive

The role of typographic experimentation is to
extend the boundaries of language by
probing visual and verbal syntax
and the relationships
between word and

196 | **3.7.4** progressive

**t**y **p** e

197 | **3.7.5** combination

The role of typographic experimenta-
**tion is to extend the boundaries of**
language by freely probing visual and
**verbal syntax and the relationships**
between word and image. Syntactic

198 | **3.7.5** combination

**t** t **y** y **p** p **e** e

199 | **3.7.5** combination

The role of typographic experimentation is to
extend the boundaries of language by
probing visual and verbal syntax
and the relationships
between word and

200 | **3.7.5** combination

## .8 Rotation

Rotating type seems a rather basic exercise, but the effect of angling type and thereby removing it from the safety of its conventional, horizontal baseline can powerfully influence type's energy and emotion. As rotations progress from slight (figs. **201-202**) to extreme (figs. **205-206**), dynamic forces and emotional impact increase. Juxtaposing typographic elements at different angles can produce intriguing visual results (figs. **207-208**).

201 | **3.8.1** slight

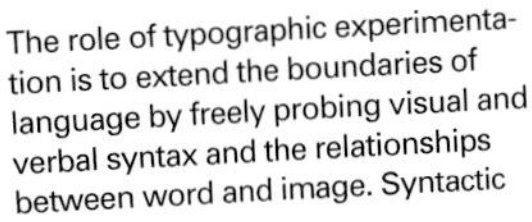


202 | **3.8.1** slight

203 | **3.8.2** moderate

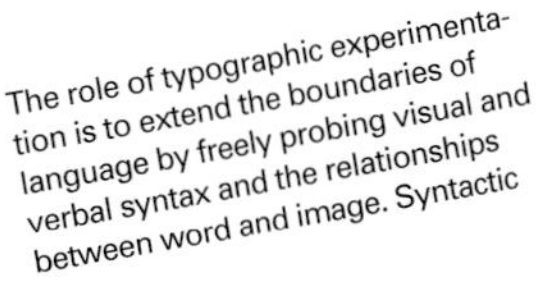


204 | **3.8.2** moderate

205 | **3.8.3** extreme

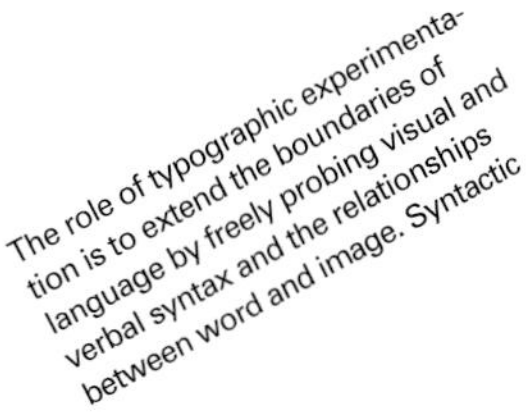


206 | **3.8.3** extreme

207 | **3.8.4** combination

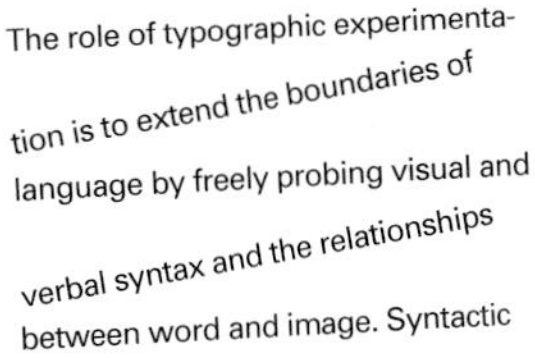


208 | **3.8.4** combination

## 4.1 Ruled lines

Referred to as typographic support elements, ruled lines serve as visual punctuation. Deliberately placed ruled lines can emphasize thoughts, separate units of information for hierarchical clarity, and contribute to type's throbbing presence. A simple underline (figs. **221, 222**) makes an emphatic statement. More complex variations connote architectonic spaces, for they divide and define typographic space. Consider the stair-stepped architectural motifs (figs. **217, 218**). In combination, type and ruled lines are also capable of evoking musical attributes by entering into a rhythmic dialogue (figs. **223, 224**). Not shown here, but equally important to consider for exploration are other varieties of ruled lines such as swelled, dotted, dashed, and double ruled lines.

209 | **4.1.1** horizontal

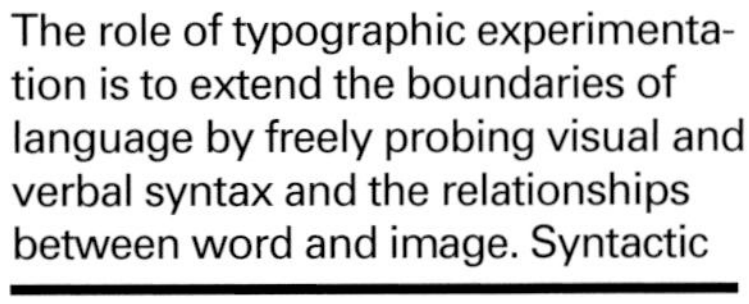


210 | **4.1.1** horizontal

211 | **4.1.2** vertical

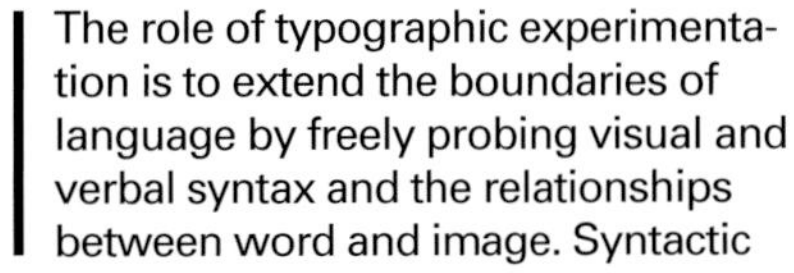


212 | **4.1.2** vertical

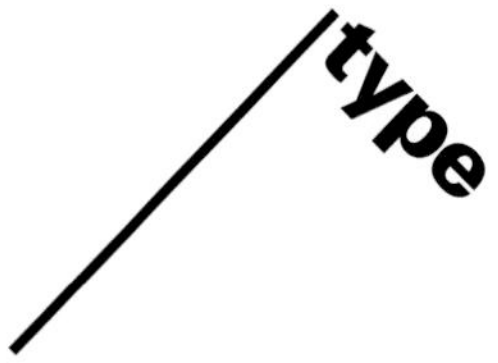


213 | **4.1.3** diagonal

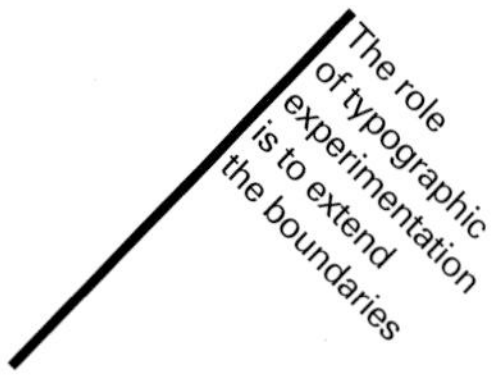


214 | **4.1.3** diagonal

215 | **4.1.4** curved

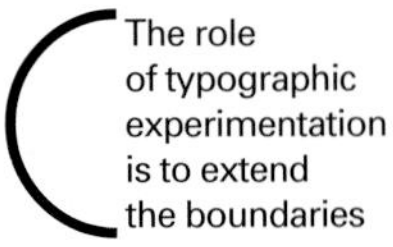


216 | **4.1.4** curved

type

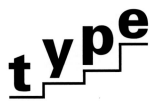

217 **4.1.5** stair-stepped

The role
of typographic
experimentation
is to extend
the boundaries

218 **4.1.5** stair-stepped

type

219 **4.1.6** thin

The role of typographic experimentation is to extend the boundaries of language by freely probing visual and verbal syntax and the relationships between word and image. Syntactic

220 **4.1.6** thin

type

221 **4.1.8** thick

The role of typographic experimentation is to extend the boundaries of language by freely probing visual and verbal syntax and the relationships between word and image. Syntactic

222 **4.1.8** thick

type

223 **4.1.9** combination

The role of typographic experimentation is to extend the boundaries of language by freely probing visual and verbal syntax and the relationships between word and image. Syntactic

224 **4.1.9** combination

## 4.2 Shapes

Shapes in boundless variety can be invented to create intimate spaces for typographic parts, or to highlight and separate them. As images, shapes connote meanings that potentially amplify type's content: the resolute, stable square – a room (fig. **225**); an amorphous shape – a cloud (fig. **226**). Shape may serve as a background for type (figs. **227, 228**), or as adjacent support elements (figs. **229, 230**). Intriguing dimensional environments can be created by inventively overlapping shape and type (figs. **231, 232**).

225 | **4.2.1** geometric

226 | **4.2.2** organic

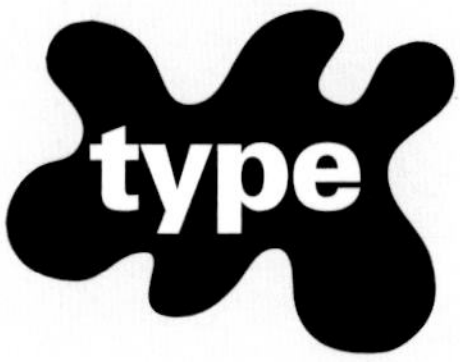


227 | **4.2.3** background

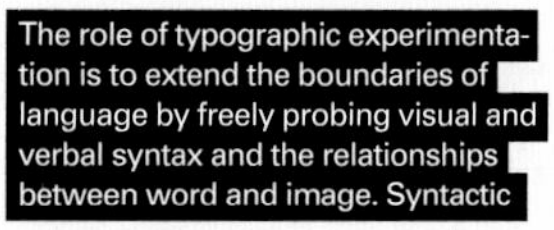


228 | **4.2.3** background

229 | **4.2.4** adjacent

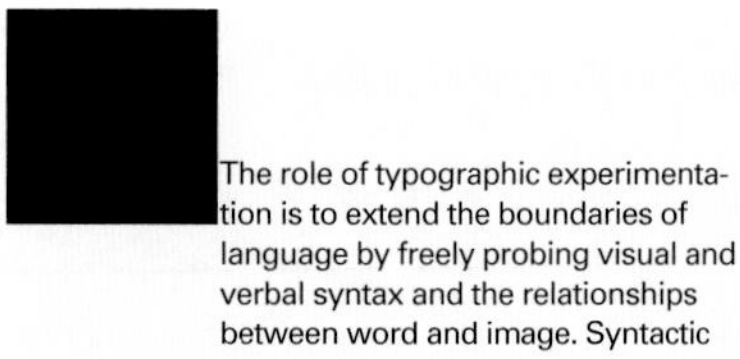


230 | **4.2.4** adjacent

231 | **4.2.5** combination

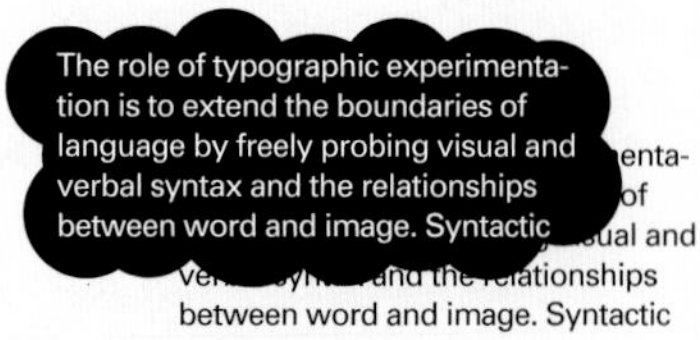


232 | **4.2.5** combination

## 4.3 Symbols

Symbols, including dingbats, fleurons, and isotypes, can be used as support elements to augment type, or to stand alone as part of a typographic composition. Symbols are often designed to accompany a specific font, and can be used with or without further computer manipulation. Inventively altering symbols with the aid of a computer provides pleasing and unexpected results.

---

**✱type**

233 | **4.3.1** normal

✱The role of typographic experimentation is to extend the boundaries of language by freely probing visual and verbal syntax and the relationships between word and image. Syntactic

234 | **4.3.1** normal

**✱type**

235 | **4.3.2** manipulated

✱ The role of typographic experimentation is to extend the boundaries of language by freely probing visual and verbal syntax and the relationships between word and image. Syntactic

236 | **4.3.2** manipulated

**"type"**

237 | **4.3.1** normal

"The role of typographic experimentation is to extend the boundaries of language by freely probing visual and verbal syntax and the relationships between word and image."

238 | **4.3.1** normal

**"type"**

239 | **4.3.2** manipulated

" The role of typographic experimentation is to extend the boundaries of language by freely probing visual and verbal syntax and the relationships between word and image. "

240 | **4.3.2** manipulated

## 4.4 Images

Images may appear as backgrounds (figs. **241, 242**), or adjacent elements (figs. **243, 244**), or may be contained within letters and words (figs. **245, 246**). They may be presented normally, distorted in various ways by means of computer software, and/or color manipulated. For comparison, figures **247-256** illustrate various computer manipulations of the same photograph.

241 **4.4.1** background

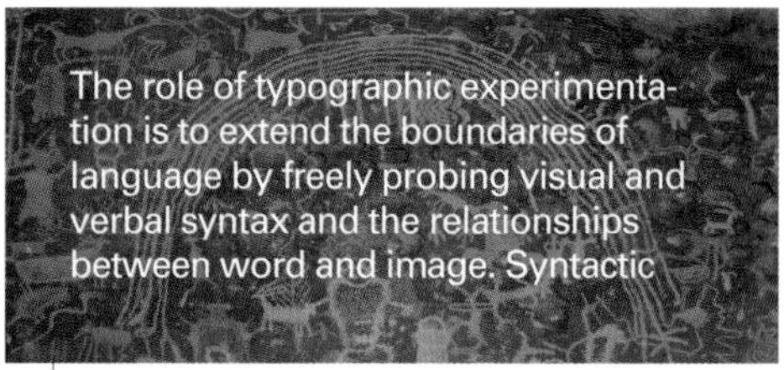


242 **4.4.1** background

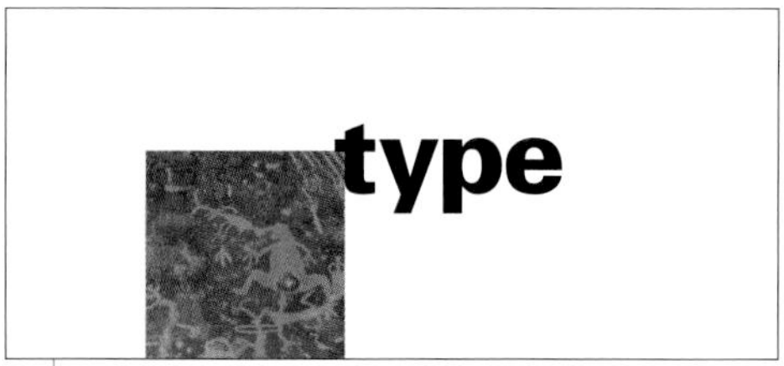


243 **4.4.2** adjacent

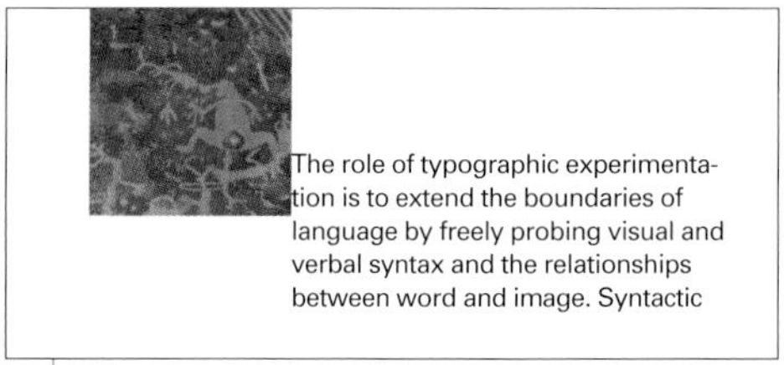


244 **4.4.2** adjacent

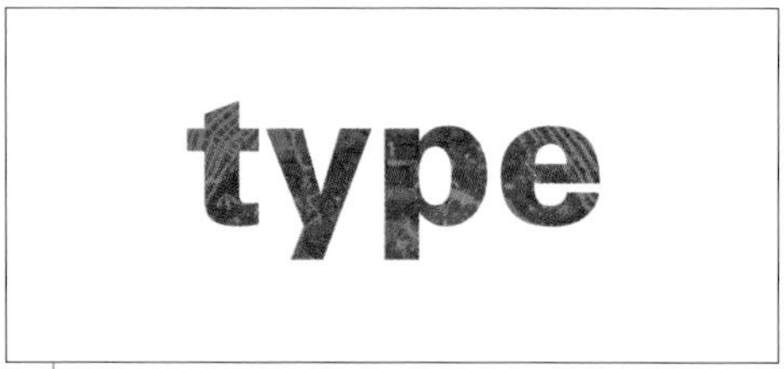


245 **4.4.3** contained

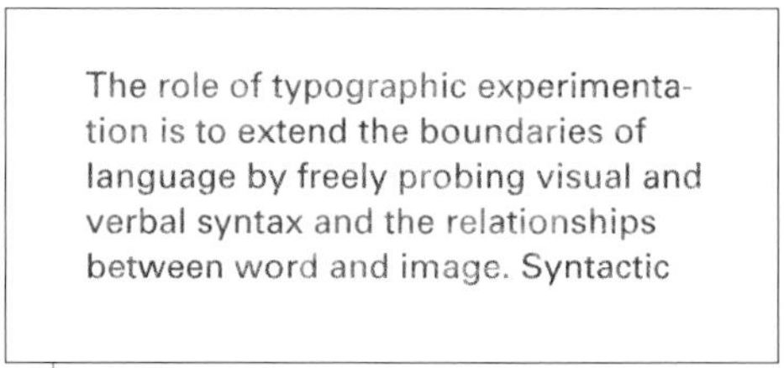


246 **4.4.3** contained

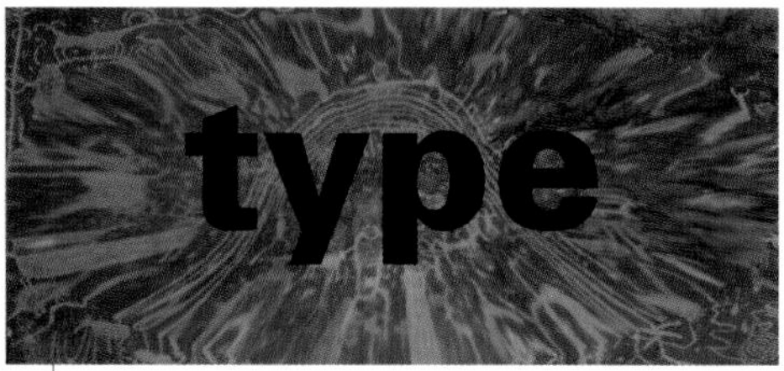


247 **4.4.4** manipulated

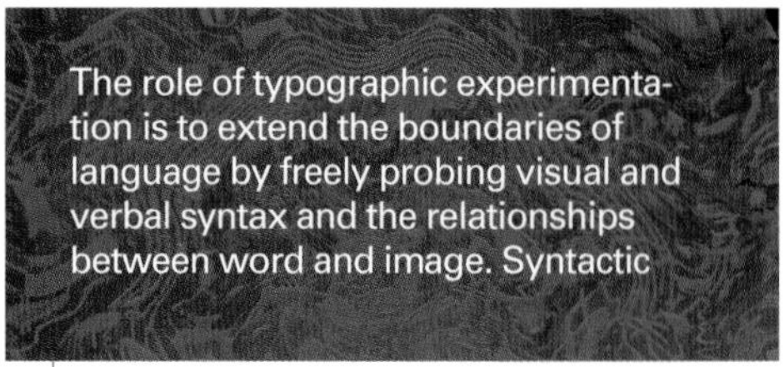


248 **4.4.4** manipulated

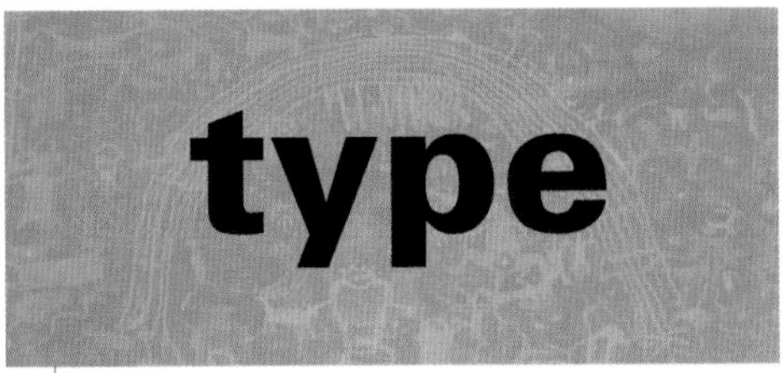


249 **4.4.4** manipulated

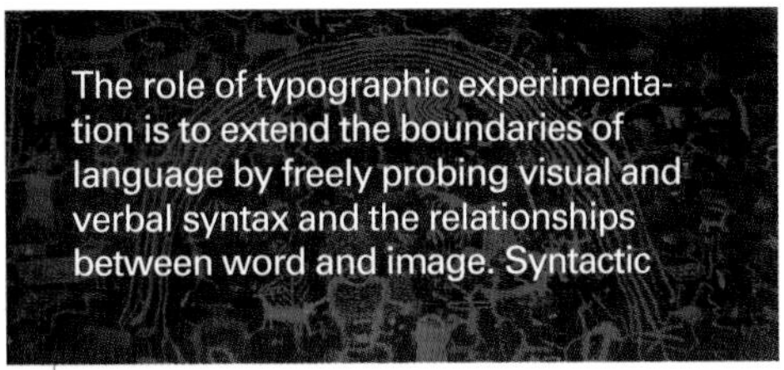


250 **4.4.4** manipulated

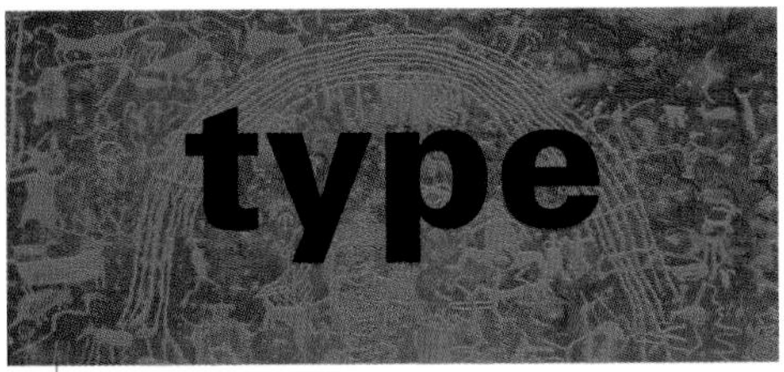


251 **4.4.4** manipulated

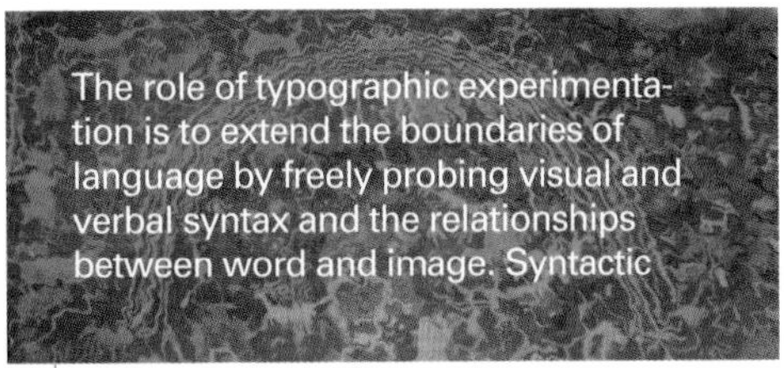


252 **4.4.4** manipulated

253 **4.4.4** manipulated

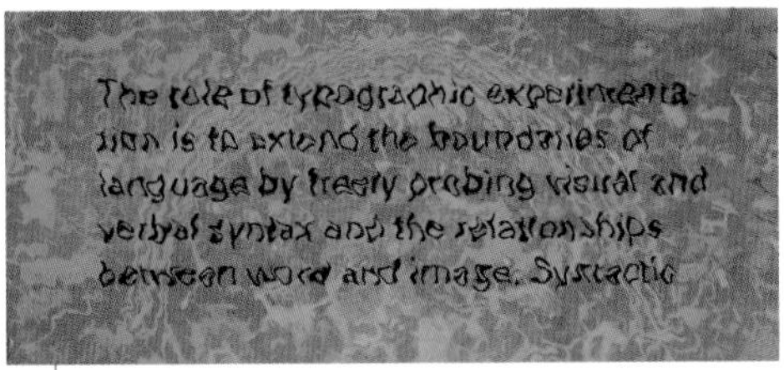

254 **4.4.4** manipulated

255 **4.4.5** combination

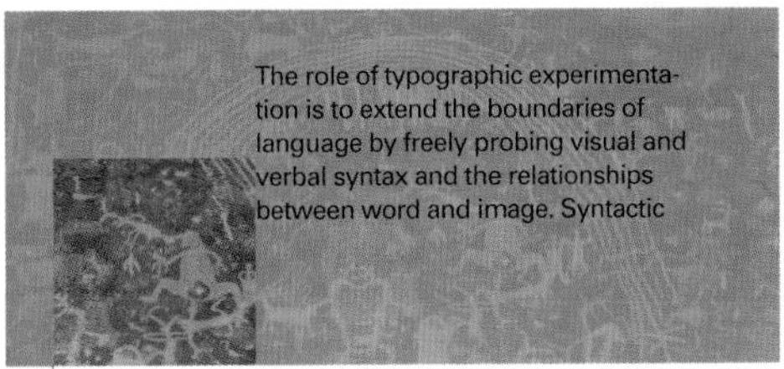


256 **4.4.5** combination

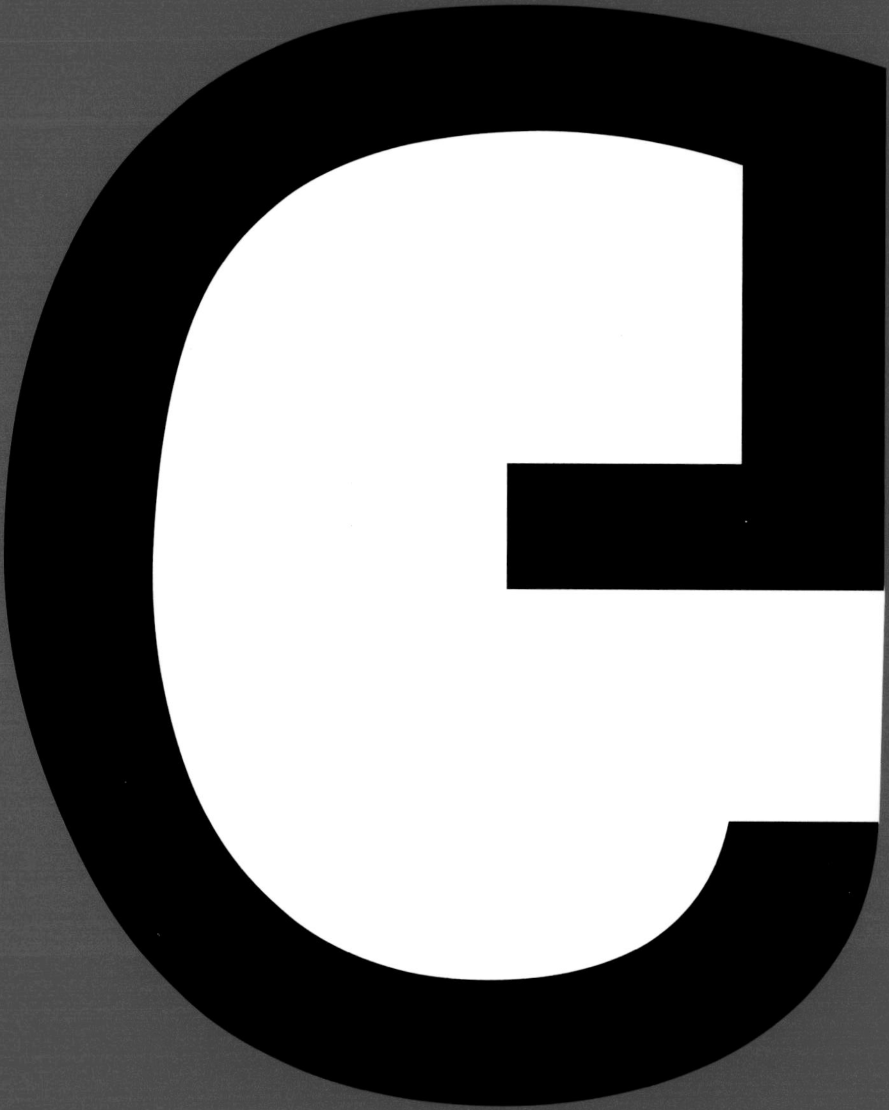

# Typographical journey

3

# Typographical journey

An experimental typography course taught by the author at Virginia Commonwealth University is the focus of this chapter. You will observe how the morphological factors presented in the previous chapter are interpreted and investigated by individual students. Only the most significant factors of each investigation are mentioned, and these are cross-referenced by number to the morphology on page 25.

In the chapter's first section, student designer Minh Ta takes you on a fascinating journey of typographic exploration. The processes and thinking in which he engaged are unfolded as you move through the pages. A few things regarding the designer's journey should be mentioned. The pages contain preliminary sketches of typographic explorations as well as final computer realizations. Students are encouraged to make trace sketches of ideas before going to the computer. It is interesting to compare the sketches with final computer output. The designer identifies his sketches, which appear in black and white, with broken outlines. The final computer-generated plates are printed in full color and are bordered by solid ruled lines. Numerals referencing the morphological chart are connected to the plates by dotted lines. Significant details are explained with descriptive captions. Finally, this journey is a typographic exploration in and of itself. Be prepared for challenging, unconventional reading and a kinetic visual experience.

The second part of the chapter features a portfolio of experiments by selected students from the class. These also are keyed to the morphology in Chapter 2.

Project brief:

explore

unfamiliar regions

pioneer the unknown

[maps not necessary]

word as image

see/feel/hear/touch:

the sensuous curve of an s

the intersection of an x

nuance of

point

line

plane

surface

edge

texture

modulation

type as metaphor:

love song

city

galaxy

jazz orchestra

threering circus

starry night

meandering river

scream

whisper

new form +

new content +

new expression

Make 20 typographical explorations based on the factors in the accompanying morphology. Freely explore all of the factors in each of the four categories, but for each composition, focus specifically upon selected variables. One exploration, for example, might focus upon 1.3.1, 2.7.2, and 3.1.2, while another might concentrate upon 1.1.1, 1.6.3, 2.5.2, and 3.4.3. Strive for as much diversity in your investigations as possible.

Use three elements for all explorations:

single letter (point): any
word (line): "type"
text (plane): as provided.

The size of the compositional space for each investigation is 8 x 8 inches.

Make preliminary idea sketches on trace as well as on the computer. Select and use software as appropriate.

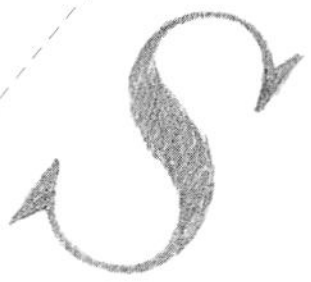

3.1.2

1.2.1

1.4.2

The role of typographic experimentation is to extend the boundaries of language by freely probing visual and verbal syntax and the relationships between word and image.
As in other forms of language typography is capable of infinite expression.
Syntactic exploration enables designers to discover among typographic media an enormous potential to edify, entertain and surprise.
S
type
The only limits to typographic discovery are those imposed by the designer herself

This plate focuses on visual clarity, where concentration is reserved for the experimentation of lower- and upper-case letters, a serif typeface, and various type sizes.

1.3.4

1.1.3

1.2.1

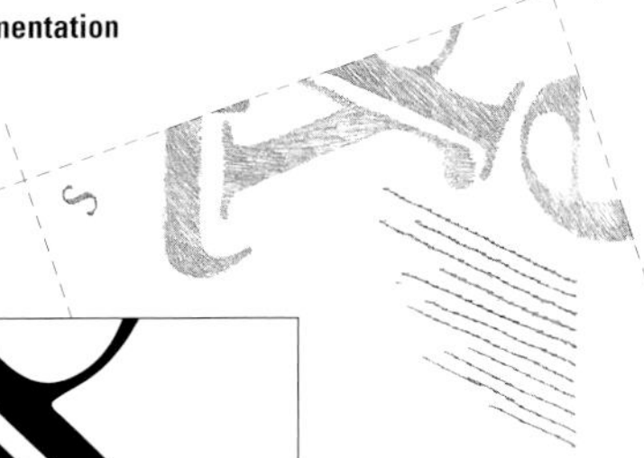

the role of typographic experimentation is to extend
the boundaries of language by freely probing
visual and verbal syntax and the
relationships between word and image
syntactic exploration enables designers to discover
among typographic media an enormous potential
to edify, entertain and surprise
as in other forms of language typography
is capable of infinite expression
the only limits to typographic discovery are
those imposed by the designer herself

This composition relies on the formal qualities of a serif face to establish the structure of the word *type* and in turn, to influence the placement of the letter *s* and the supporting text. Moderately slanting these elements creates a subtle directional emphasis. Positioning the letters to the upper right encourages asymmetrical balance and a restful negative space.

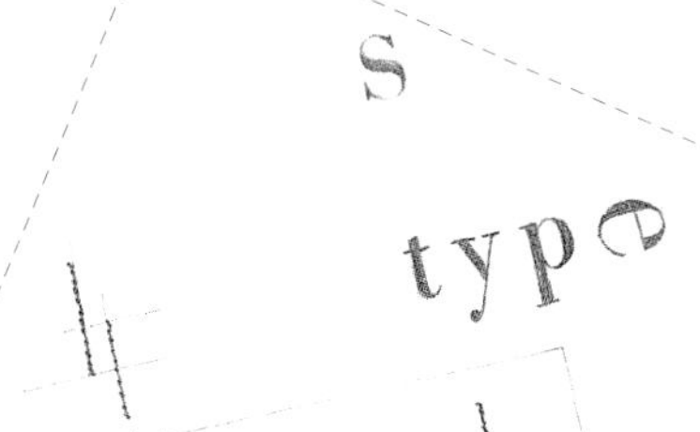

Adhering to a diagonal grid creates a format that is regular and consistent.

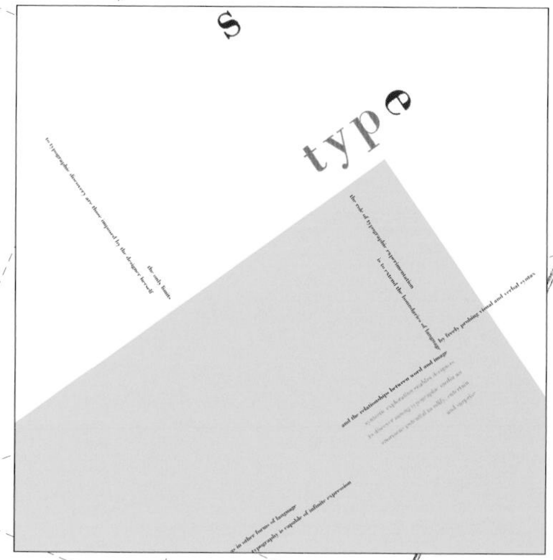

Diagonal direction is not only evident in this study, but a visual depth is also perceived. This dimensionality is established by applying an extreme slant and a moderate rotation to the visual components.

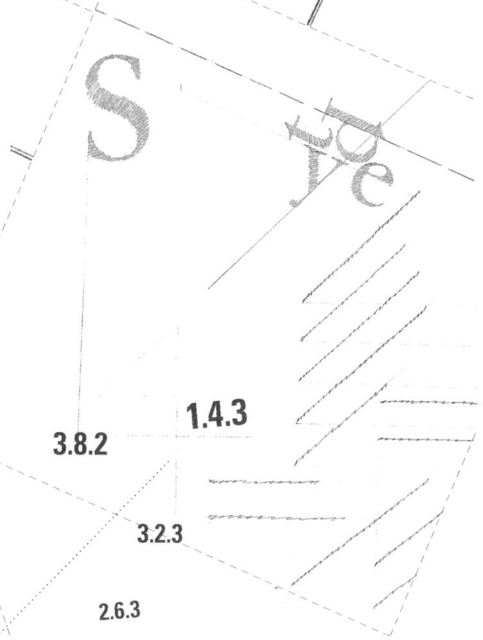

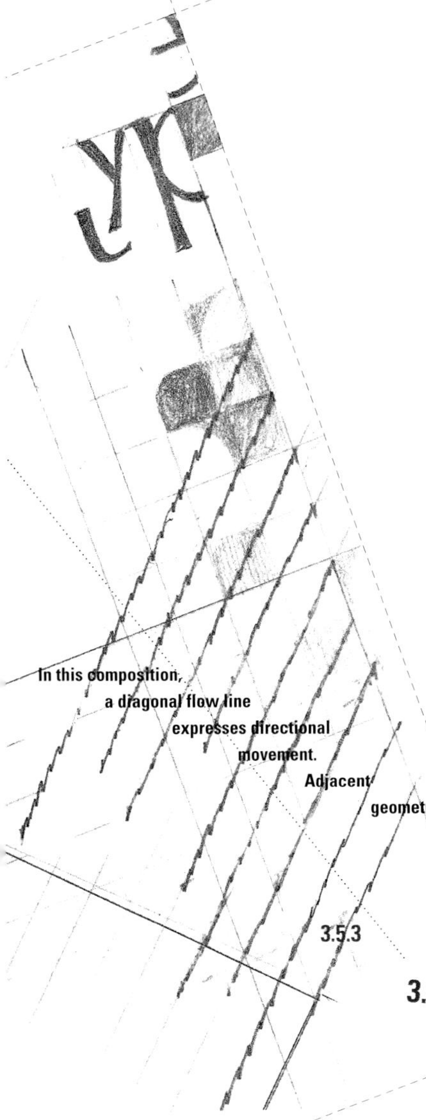

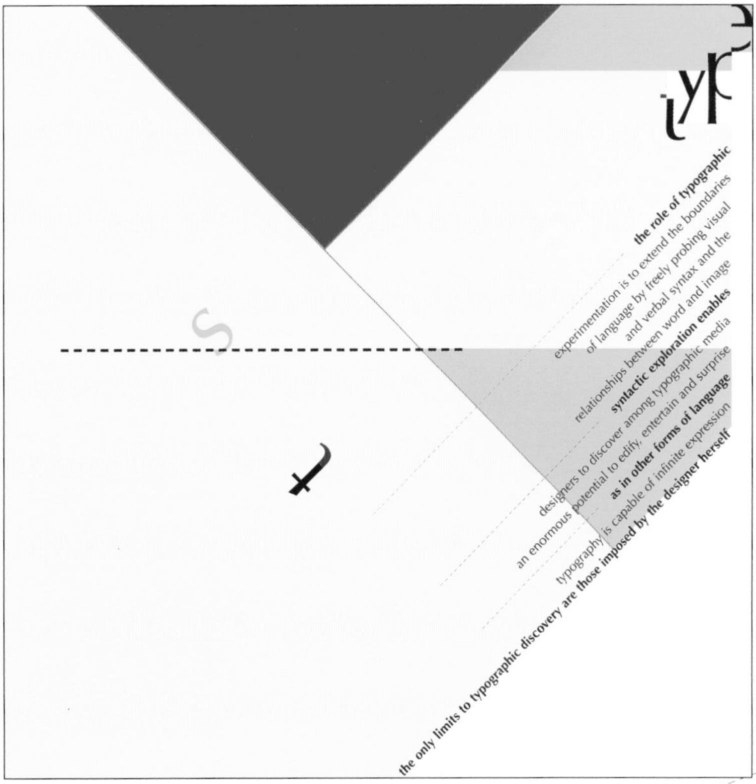
ype
s
t
the role of typographic
experimentation is to extend the boundaries
of language by freely probing visual
and verbal syntax and the
relationships between word and image
syntactic exploration enables
designers to discover among typographic media
an enormous potential to edify, entertain and surprise
as in other forms of language
typography is capable of infinite expression
the only limits to typographic discovery are those imposed by the designer herself

In this composition, a diagonal flow line expresses directional movement. Adjacent geometric shapes provide the foundation for the composition's structure, while lines are used as support elements. A counterpoint to the directional flow of the elements is a dashed line that crosses boldly through the horizontal axis of the plane. A consequence of this action is visual spontaneity.

1.1.3

3.5.3

3.2.3

3.2.3

3.1.2

4.2.1

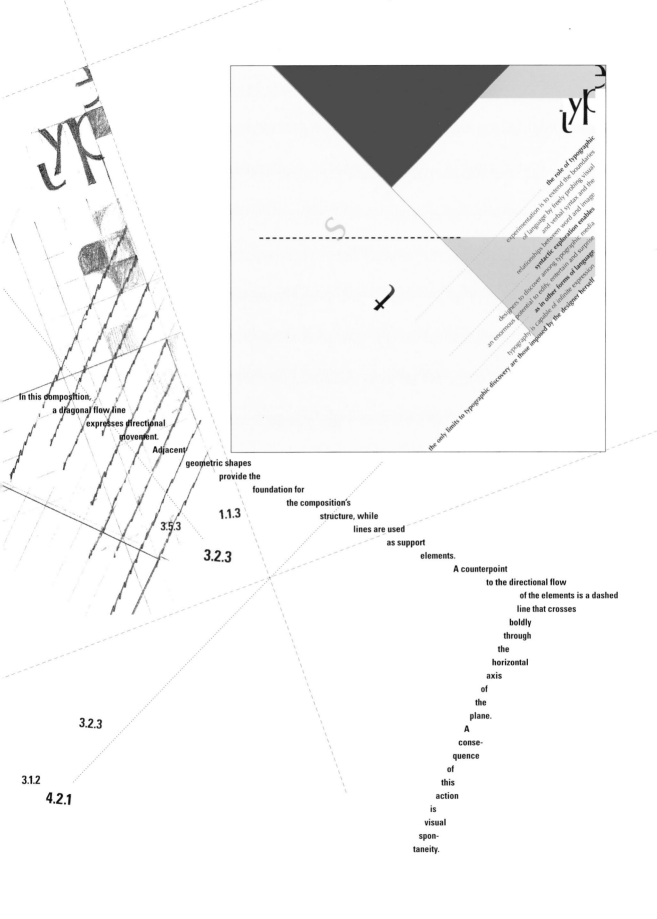

**Two different varieties of distortion appear in this work,
and are realized by means of PhotoShop software.
Mezzotinting the letter *s* and slightly blurring the word *type* add a
level of complexity to the clean design, which is shaped by its basic geometric construction
Cropping the two manipulated elements intensifies the geometry by creating imaginary
edges that divide the space**

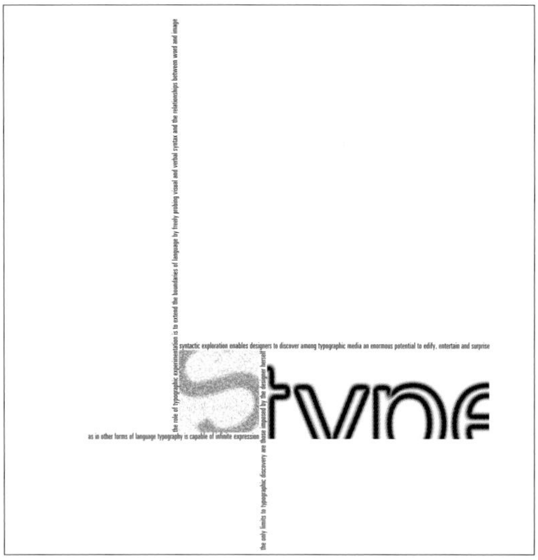
syntactic exploration enables designers to discover among typographic media an enormous potential to edify, entertain and surprise
as in other forms of language typography is capable of infinite expression
type

4.2.1

2.2.8

2.3.2

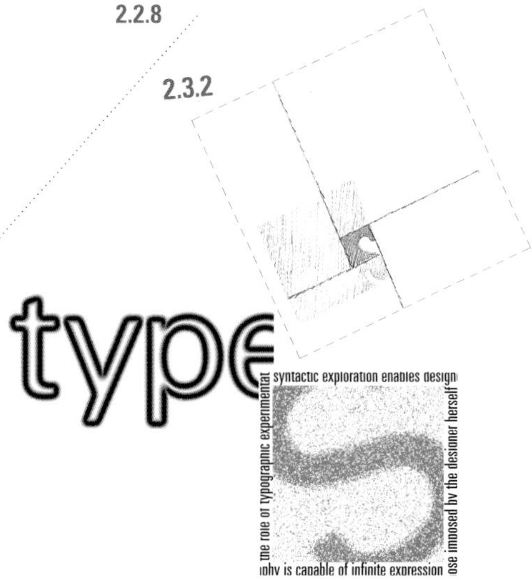


**The focal point
is the
mezzotinted *s*,
which
expresses
the
coarse
quality
of texture.**

**To manipulate a form
by the simplest gesture
and still maintain its legibility is a most basic concern.
The inversion of selected letters of various weights in this design
still permits recognition of the word *type.*
Also apparent is the irregular visual rhythm
expressed by the text through different point sizes
and vertical alignments.**

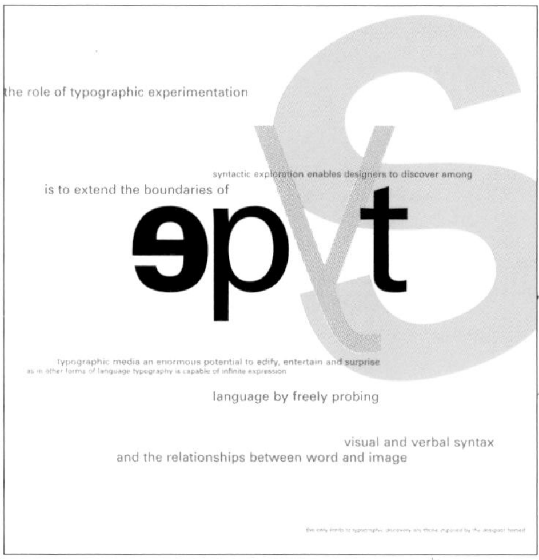

1.5.4

3.7.2

1.3.4

2.2.6

the role of typographic experimentation
freely probing visual and verbal syntax
typography
is capable of
infinite expression
the only limits to
typographic discovery
are those imposed by the designer

**A harmonious relationship between progressive rhythm and circular motion is realized in the study. Diagonal ruled lines differing in weight and length intensify the rhythmic progression, while the thin, outlined *s* kinetically unites the composition with organic arcs.**

**2.4.1**

**3.7.4**

**3.2.4**

**4.1.9**

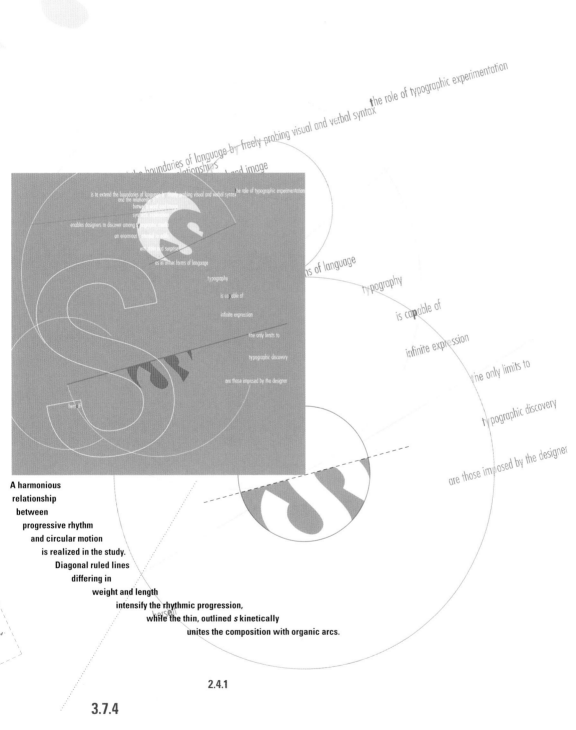

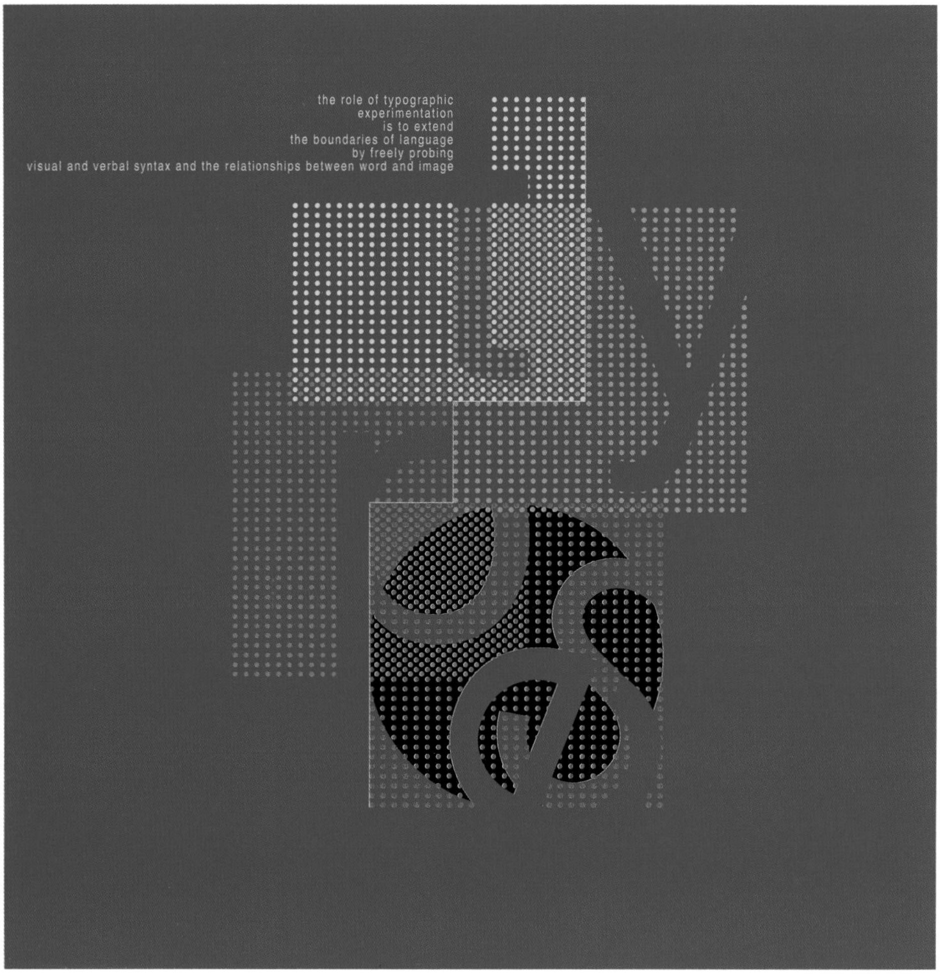
the role of typographic
experimentation
is to extend
the boundaries of language
by freely probing
visual and verbal syntax and the relationships between word and image

This study is derived from
a repetition of dots whose
close proximity
shapes the squares.
The result is a
geometric pattern
combined with
typographic
characters.
The complexity
of the structure
is organized
and unified
by a stair-
stepped line
that divides
the composition
into halves.

3.2.3

3.4.1

4.4.1

4.2.1

3.5.1

4.1.5

3.1.3

# type

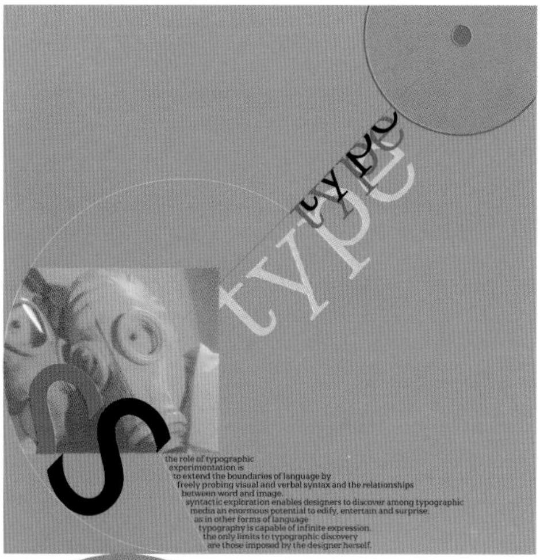
type
type
s
the role of typographic
experimentation is
to extend the boundaries of language by
freely probing visual and verbal syntax and the relationships
between word and image.
syntactic exploration enables designers to discover among typographic
media an enormous potential to edify, entertain and surprise.
as in other forms of language
typography is capable of infinite expression.
the only limits to typographic discovery
are those imposed by the designer herself.

**A unification of type and image is achieved by means of a linear arc that connects the elements. The mysterious figures in the photo are accented and mimicked by a pair of *s* letterforms; one is cropped, the other is seen in its entirety.**

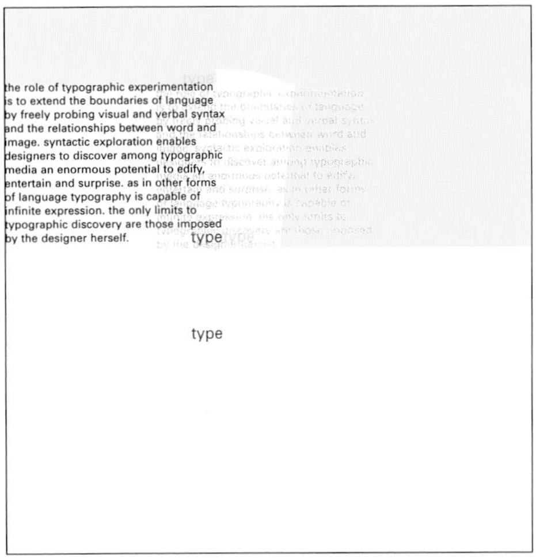
the role of typographic experimentation is to extend the boundaries of language by freely probing visual and verbal syntax and the relationships between word and image. syntactic exploration enables designers to discover among typographic media an enormous potential to edify, entertain and surprise. as in other forms of language typography is capable of infinite expression. the only limits to typographic discovery are those imposed by the designer herself.
type
type

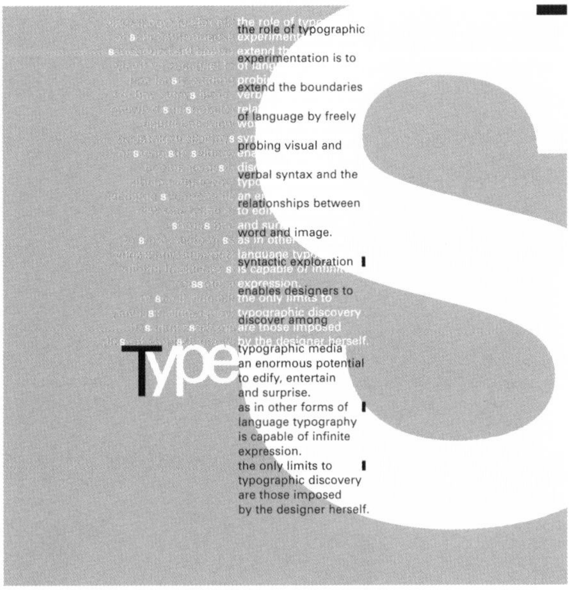
Type
the role of typographic experimentation is to extend the boundaries of language by freely probing visual and verbal syntax and the relationships between word and image.
syntactic exploration enables designers to discover among typographic media an enormous potential to edify, entertain and surprise.
as in other forms of language typography is capable of infinite expression.
the only limits to typographic discovery are those imposed by the designer herself.

All compositions are a blend of spatial articulation and form manipulation. In this example, text is repeated to touch and overlap the fragmented *s*. The irregular background shape divides the space into two distinct regions.

This design's utter dedication to consonant grouping is evident. Each constituent element is aligned to the next for a centralized unity. The informal field of *s* letters stands in contrast to the more rigid column of text. Alternative rhythm is achieved by modifying the leading in the body of text.

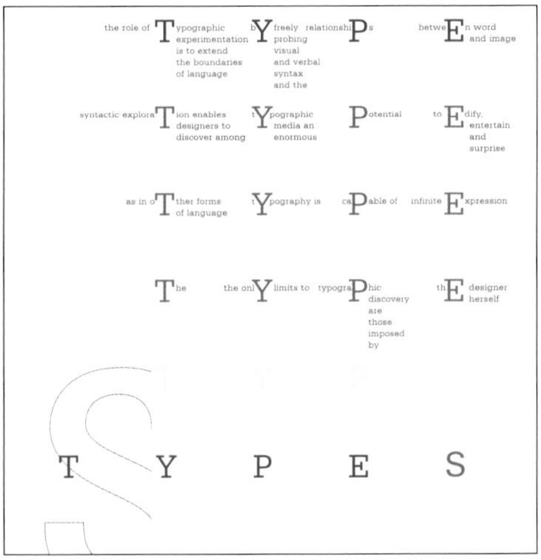
T Y P E S

Typographic elements are organized by separating them into ordered groups. The square shape formed by the repeated word *type* casts a soft shadow, seen below and to the left as a color tint. Identical in size, this device implies dimensionality. The use of upper-case and lower-case letters accentuates the division between top and bottom layers.

2.2.1
4.2.1
3.5.4
3.6.1
3.1.1
3.5.1
4.1.2
2.2.8
1.1.3
3.5.3
2.6.2

3.7.4

2.2.1 **3.2.4**

3.1.3

**In this study, dynamic symmetry is a manifestation of the concentric circles. The circular paths of text zoom progressively out from a center point in the composition.**

3.6.2

3.4.1

3.7.3

**The asymmetrical placement of the secondary components is significant, for it counterbalances the strong circular pattern.**

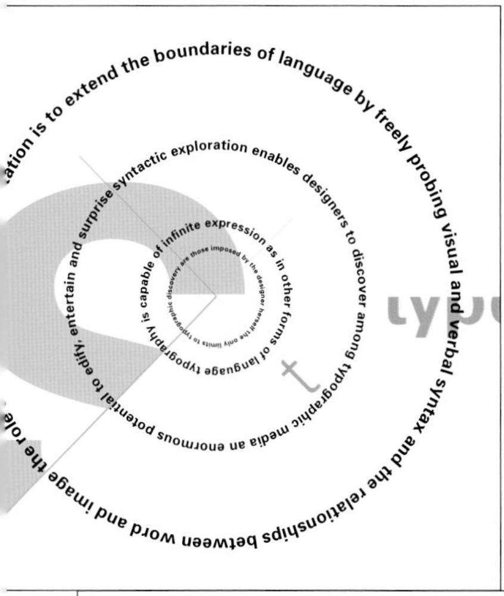

the role of typographic experimentation is to extend the boundaries of language by freely probing visual and verbal syntax and the relationships between word and image
syntactic exploration enables designers to discover among typographic media an enormous potential to edify, entertain and surprise
as in other forms of language typography is capable of infinite expression
type

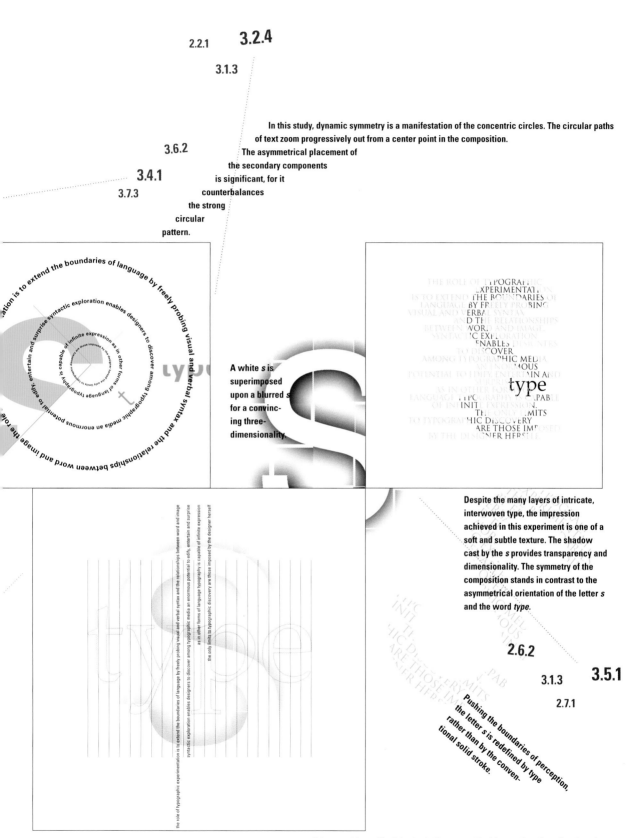

**A white *s* is superimposed upon a blurred *s* for a convincing three-dimensionality.**

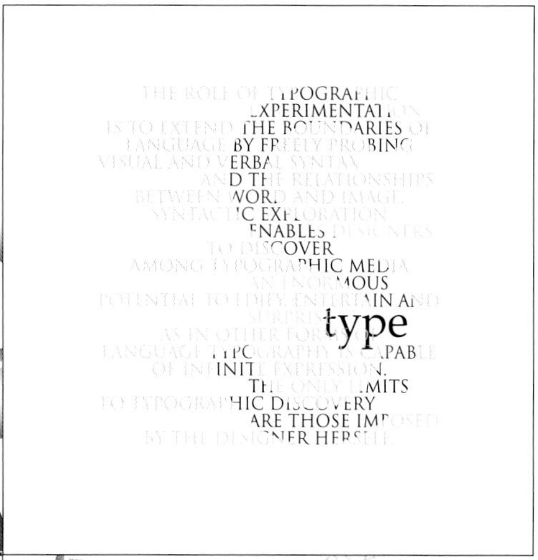

type

**Despite the many layers of intricate, interwoven type, the impression achieved in this experiment is one of a soft and subtle texture. The shadow cast by the *s* provides transparency and dimensionality. The symmetry of the composition stands in contrast to the asymmetrical orientation of the letter *s* and the word *type*.**

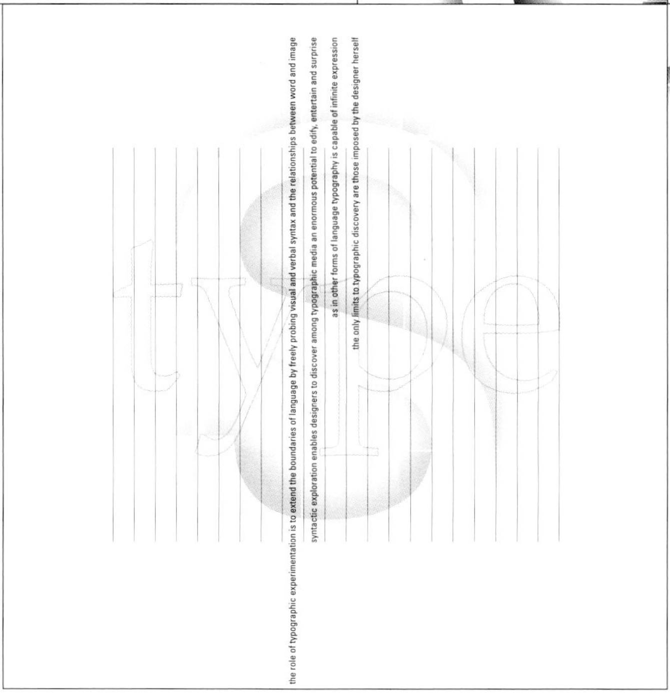

the role of typographic experimentation is to extend the boundaries of language by freely probing visual and verbal syntax and the relationships between word and image
syntactic exploration enables designers to discover among typographic media an enormous potential to edify, entertain and surprise
as in other forms of language typography is capable of infinite expression
the only limits to typographic discovery are those imposed by the designer herself
type

2.6.2

3.1.3 **3.5.1**

2.7.1

**Pushing the boundaries of perception, the letter *s* is redefined by type rather than by the conventional solid stroke.**

**A typographic motif originates in the symmetrical interaction of overlapping elements. A transparent screen of ruled lines mingles with the tiles in the background, suggesting the existence of a second ground.**

2.1.1

3.1.2

3.6.1

3.5.4

A visual constellation consists of interdependent parts that, when suspended in space, form a Gestalt. The constellation in the adjacent experiment consists of a relaxed text block and a rigid repetition of words that form a harmonious duet.

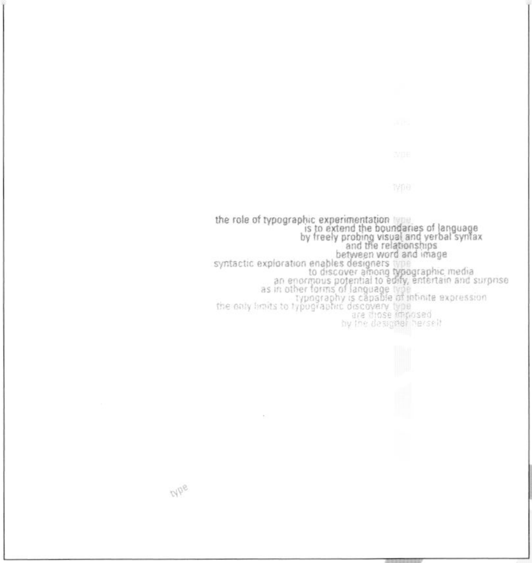


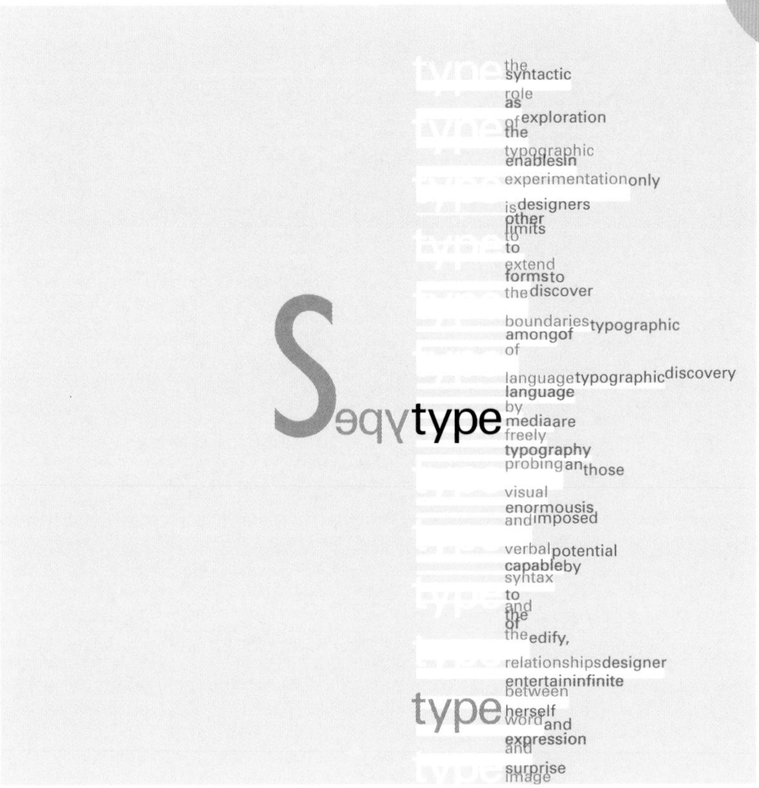


Unique design can arise from the simplest of devices.

As in this example, flushing text to the left and severely reducing the number of words per line arouse visual interest.

Compositional tension increases as sentences are aligned along a vertical reading path.

**Typographic rhythms are established by controlling the spatial intervals between letters, words and lines. Progressive rhythms result when spatial intervals between typographic elements assume a graded arrangement.**

2.7.1

3.1.2

3.4.3

3.5.4

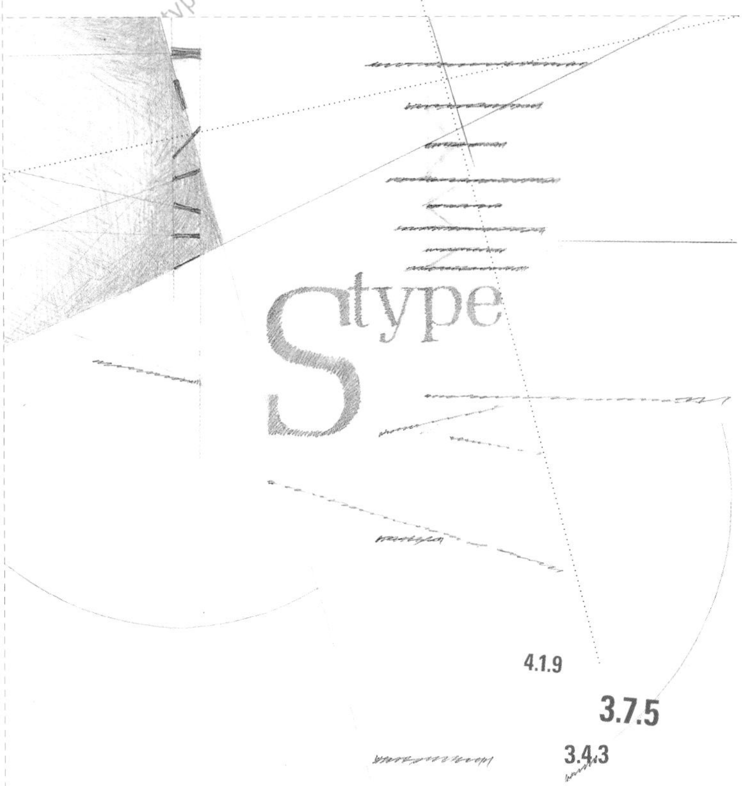


4.1.9

3.7.5

3.4.3

3.1.3

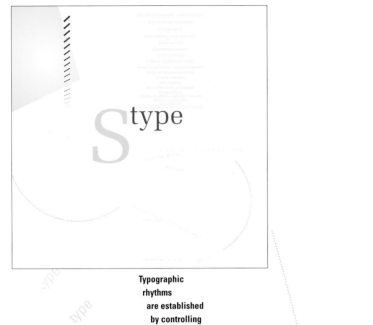

2.1.2

3.1.2

3.2.3

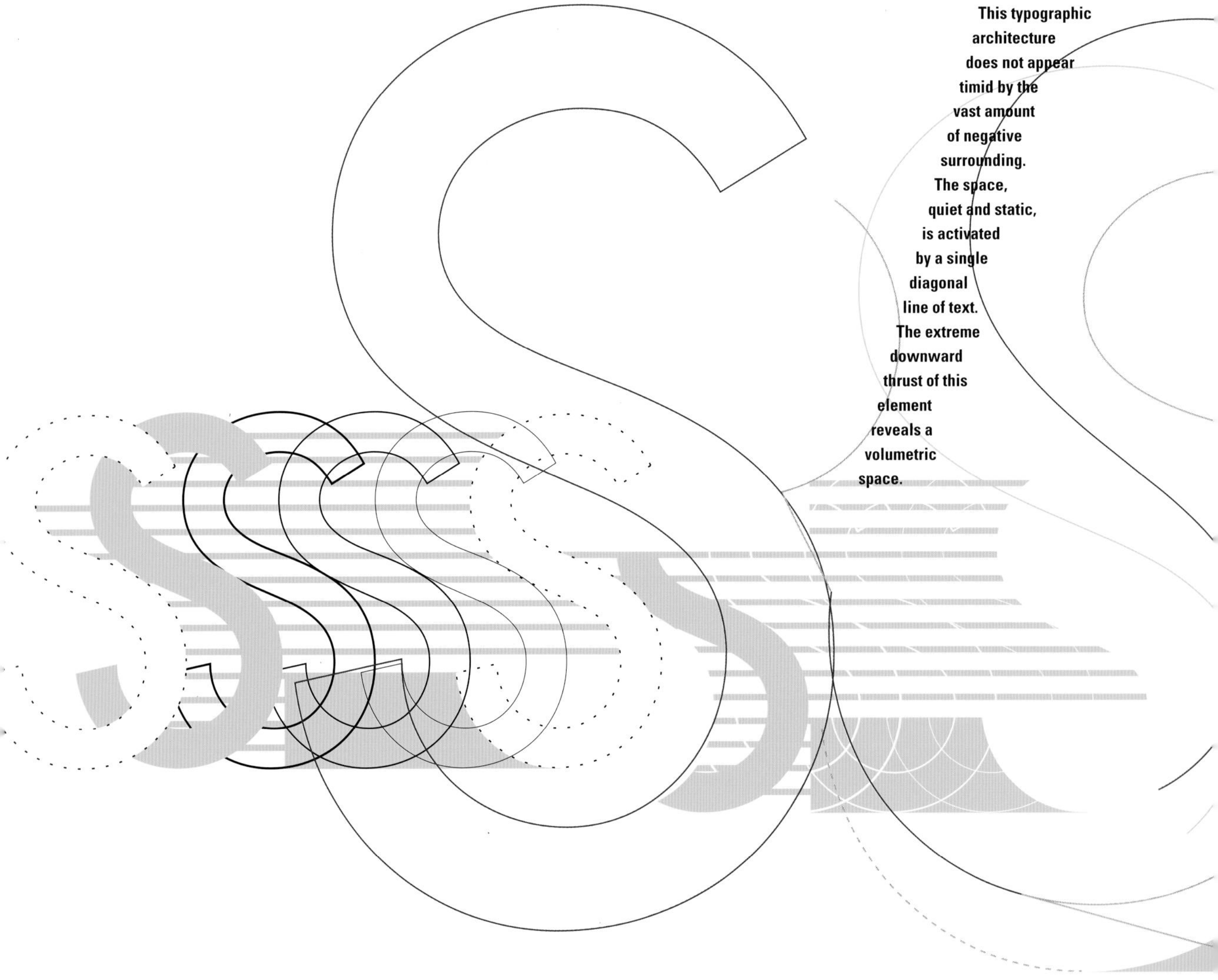

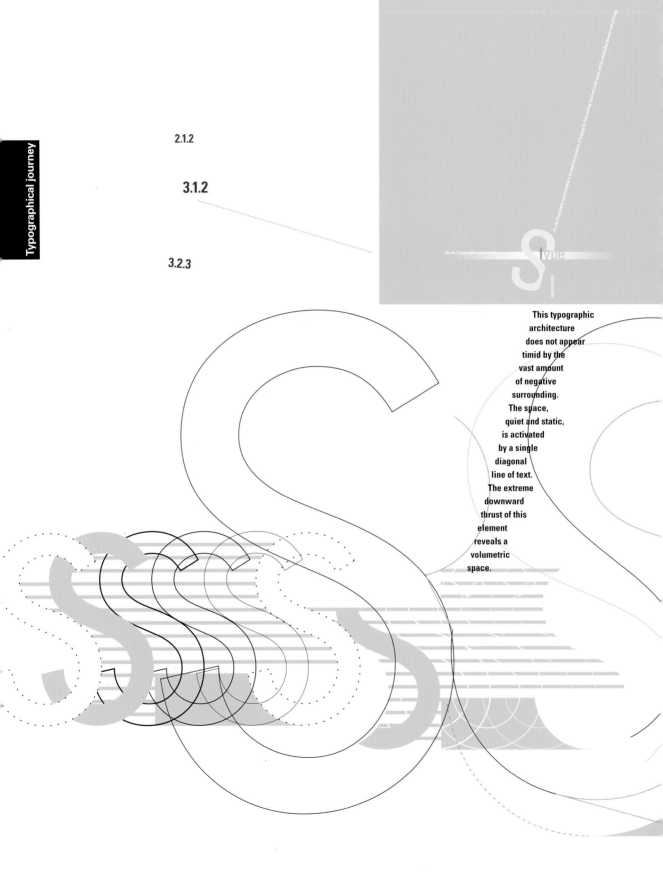

This typographic architecture does not appear timid by the vast amount of negative surrounding. The space, quiet and static, is activated by a single diagonal line of text. The extreme downward thrust of this element reveals a volumetric space.

Text and ruled lines
separated by equal
intervals of space
are densely
packed to
reveal an
irregular
texture
and
rhythm.
The effect is pleasingly ambiguous;
one senses order amidst the chaos.

type

3.6.3

2.5.4

3.5.1

2.3.4

Though the
characters
in the
word *type*
are frag-
mented,
reduced,
and sub-
stituted
with mathe-
matical
symbols,
the word
remains
readable.
The *y* is
a curious
combination
of a symbol
and a
curving
line of text.

the only limits to typographic discovery are those imposed by the designer herself

3.4.3

2.3.2

2.2.1

3.1.2

4.3.1

2.3.2

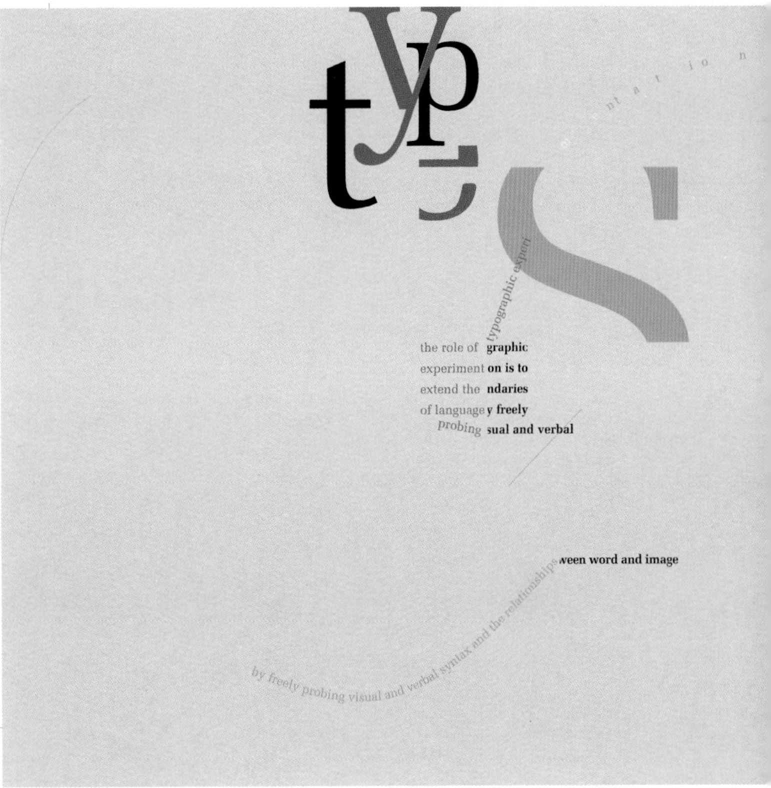

typographic experi
the role of graphic
experiment on is to
extend the ndaries
of language y freely
probing sual and verbal
ween word and image
by freely probing visual and verbal syntax and the relationships


While at first glance
this composition
appears fragmented
and discordant,
further observation
reveals a deliberate
positioning of parts.
The alignment of the
edges of the characters
and text provides an
orderly structure that
belies the disheveled
appearance. The directional
attributes of the elements move
the eye in a circular path through the
composition.

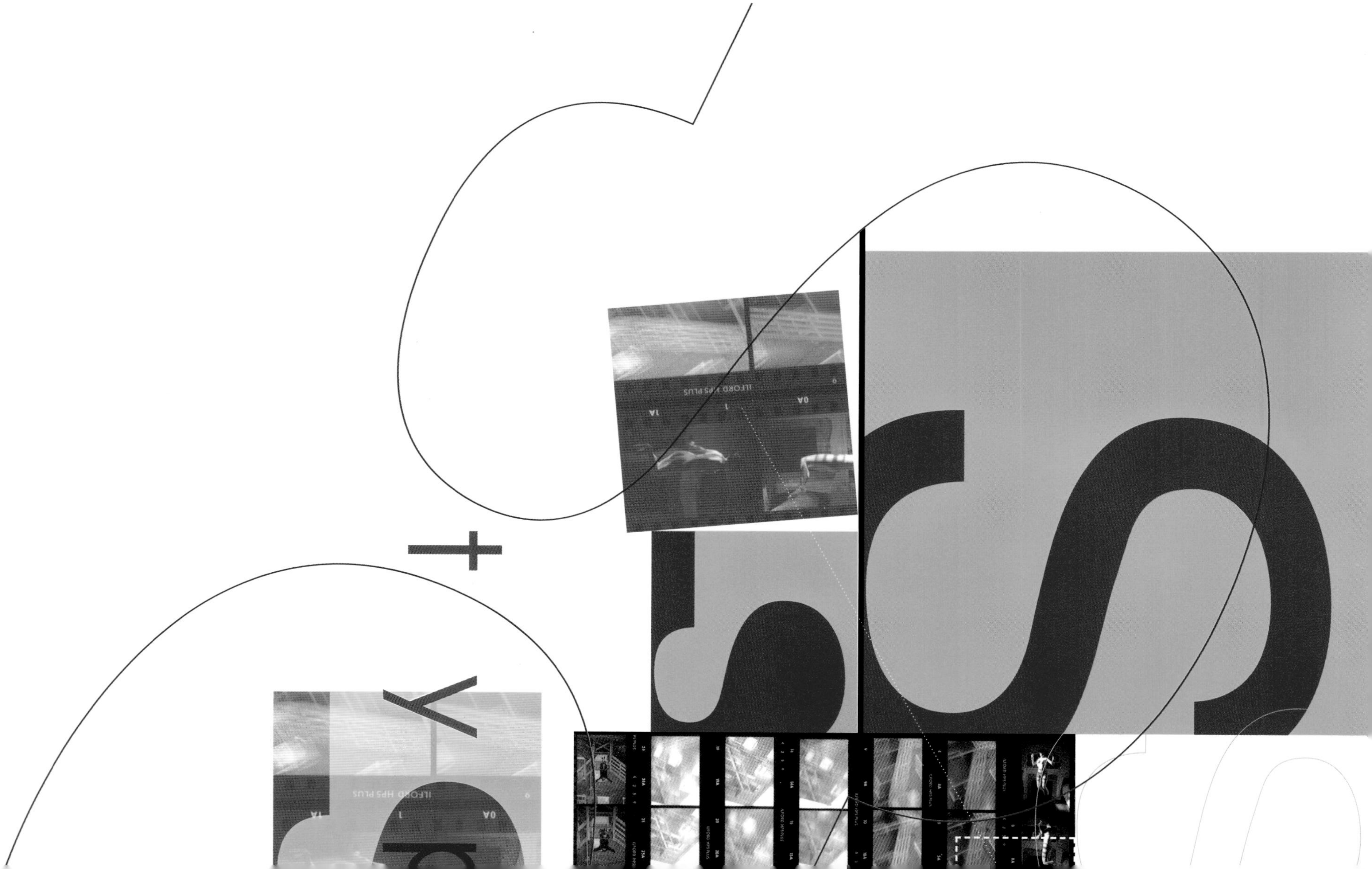
ILFORD HP5 PLUS

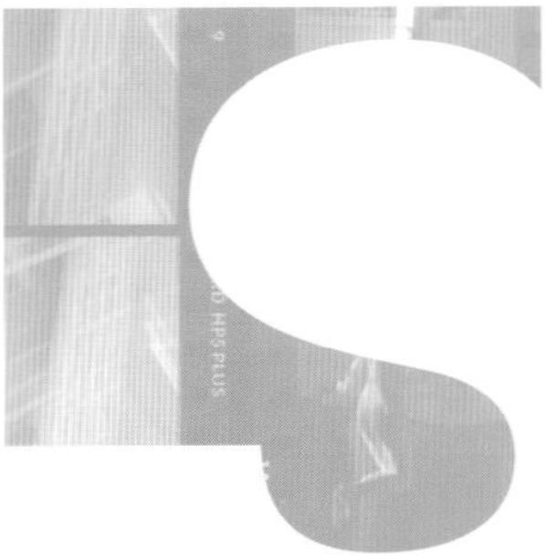

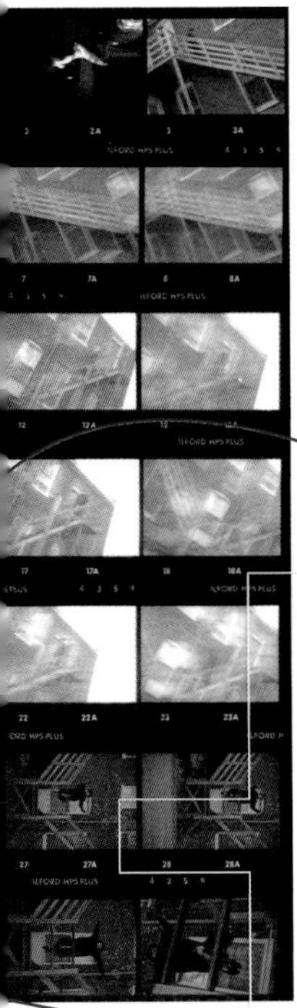

the role of typographic experimentation is to extend the boundaries of language by freely probing visual and verbal syntax and the relationships between word and image
syntactic exploration enables designers to discover among typographic media an enormous potential to edify, entertain and surprise
as in other forms of language typography is capable of infinite expression
the only limits to typographic discovery are those imposed by the designer herself
ILFORD HP5 PLUS

e

**Dependent on the sensuous silhouetted *s* as the foundation from which organic shapes evolve, this experiment explores elaboration as the primary design factor. Not only is the *s* form reduced from its original structure, its final shape is resolved with the addition of transparent imagery.**

4.2.2

2.5.1

2.3.4

4.4.1

Computer manipulation energizes the letterform.

Rippling and blurring effects.

Here, the procedure is to produce an active plane of type by separating the text into active groups. Repetition of vertical dashes, progressing from thick to thin, rhythmically slice through the space. The dissonant grouping of words and lines produces an energetic and irregular visual field.

3.7.2

3.5.1

2.5.2

A font possessing a boxed frame for each of its individual letters comprises the main text. The diagonal placement of the text is reminiscent of an architectural layout. Supporting this angular layout is a square of moving cubes with an imprinted *s*. A thin vertical line plays off the predictability of the composition's directional structure.

typographic experimentation

3.6.2

3.7.2 3.5.3 4.1.2

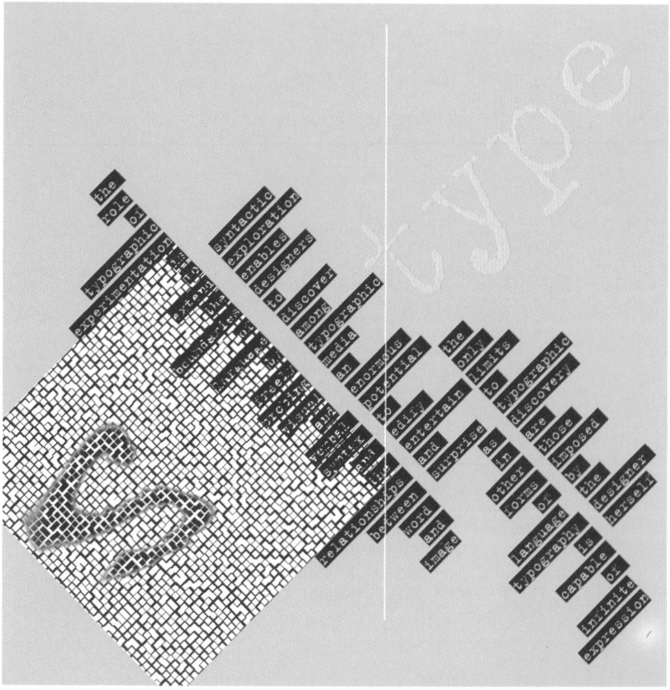

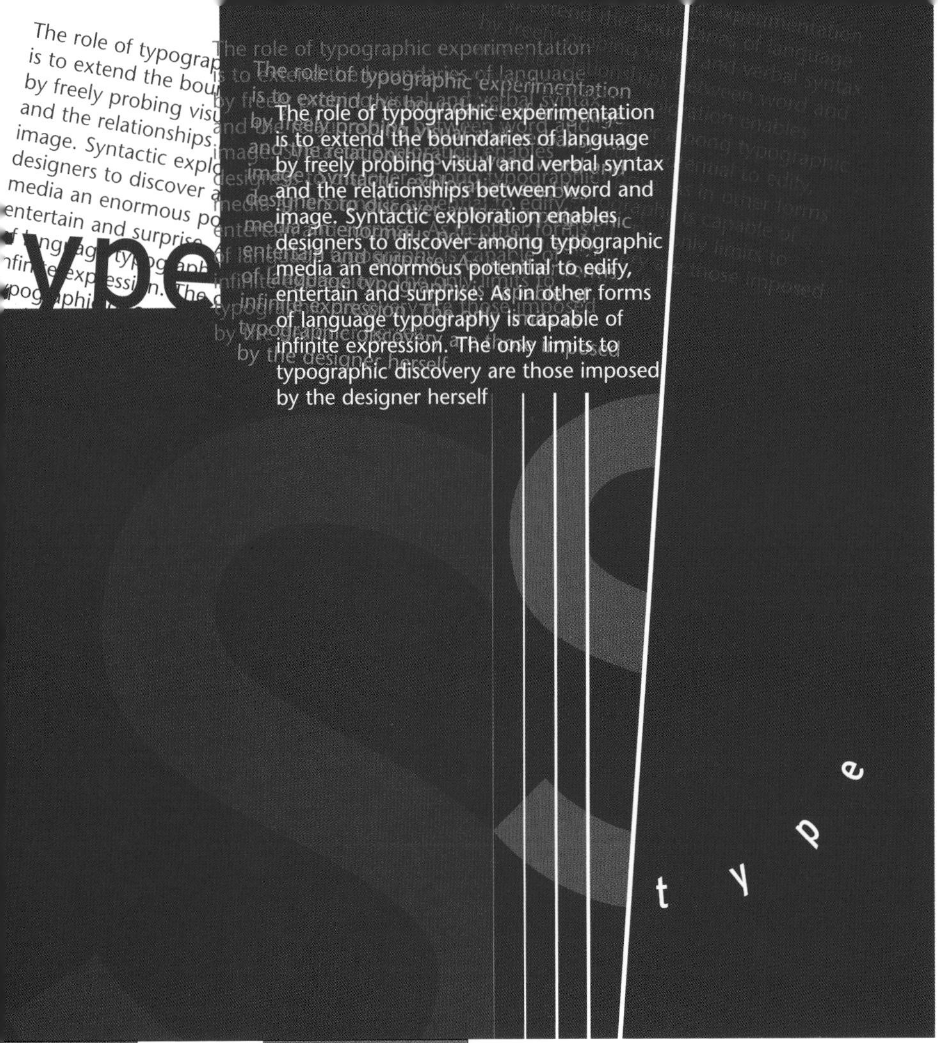
The role of typographic experimentation is to extend the boundaries of language by freely probing visual and verbal syntax and the relationships between word and image. Syntactic exploration enables designers to discover among typographic media an enormous potential to edify, entertain and surprise. As in other forms of language typography is capable of infinite expression. The only limits to typographic discovery are those imposed by the designer herself
type
type

Overlapping text generally provides a design with a tactile quality. Here, where the text is overlaid, the texture is coarse and the rhythm is rough. The irregular sequence of the text, however, stands in contrast to the elegant spaces defined by the counterforms of the letters *s*, and the marching vertical lines.

2.2.4
3.3.3
3.1.3

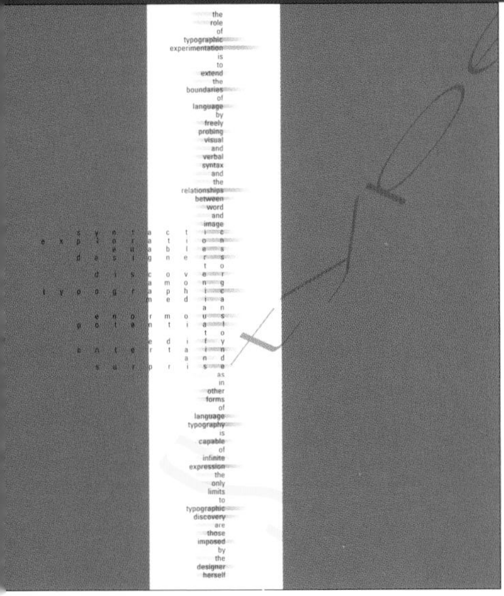

The backgrounds upon which the compositional elements cross and interrelate advance and recede. Distinguishing which ground is positive and which is negative is purposefully unresolved. Although predominantly symmetrical, the composition also implies asymmetry due to a carefully balanced placement of elements on either side of the design's central axis.

2.2.8
3.2.3
1.2.4

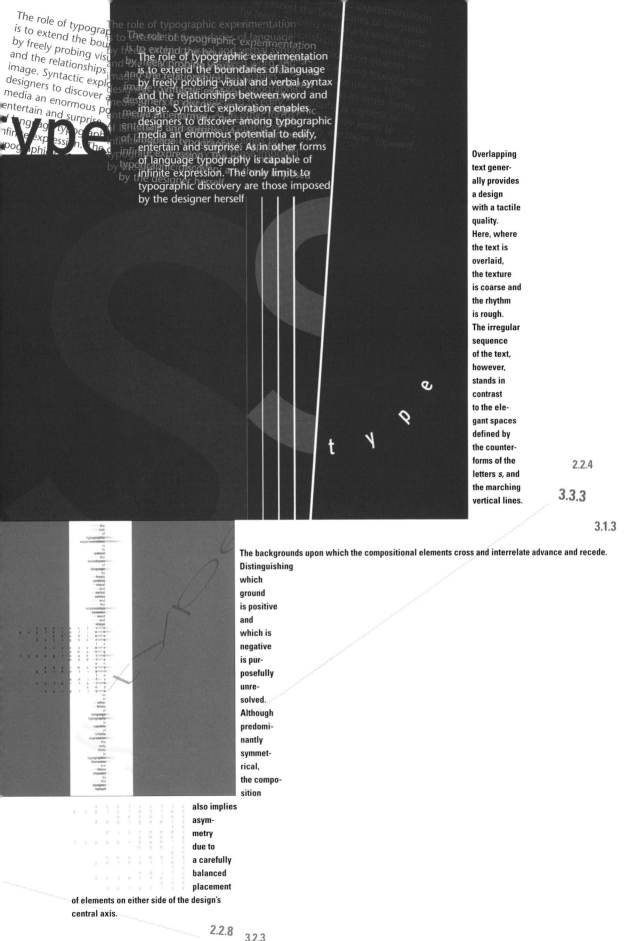

2.6.3

2.2.8

3.3.3

**The emotive qualities of type can be heightened through the manipulation of computer software filters. These powerful tools enable infinite possibilities for letter distortion. Fragmenting and blurring type add a visual dimension that challenges typographic conventions.**

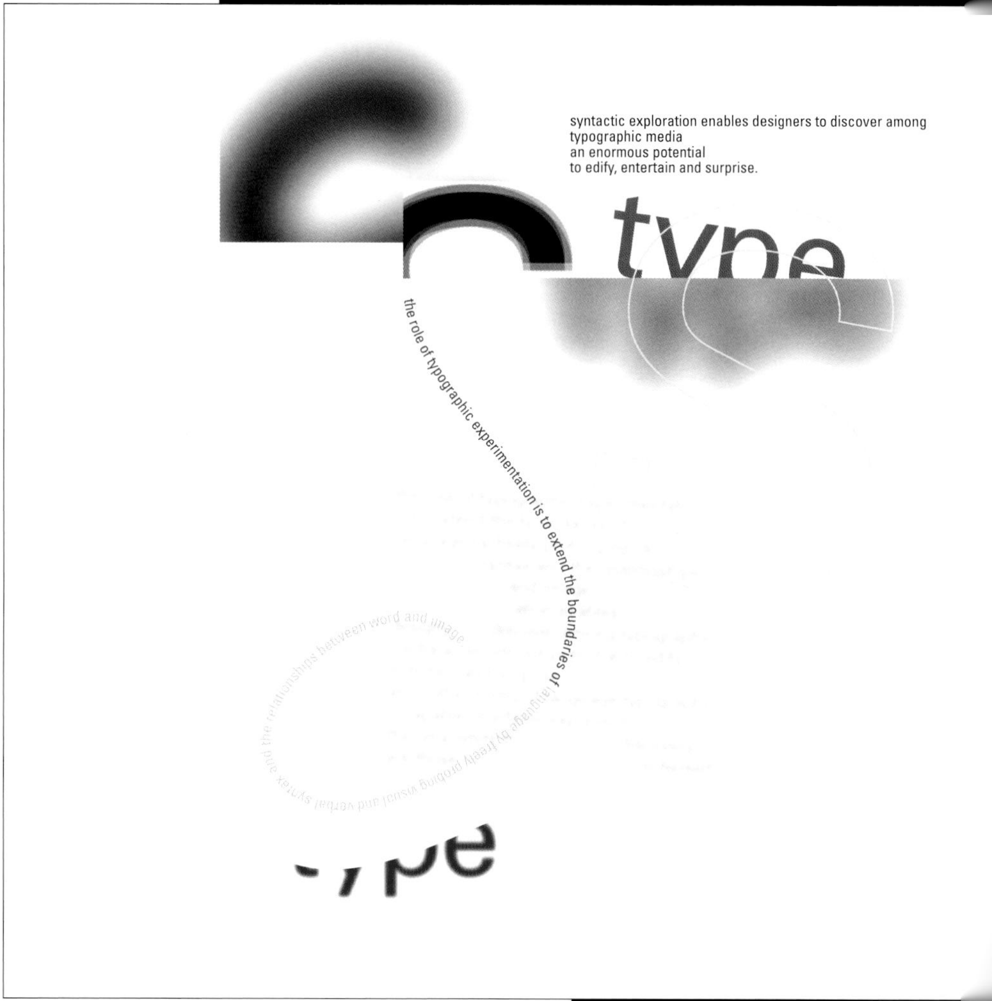
syntactic exploration enables designers to discover among
typographic media
an enormous potential
to edify, entertain and surprise.
type
the role of typographic experimentation is to extend the boundaries of language by freely probing visual and verbal syntax and the relationships between word and image

type

type

type

s

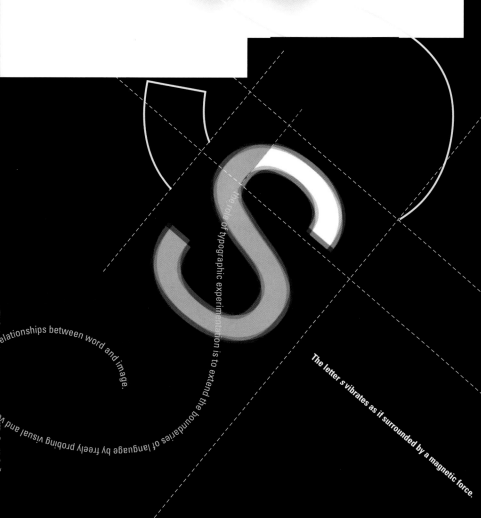

the role of typographic experimentation is to extend the boundaries of language by freely probing visual and v

elationships between word and image.

**The letter *s* vibrates as if surrounded by a magnetic force.**

**Overlapping type and ruled lines create a complex field of visual information. Dashed lines form the positive shapes as well as the negative white spaces. The interaction between foreground and background appears ambiguous as the components weave in and out of one another.**

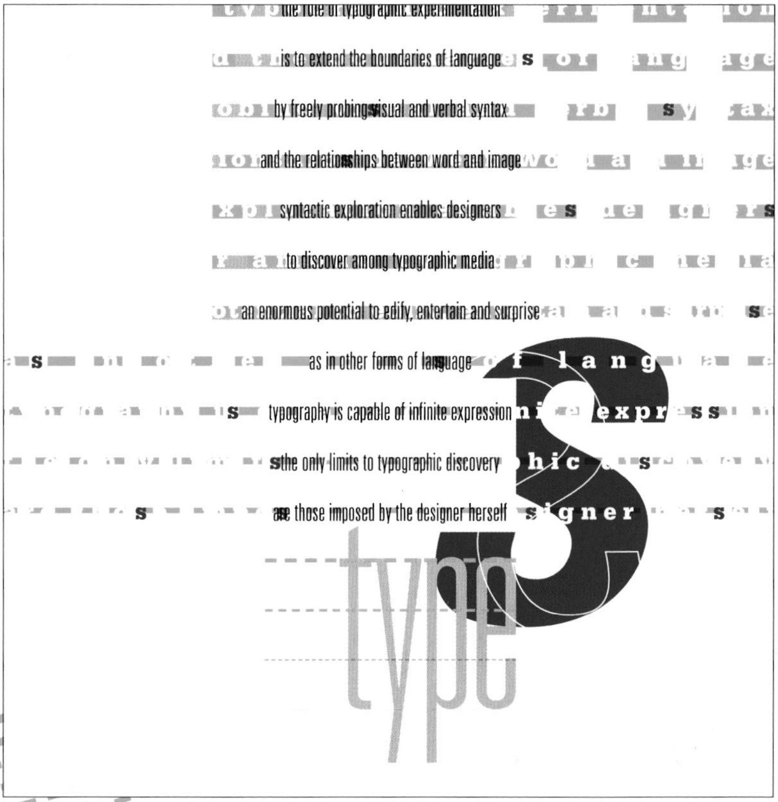
the role of typographic experimentation
is to extend the boundaries of language
by freely probing visual and verbal syntax
and the relationships between word and image
syntactic exploration enables designers
to discover among typographic media
an enormous potential to edify, entertain and surprise
as in other forms of language
typography is capable of infinite expression
the only limits to typographic discovery
are those imposed by the designer herself
type

4.2.1
3.5.3
2.5.2
2.3.4
the role of typographic experimentation
is to extend the boundaries of language
by freely probing visual and verbal syntax
and the relationships between word and image
syntactic exploration enables designers
to discover among typographic media
an enormous potential to edify, entertain and surprise
as in other forms of language
typography is capable of infinite expression
the only limits to typographic discovery
are those imposed by the designer herself

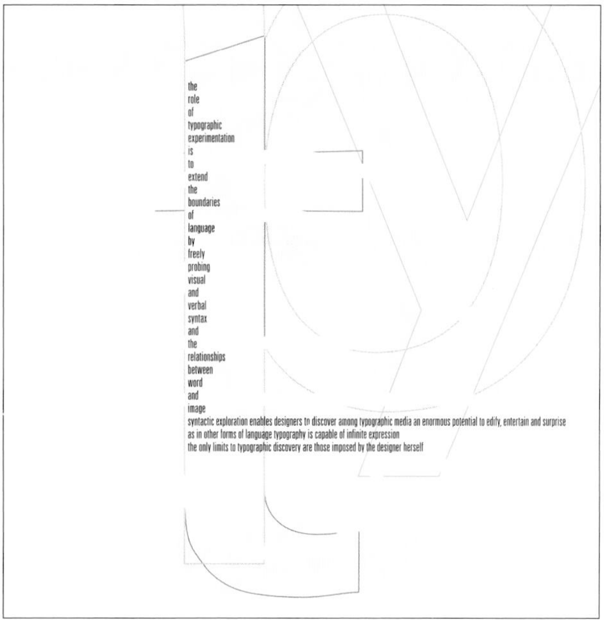
the
role
of
typographic
experimentation
is
to
extend
the
boundaries
of
language
by
freely
probing
visual
and
verbal
syntax
and
the
relationships
between
word
and
image
syntactic exploration enables designers to discover among typographic media an enormous potential to edify, entertain and surprise
as in other forms of language typography is capable of infinite expression
the only limits to typographic discovery are those imposed by the designer herself

**Letterform design and constructed texture are the basis of this typographic design. Individual letters of varying outlined strokes are abstracted to compose a series of shapes. Repeated triangular stars establish a dazzling kinetic pattern.**

3.5.4

2.2.8

2.5.5

**Distortion is an essential extension of typographic language, and the free expression of typographic form contributes to contemporary visual culture. At the same time, sensitivity to typographic tradition remains a critical concern, for without harmony there is no beauty.**

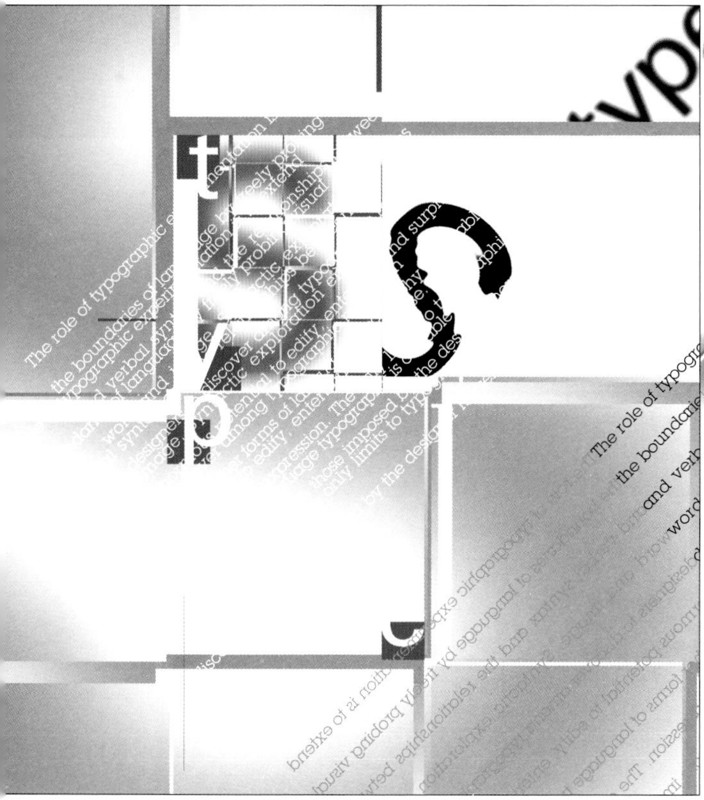

**The rippling filter offers a letter a malleable characteristic.**

2.5.1

2.7.1

2.4.5

3.5.1

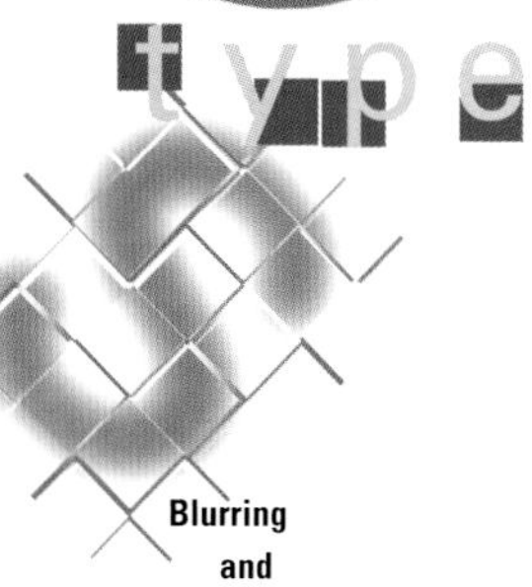


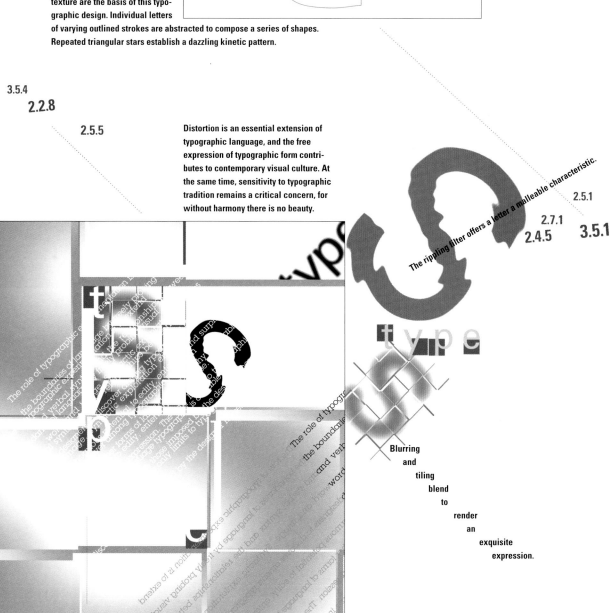

**Blurring and tiling blend to render an exquisite expression.**

## Portfolio

**Note:** As you study the work in this portfolio, be mindful that the student designers pinpointed specific factors from the morphology in Chapter 2 for investigation. Though you may discover that other factors also play some role in the experiments, only the prominent ones are mentioned.

1
Factors:
**1.1.1** case *upper*
**2.6.1** dimensionality *volumetric*
**4.2.2** shapes *organic*
Designer: **Veronica Ledford**

2
Factors:
**2.2.1** distortion *fragmenting*
**2.4.5** outline *combination*
**3.7.4** rhythm *progressive*
Designer: **Timea Adrian**

3
Factors:
**1.3.3** size *large*
**3.7.4** rhythm *progressive*
**4.1.9** ruled lines *combination*
**4.2.3** shapes *combination*
Designer: **Joshua Sandage**

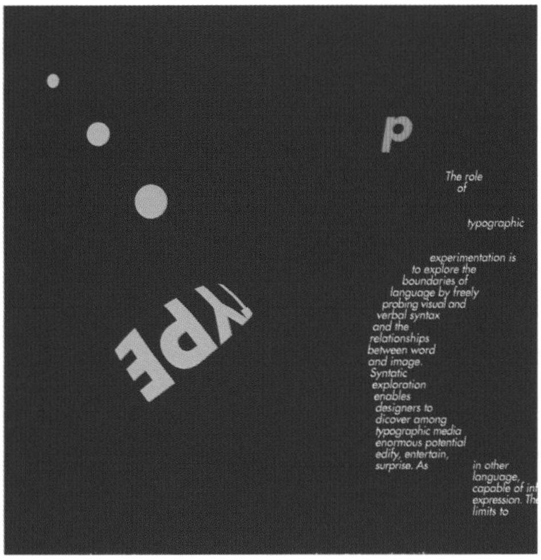

p
The role of typographic experimentation is to explore the boundaries of language by freely probing visual and verbal syntax and the relationships between word and image. Syntatic exploration enables designers to dicover among typographic media enormous potential edify, entertain, surprise. As

1

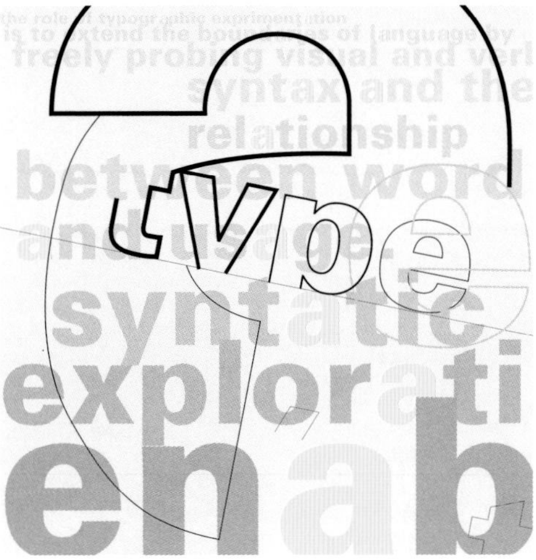

syntax and the
relationship
between word
syntatic

2

type

3

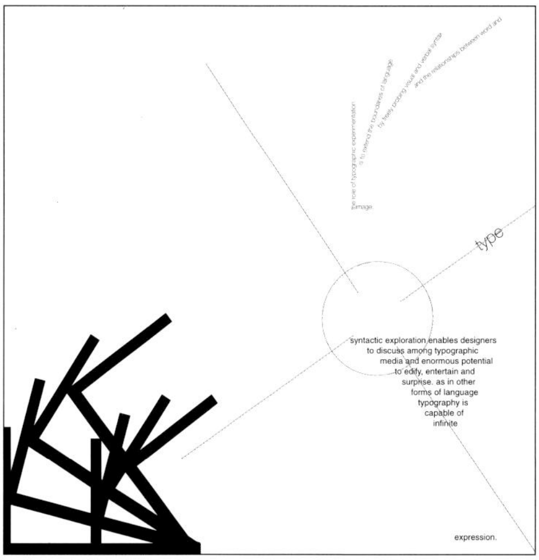
type
syntactic exploration enables designers to discuss among typographic media and enormous potential to edify, entertain and surprise. as in other forms of language typography is capable of infinite
expression.

4

the ro typographic xperimentation is to extend the
boundaries of language by freely probing visual and
verbal syntax and the relationship between word and
usage. syntactic exploration enables designers to discover
among typographic media an enormous potential to edify,
entertain and surprise. as in other forms of
language typography is capable of infinite expression. the
only limits to typographic discovery are those
imposed by the designer herself.

5

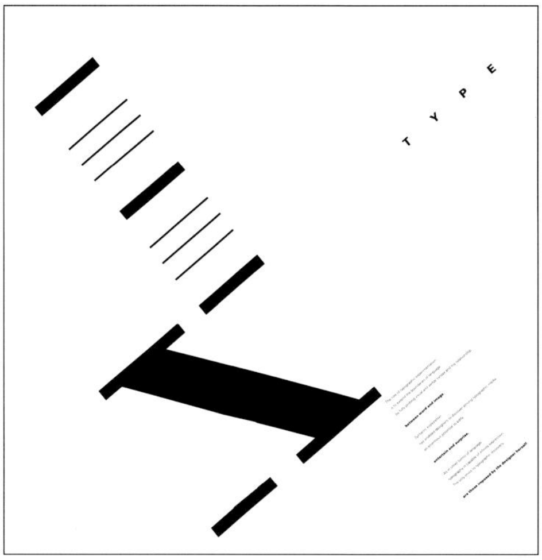
TYPE

6

type

7

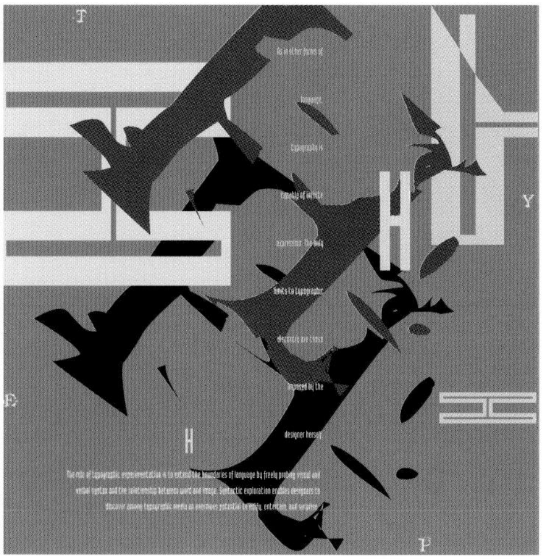

8

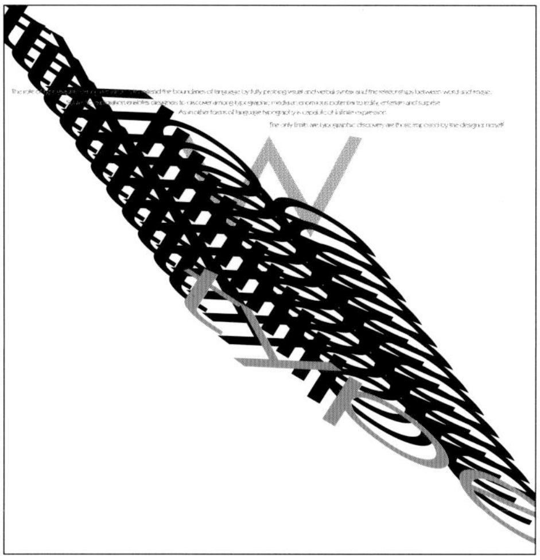

9

4
Factors:
**1.3.3** size *combination*
**3.2.5** direction *combination*
**3.6.1** repetition *few*
**4.1.3** ruled lines *diagonal*
Designer: **Ginger Cho**

5
Factors:
**1.3.3** size *combination*
**3.1.3** balance *combination*
**3.8.2** rotation *moderate*
Designer: **Timea Adrian**

6
Factors:
**3.2.3** direction *diagonal*
**3.7.3** rhythm *alternating*
**3.8.2** rotation *moderate*
**2.3.2** elaboration *subtraction*
Designer: **Rosemary Sabatino**

7
Factors:
**1.2.1** face *serif*
**3.5.2** proximity *touching*
**3.8.2** rotation *combination*
**4.2.2** shapes *organic*
Designer: **Joshua Sandage**

8
Factors:
**1.3.4** size *combination*
**2.2.7** distortion *mutilating*
**2.4.5** outline *combination*
Designer: **Chris Raymond**

9
Factors:
**2.2.4** distortion *stretching*
**3.2.3** direction *diagonal*
**3.6.4** repetition *pattern*
Designer: **Ann Ford**

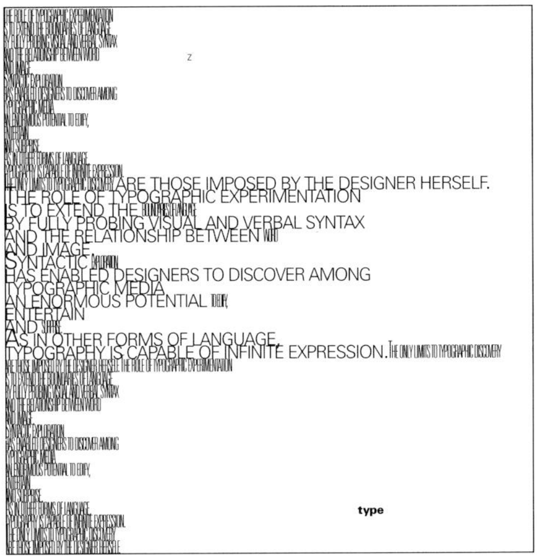
ARE THOSE IMPOSED BY THE DESIGNER HERSELF.
THE ROLE OF TYPOGRAPHIC EXPERIMENTATION
IS TO EXTEND THE
BY FULLY PROBING VISUAL AND VERBAL SYNTAX
AND THE RELATIONSHIP BETWEEN
AND IMAGE
SYNTACTIC
HAS ENABLED DESIGNERS TO DISCOVER AMONG
TYPOGRAPHIC MEDIA
AN ENORMOUS POTENTIAL
ENTERTAIN
AND
AS IN OTHER FORMS OF LANGUAGE,
TYPOGRAPHY IS CAPABLE OF INFINITE EXPRESSION.
type

10

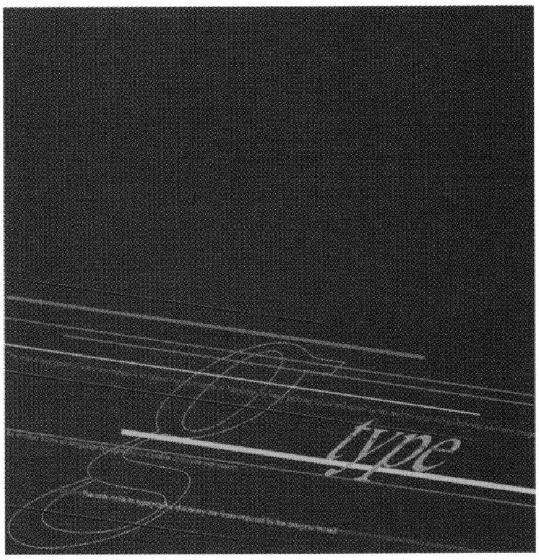
type

11

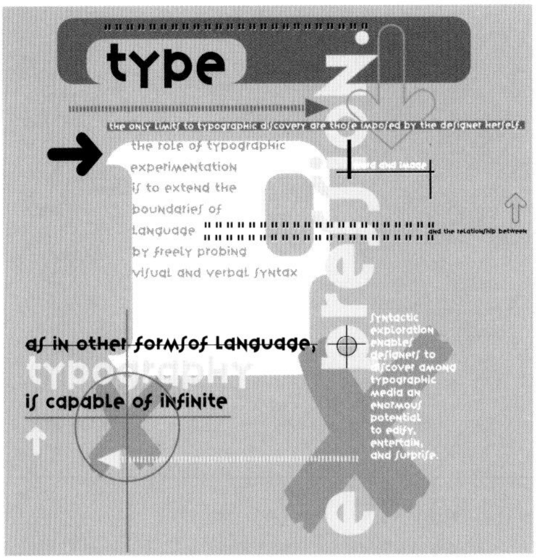
type
the only limits to typographic discovery are those imposed by the designer herself.
the role of typographic experimentation is to extend the boundaries of language by freely probing visual and verbal syntax
as in other forms of language,
typography
is capable of infinite
syntactic exploration enables designers to discover among typographic media an enormous potential to edify, entertain, and surprise.

12

type

13

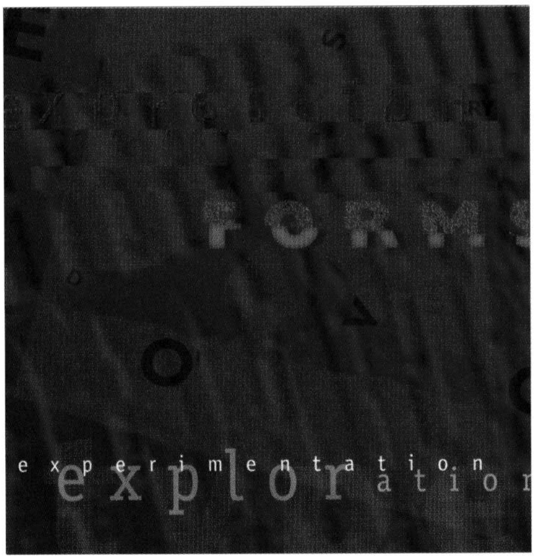
FORMS
e x p e r i m e n t a t i o n
exploration

14

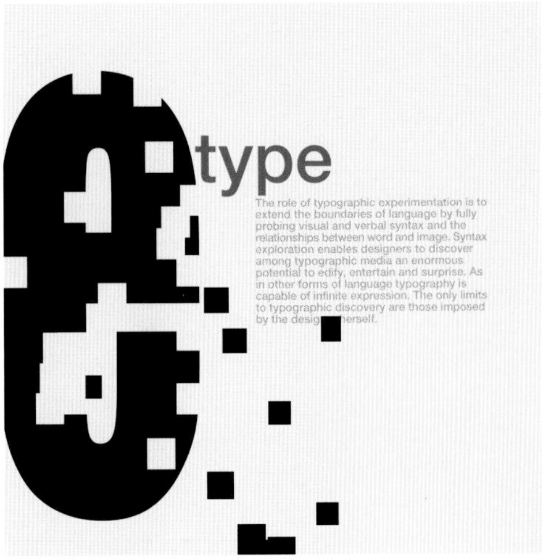
type
The role of typographic experimentation is to extend the boundaries of language by fully probing visual and verbal syntax and the relationships between word and image. Syntax exploration enables designers to discover among typographic media an enormous potential to edify, entertain and surprise. As in other forms of language typography is capable of infinite expression. The only limits to typographic discovery are those imposed by the designer herself.

15

10
Factors:
**1.6.4** width *combination*
**2.5.5** texture *combination*
**2.7.4** tonality *combination*
**3.2.1** direction *horizontal*
Designer: **Rosemary Sabatino**

11
Factors:
**2.2.2** distortion *skewing*
**3.2.3** direction *diagonal*
**4.1.9** ruled lines *combination*
Designer: **Joshua Sandage**

12
Factors:
**3.4.2** grouping *dissonant*
**1.2.4** face *eccentric*
**3.5.1** proximity *overlapping*
**4.3.1** symbols *normal*
Designer: **Krysta Higham**

13
Factors:
**1.3.3** size *large*
**3.2.4** direction *circular*
**3.4.1** grouping *consonant*
**4.2.3** shapes *combination*
Designer: **Joshua Sandage**

14
Factors:
**2.2.8** distortion *combination*
**3.5.1** proximity *overlapping*
Designer: **Chris Raymond**

15
Factors:
**1.3.3** size *large*
**1.5.1** width *narrow*
**2.2.1** distortion *fragmenting*
**4.2.3** shapes *combination*
Designer: **Ann Ford**

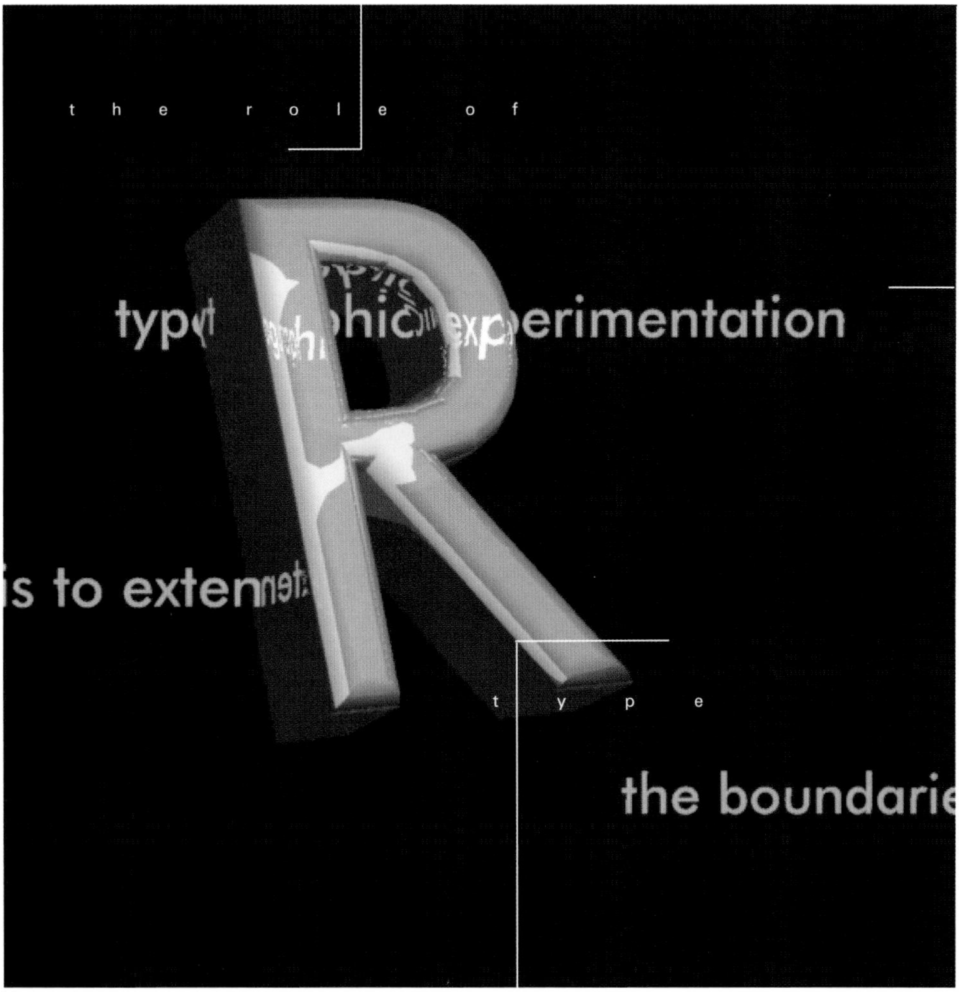
t h e r o l e o f
typographic experimentation
is to extend
t y p e
the boundarie

16
Factors:

**2.6.1** dimensionality *volumetric*
**3.5.1** proximity *overlapping*
**4.1.9** ruled lines *combination*

Designer: **San Van**

Portfolio

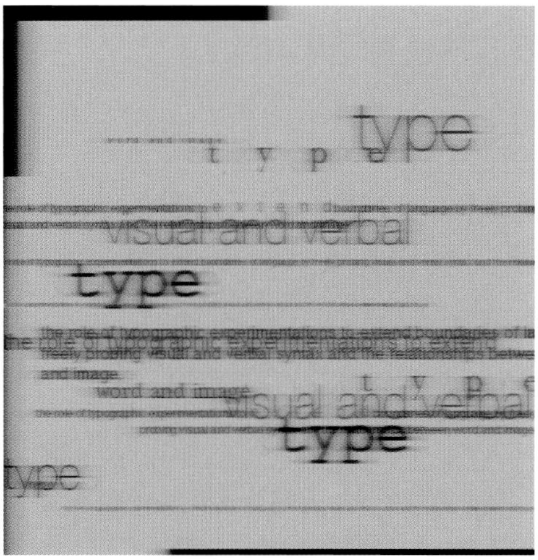

17

18

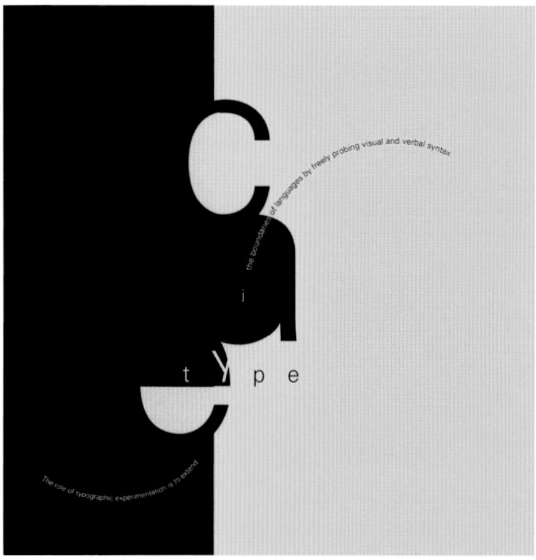

19

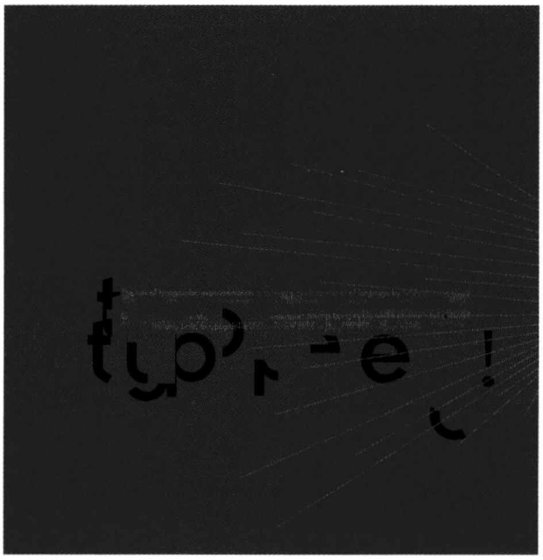
20

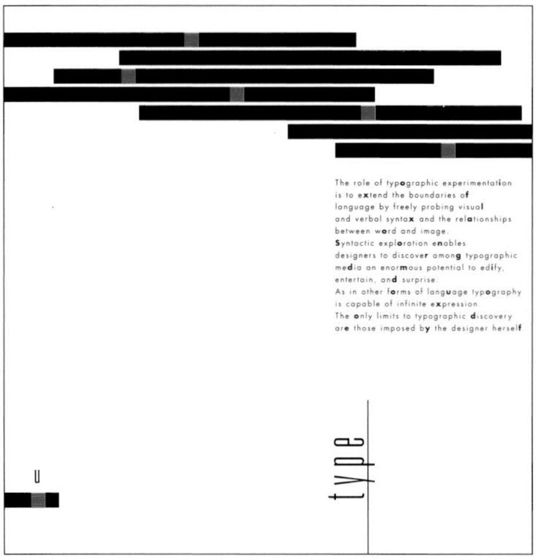

21

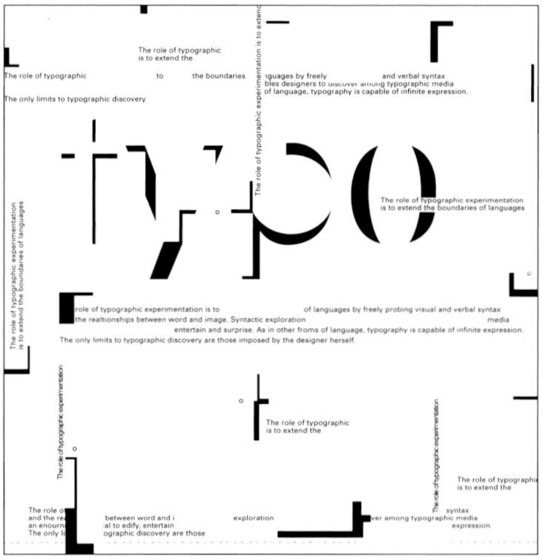

22

17
Factors:
**1.2.5** face *combination*
**2.2.5** distortion *blurring*
**3.2.1** direction *horizontal*
**3.5.1** proximity *overlapping*
Designer: **Ginger Cho**

18
Factors:
**2.2.1** distortion *fragmenting*
**3.2.3** direction *diagonal*
**3.7.1** rhythm *regular*
**4.1.8** ruled lines *thick*
Designer: **Chris Raymond**

19
Factors:
**2.3.1** elaboration *addition*
**3.2.4** direction *circular*
**3.3.1** ground *advancing*
**4.2.2** shapes *organic*
Designer: **Chris Raymond**

20
Factors:
**2.3.2** elaboration *subtraction*
**3.7.2** rhythm *irregular*
**4.1.3** ruled lines *diagonal*
Designer: **Priya Rama**

21
Factors:
**3.7.2** rhythm *irregular*
**4.1.8** ruled lines *thick*
Designer: **Priya Rama**

22
Factors:
**2.2.1** distortion *fragmenting*
**2.3.2** elaboration *subtraction*
**3.7.2** rhythm *irregular*
**4.2.1** shapes *geometric*
Designer: **San Van**

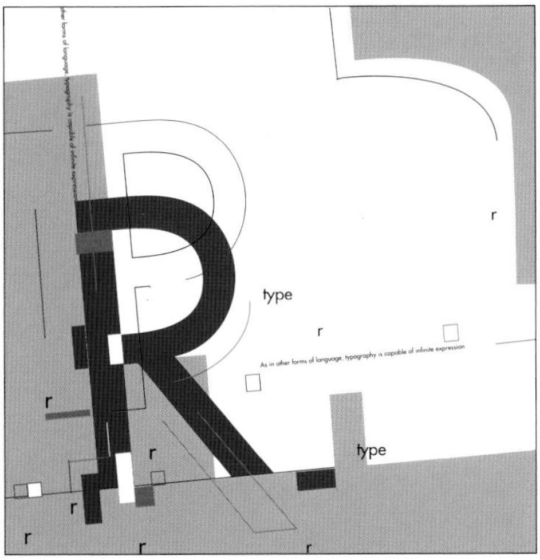
type
type

23

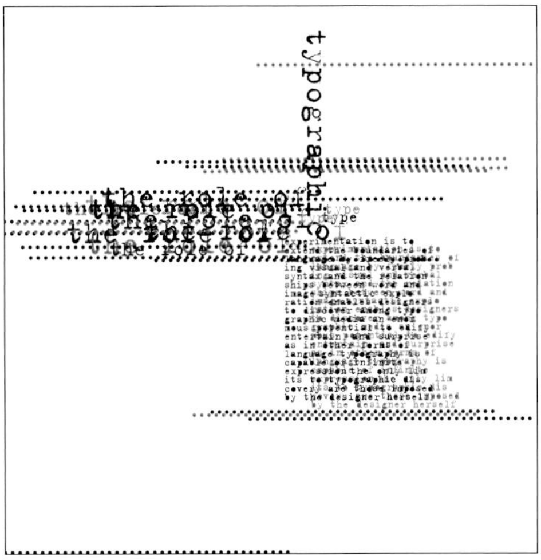
typography

24

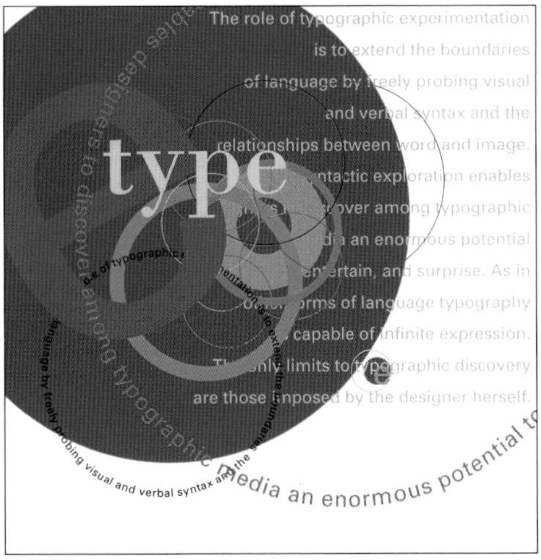
The role of typographic experimentation
is to extend the boundaries
of language by freely probing visual
and verbal syntax and the
relationships between word and image.
type
are those imposed by the designer herself.

25

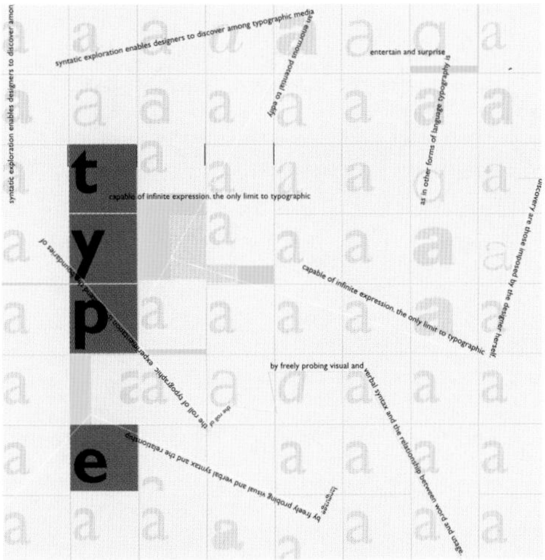
t
y
p
e

26

ty
pe

27

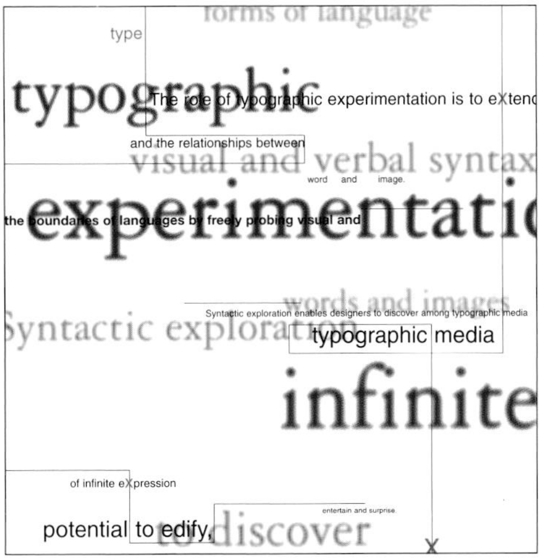
type
typographic
The role of typographic experimentation is to eXtend
and the relationships between
visual and verbal syntax
experimentatio
infinite
typographic media
of infinite eXpression
potential to edify, discover

28

23
Factors:
**1.2.5** elaboration *combination*
**3.5.1** proximity *overlapping*
**2.4.1** outline *thin*
**4.1.6** ruled lines *thin*
**4.2.1** shapes *geometric*
Designer: **San Van**

24
Factors:
**2.5.4** texture *irregular*
**3.5.1** proximity *overlapping*
**4.1.1** ruled lines *horizontal*
Designer: **Priya Rama**

25
Factors:
**3.2.4** direction *circular*
**3.5.1** proximity *overlapping*
**3.8.2** rotation *moderate*
**4.1.4** ruled lines *circular*
Designer: **Joshua Sandage**

26
Factors:
**3.2.3** direction *diagonal*
**3.6.2** repetition *many*
**4.2.1** shapes *geometric*
Designer: **Timea Adrian**

27
Factors:
**3.1.2** balance *asymmetrical*
**3.3.1** ground *advancing*
**3.4.2** grouping *dissonant*
**4.2.1** shapes *geometric*
Designer: **Ginger Cho**

28
Factors:
**2.2.5** distortion *blurring*
**3.2.1** direction *horizontal*
**3.5.1** proximity *overlapping*
**4.1.6** ruled lines *thin*
Designer: **San Van**

29
Factors:

**2.3.1** elaboration *addition*
**3.2.2** direction *vertical*
**3.7.2** rhythm *irregular*

Designer: **San Van**

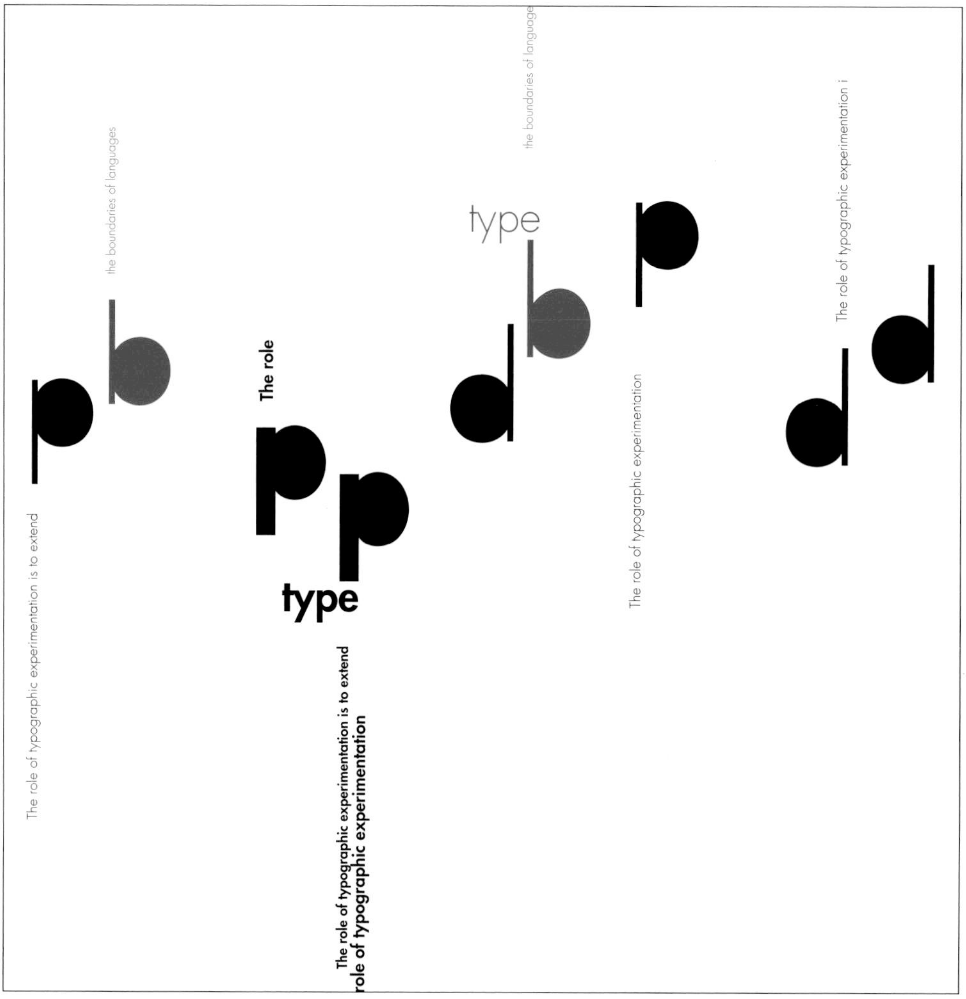
The role of typographic experimentation is to extend
the boundaries of languages
The role
type
The role of typographic experimentation is to extend
role of typographic experimentation
type
the boundaries of language
The role of typographic experimentation
The role of typographic experimentation i

29

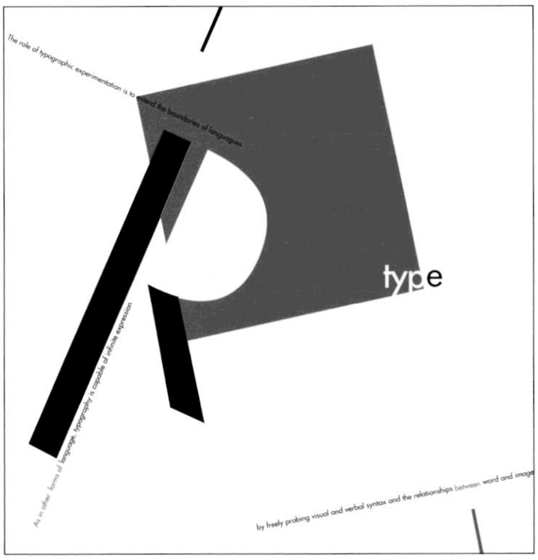
The role of typographic experimentation is to extend the boundaries of languages
type
by freely probing visual and verbal syntax and the relationships between word and image

30

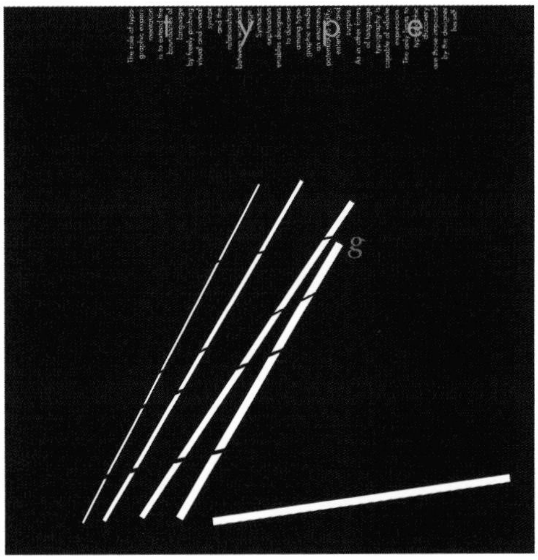

31

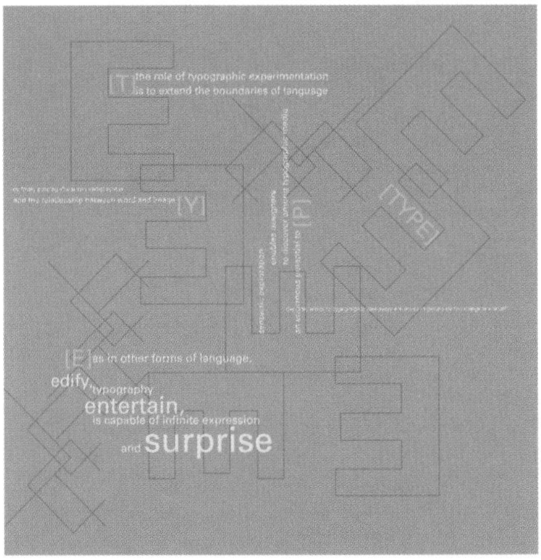
[T] the role of typographic experimentation is to extend the boundaries of language
[TYPE]
[E] as in other forms of language,
edify,
typography
entertain,
is capable of infinite expression
and surprise

32

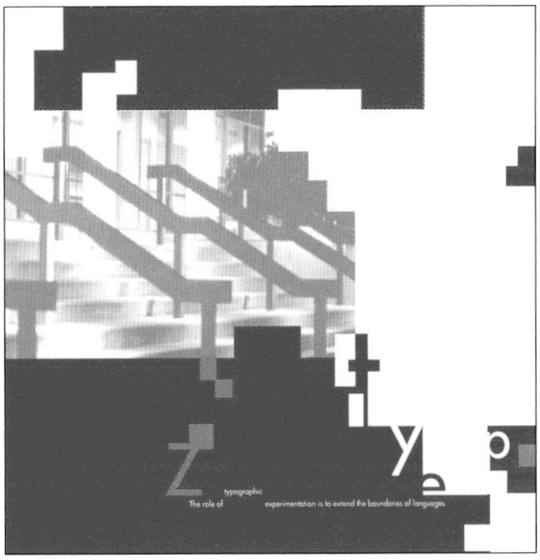
typographic
The role of experimentation is to extend the boundaries of languages

33

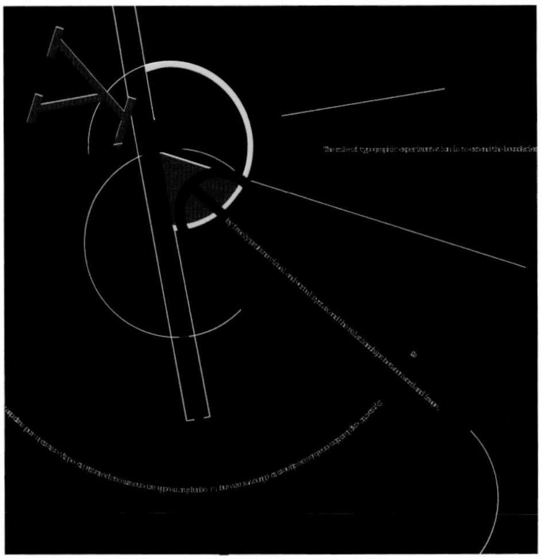

34

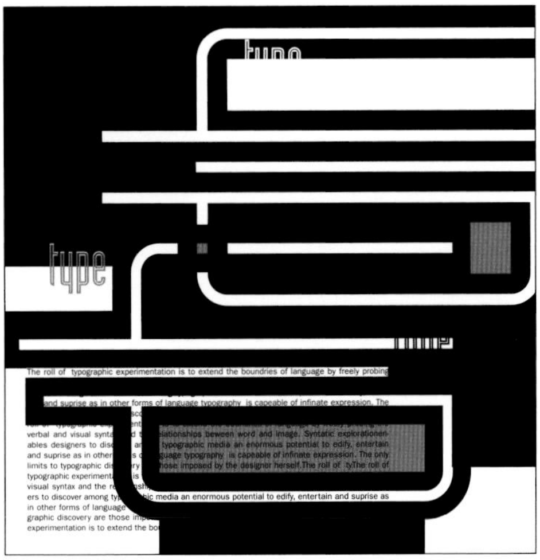
type
The roll of typographic experimentation is to extend the boundries of language by freely probing

35

30
Factors:
**2.2.8** distortion *combination*
**3.1.2** balance *asymmetrical*
**3.3.3** ground *combination*
**4.2.3** shapes *combination*
Designer: **San Van**

31
Factors:
**1.3.4** size *combination*
**3.7.5** rhythm *combination*
**4.1.3** ruled lines *diagonal*
Designer: **Priya Rama**

32
Factors:
**2.4.1** outline *thin*
**3.4.2** grouping *dissonant*
**3.5.1** proximity *overlapping*
**3.7.4** rhythm *progressive*
Designer: **Krysta Higham**

33
Factors:
**1.2.2** face *sans serif*
**4.2.1** shapes *geometric*
**4.4.5** images *combination*
Designer: **San Van**

34
Factors:
**1.3.1** size *small*
**2.3.2** elaboration *subtraction*
**3.4.2** grouping *dissonant*
**4.1.9** ruled lines *combination*
**4.2.3** shapes *combination*
Designer: **San Van**

35
Factors:
**1.2.4** face *eccentric*
**3.5.1** proximity *overlapping*
**3.7.2** rhythm *irregular*
**4.2.1** shape *geometric*
Designer: **Kelly Perkins**

36
Factors:
**1.2.4** face *eccentric*
**2.6.1** dimensionality *volumetric*
**4.2.5** shapes *combination*
Designer: **Jesus Palacios**

37
Factors:
**1.3.4** size *combination*
**1.2.5** face *combination*
**2.2.2** distortion *skewing*
**4.2.1** shapes *geometric*
Designer: **Ginger Cho**

38
Factors:
**1.2.4** face *eccentric*
**2.6.1** dimensionality *volumetric*
**3.5.1** proximity *overlapping*
**4.2.2** shapes *organic*
Designer: **Kelly Perkins**

39
Factors:
**1.2.5** face *combination*
**2.2.2** distortion *skewing*
**3.8.4** rotation *combination*
**4.2.2** shapes *organic*
Designer: **Jesus Palacios**

40
Factors:
**1.3.4** size *combination*
**3.5.3** proximity *separating*
**2.2.7** distortion *mutilating*
Designer: **Rosemary Sabatino**

41
Factors:
**1.2.5** face *combination*
**2.2.8** distortion *combination*
**2.4.1** outline *thin*
**3.5.4** proximity *combination*
Designer: **Timea Adrian**

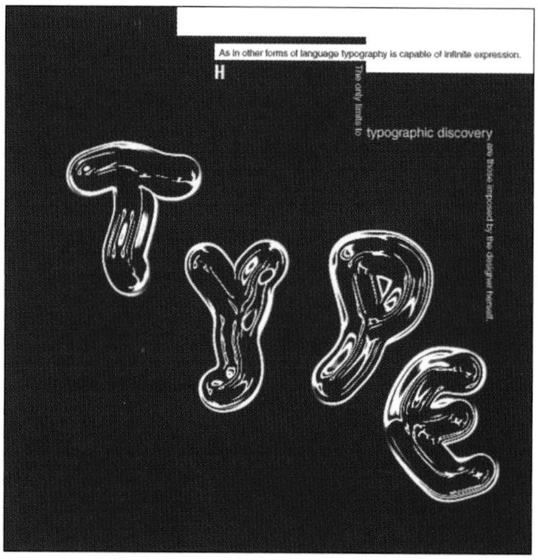

As in other forms of language typography is capable of infinite expression.
H
The only limits to
typographic discovery
are those imposed by the designer herself.
Type

36

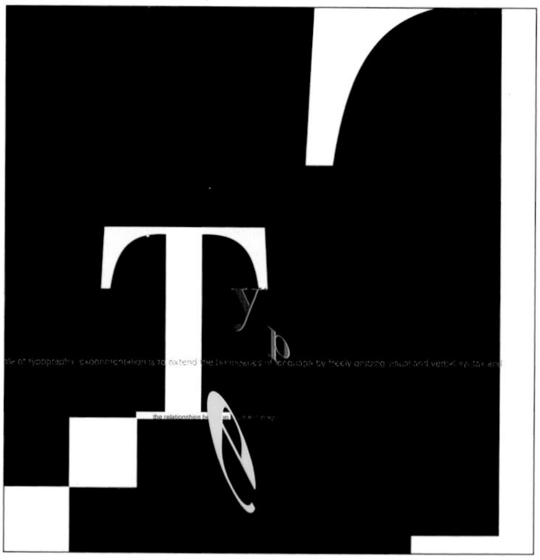

37

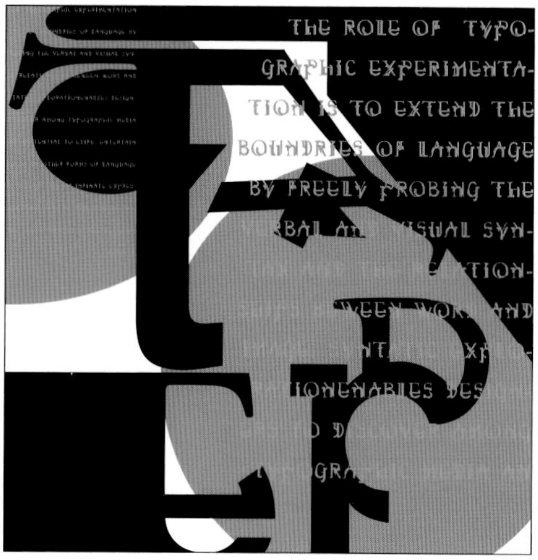

38

39

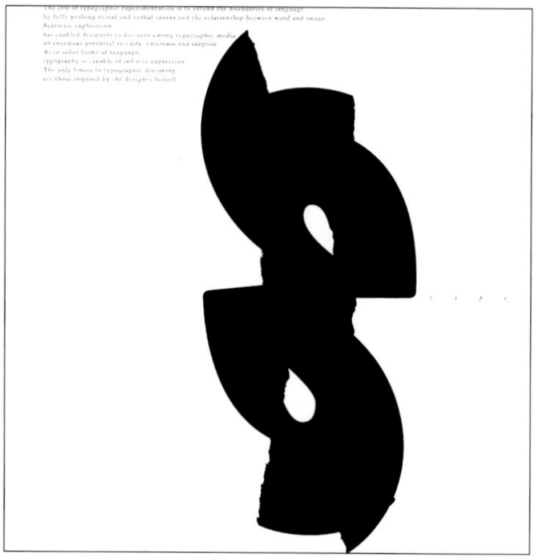
40

41

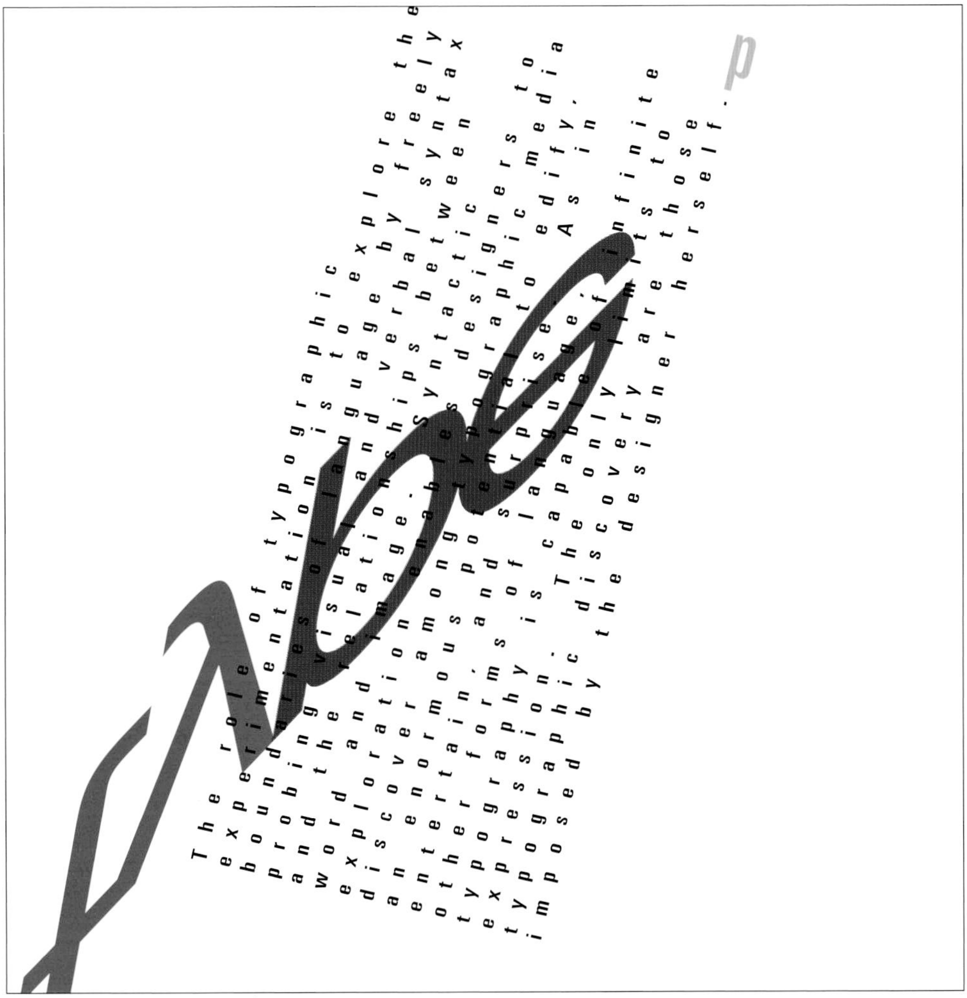

42

Factors:

**1.1.2** case *lower*

**2.2.8** distortion *combination*

**2.5.3** texture *regular*

Designer: **Veronica Ledford**

43

Factors:

**1.3.4** size *combination*
**2.3.2** elaboration *reduction*
**3.6.5** repetition *combination*
**4.2.2** shapes *organic*

Designer: **Joshua Sandage**

43

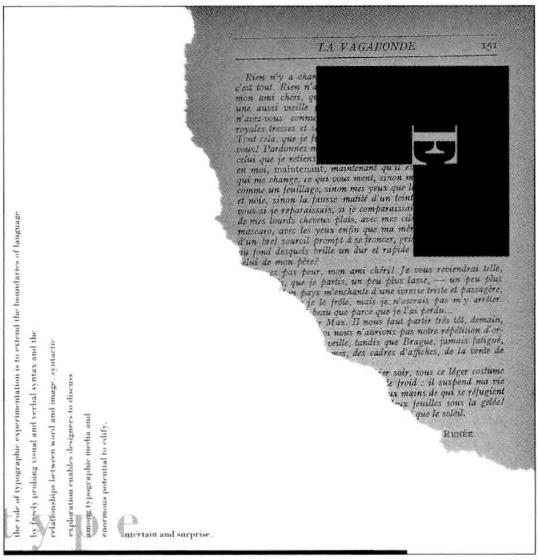


44

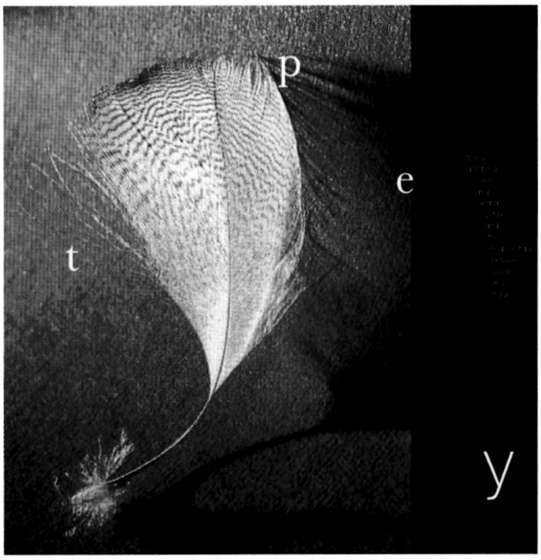


45

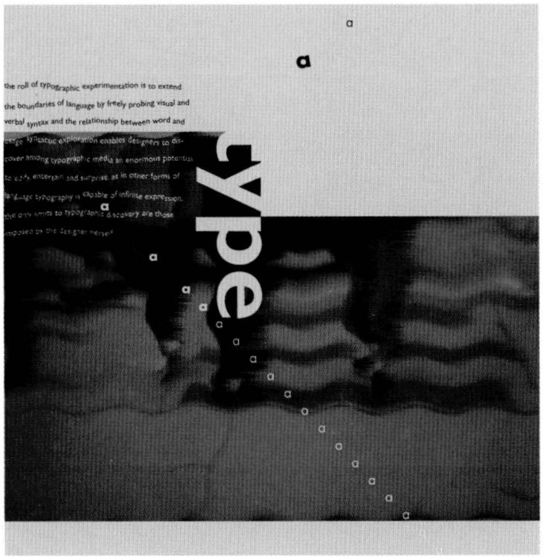


46

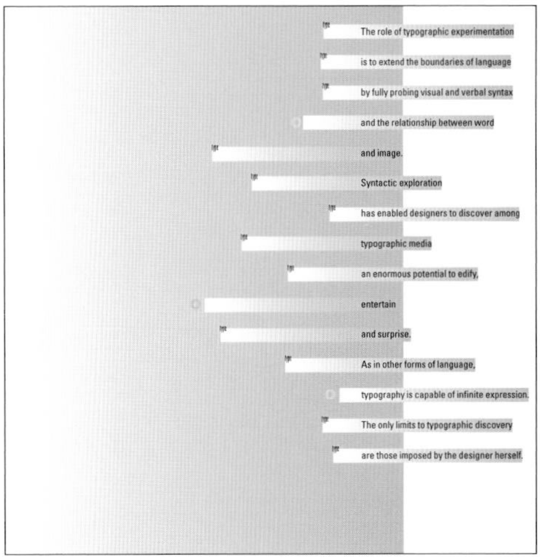


47

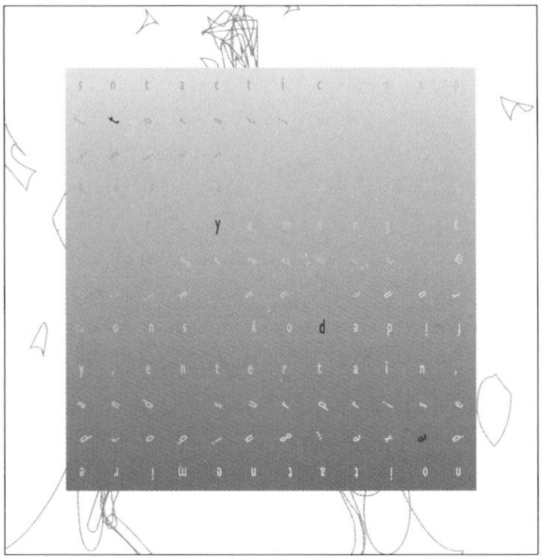

48

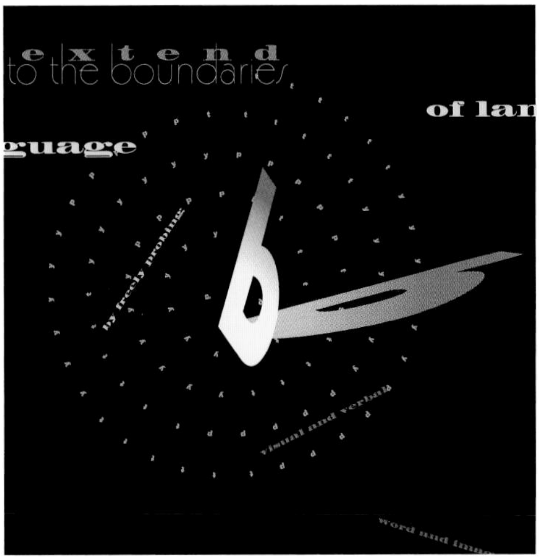


49

44
Factors:
**1.3.4** size *combination*
**3.5.1** proximity *overlapping*
**4.1.1** ruled lines *horizontal*
**4.4.4** images *manipulated*
Designer: **Ginger Cho**

45
Factors:
**1.3.4** size *combination*
**3.2.4** direction *circular*
**4.4.1** images *background*
Designer: **Ginger Cho**

46
Factors:
**1.3.4** size *combination*
**2.2.3** distortion *bending*
**3.7.4** rhythm *progressive*
Designer: **Timea Adrian**

47
Factors:
**1.3.1** size *small*
**2.1.1** blending *linear*
**3.7.5** rhythm *combination*
**4.2.1** shapes *geometric*
Designer: **Rosemary Sabatino**

48
Factors:
**1.3.1** size *small*
**2.1.1** blending *linear*
**2.2.7** distortion *mutilation*
**3.6.4** repetition *pattern*
**4.2.1** shapes *geometric*
Designer: **Chris Raymond**

49
Factors:
**1.2.5** face *combination*
**2.6.2** dimensionality *shadowing*
**3.4.2** grouping *dissonant*
**3.8.4** rotation *combination*
Designer: **Chris Raymond**

# Typography workshop

# 4

# Typography workshop

In April of 1997, 13 students and five teachers from the Gerrit Rietveld Academy in Amsterdam joined students and teachers from the Visual Communication program at Virginia Commonwealth University in Richmond, for a continuation of an exchange begun the previous year. The purpose of this workshop was twofold: first, to bring together an international community of people for a cross-cultural exchange of ideas; second, to create a climate for free typographic exploration and expression. The workshop consisted of presentations, films, critiques, and informal group discussions that often continued late into the night. The workshop culminated with an all-day presentation by the students. Three guest critics were invited to share their insights.

Many differences and similarities were discovered in the approaches of the two design programs. But what was learned from the shared ideas of individual participants and the resulting sense of community was most significant. At a preliminary gathering of faculty and students, Margit, a Dutch student who was visiting America for the first time, commented on how she felt like she entered a movie set when she stepped off of the airplane at Dulles International. Prior to her visit, her perception of America had been largely shaped by Hollywood films. During the two weeks of the workshop, cultural differences among the students and faculty – particularly those along social, economic, and political lines – would be revealed and discussed, a process that would melt away many preconceptions and cultural biases. Representative nationalities included Bulgarian, Dutch, Hungarian, Polish, Swiss, and American. Ironically, the foreign students would discover that America is a manifestation of many cultures, a land woven together from many different threads. The exploration of typography, a universal communication vehicle with ties to language and culture, led to the discovery of many issues that both connect and separate us as human beings.

Experimentation was guided by an open-ended project that gave impetus to exploration and interpretation of content, and provided a context for the investigation. The nucleus of the project is a poem, "In Those Years," by the influential American poet, Adrienne Rich:

**In those years, people will say, we lost track**
**of the meaning of *we*, of *you***
**we found ourselves**
**reduced to *I***
**and the whole thing became**
**silly, ironic, terrible:**
**we were trying to live a personal life**
**and yes, that was the only life**
**we could bear witness to**

**But the great dark birds of history screamed**
**and plunged**
**into our personal weather**
**They were headed somewhere else but their**
**beaks and pinions drove**
**along the shore, through the rags of fog**
**where we stood, saying *I***

What has happened to community? In technologically advanced civilizations, it appears a thing of the past. Living today is a solitary, anonymous endeavor: invisible people living in invisible cities, walking straight lines with straight backs. Eyes focused on the horizon, peripheral vision lost for lack of use. Bodies brushing but never touching; voices muffled amidst a deafening drone. What has happened to community? What has happened to "we"?

During the workshop, the I/We dichotomy was evident in the way the students interacted with or isolated themselves from others, and in the way the project was interpreted. Generally, some of the students (especially the Dutch, and a small minority of Americans) questioned every aspect of the project brief or ignored some of the constraints. Their quest was for absolute individuality (the "I"). Others felt obligated to precisely follow the brief, to conform (the "We"). These varying attitudes inevitably led to a wide range of solutions, and a dynamic creative environment. The experiments shown on the following pages represent a small but informative cross-section of the total work produced. Examples span the entire design process, from preliminary investigations to final solutions.

As the dust of the workshop has settled, one significant question arises: what is the role of typography in the global communication frenzy?

Project brief:

The departure point of this project is an interview by Bill Moyers of poet Adrienne Rich. Here you will find three voices: the voice of Moyers as interviewer; the voice of Rich as interviewee; the voice of Rich's poetry. In the process of everyday living we hear voices that shape our individual worlds, and together these voices shape culture.

During the course of this project you will typographically interpret your voice as it converses with the voices of the interview. Your voice will be discovered as it emanates from workshop experiences, observations, and travels.

Process:
Several considerations will guide this project, including the manifestations of culture as represented by the participants of the workshop; viewing the content from different/many perspectives; personal background; world view; personal values; and the social, economic, and political forces that ultimately define culture.

Maintain a sketch-book/journal to record your experiences and observations, and the voices that inform you during the workshop experience. The poem is typeset in many variations for your use. Other typographic material, including found typography, can be appropriated and integrated as needed.

Considerations:
Self discovery and
Self expression
Problem seeking and solving
Permutation
Transformation
Shifting problem boundaries
Message clarity
Type as word and image

Possible realization:
2-d typography
3-d typography
Type as object
Environmental typography
Projected typography
Time-based typography
Kinetic typography

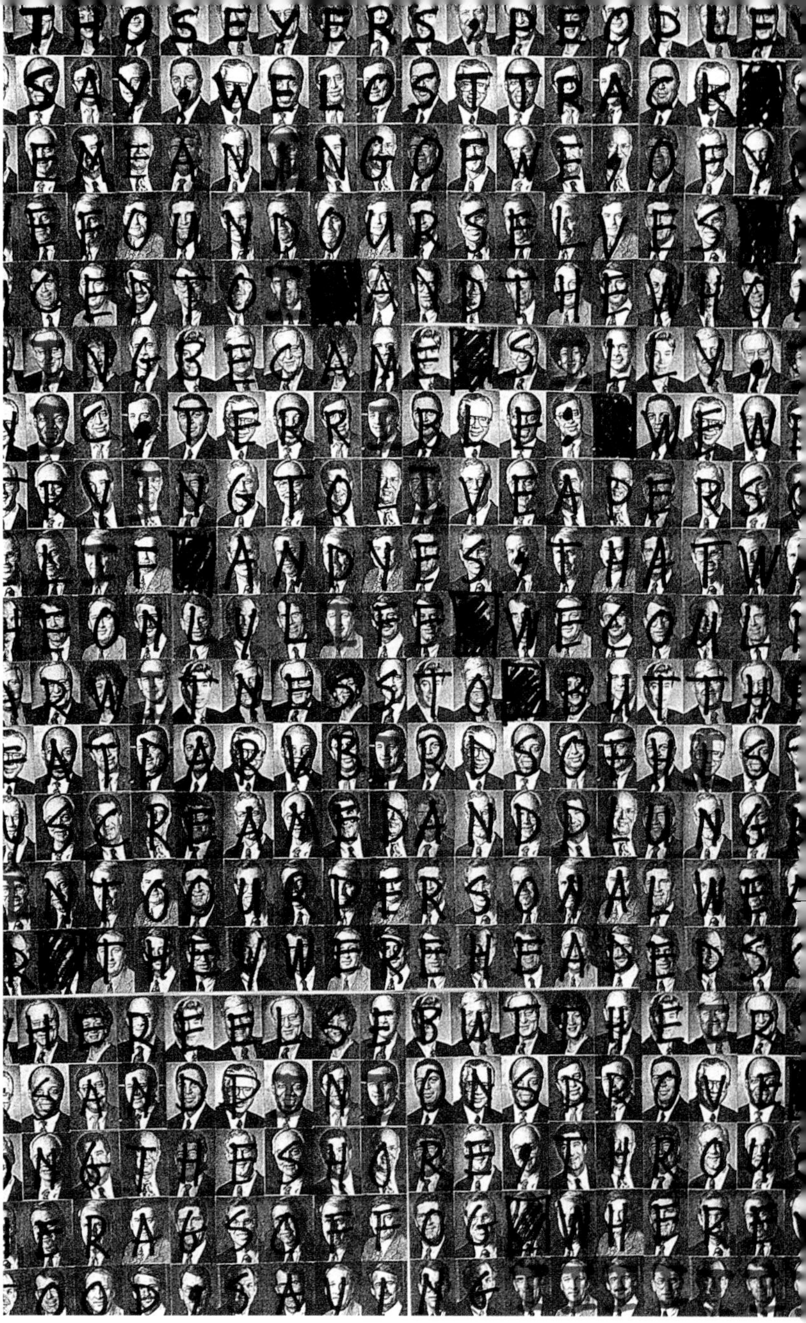

1

1
**Letters of the poem, "In Those Years," by Adrienne Rich are superimposed upon a rigid field of men in business suits. Hardly representative of the ideal community, which shows no bias towards gender, race, or religion, this image is exemplary of concerns that arose during workshop. The red letters / suggest that there are individuals within this robotic group.**
1: Nicolet Schouten

**"It seems as though the Rietveld** students bring a sense of humor to their work that really comes across. I don't have a sense of humor when it comes to design. I can't do that, so I really respect this ability, and I am in awe of it. I wish I could be funny when I design, but I can't. As a former graduate of the program here, I would say that the students are very process oriented, very methodological in their approach."
**N.D.**

2

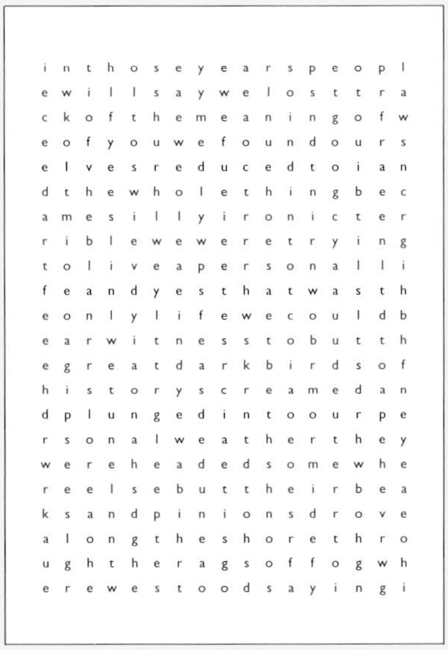


6

2
**We are many and we are all individuals.**

3
**A pictographic anthropomorph overlays a sea of people, suggesting that we all share the same ancestral roots. It also provides a primitive signature that states "I am me."**

4
**An ordinary sticker containing an advertising slogan is repeated and thus reinterpreted to suggest American consumerism.**

5
**As individuals, we have ears but we don't always hear.**

6
**A typographical interpretation of the poem, with letters evenly spaced and repeated to signify individuality.**

7
**In this experiment, a photograph of corn is juxtaposed with a field of human isotypes to reference feeding the world.**

8, 9
**Pages from a sketchbook are indicative of ideas that could lead to further experimentation.**

**2-9: Nicolet Schouten**

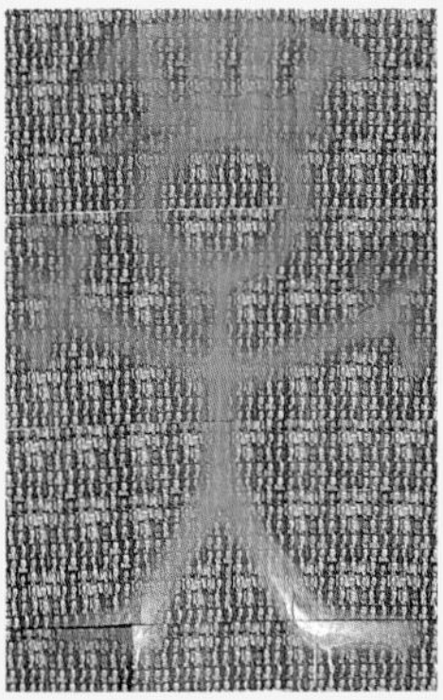

3

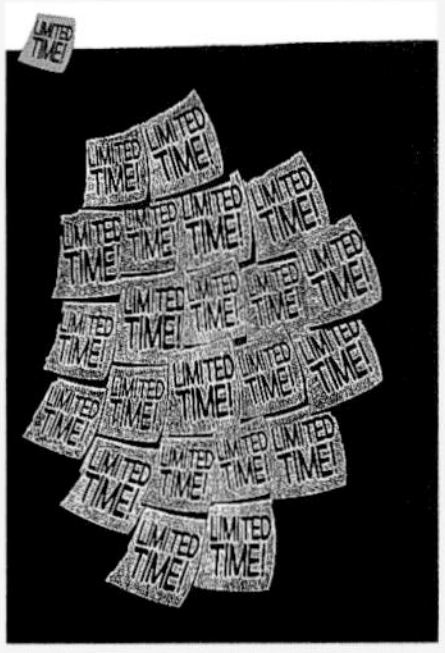


4

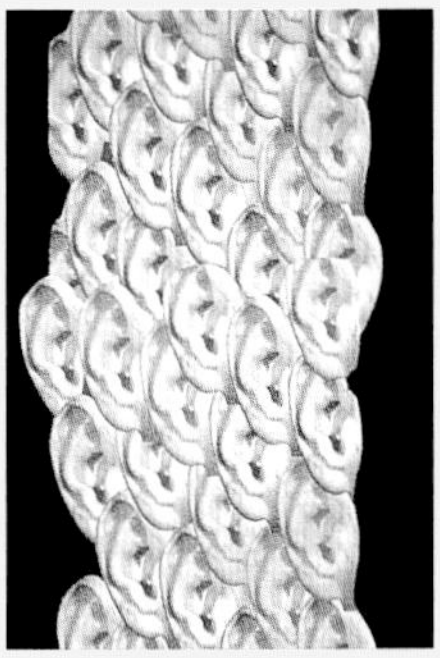

5

7

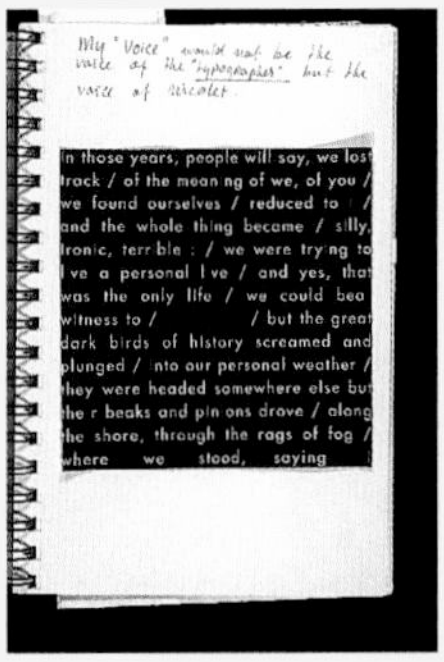

in those years, people will say, we lost
track / of the meaning of we, of you /
we found ourselves / reduced to /
and the whole thing become / silly,
ironic, terrible / we were trying to
live a personal life / and yes, that
was the only life / we could bear
witness to / / but the great
dark birds of history screamed and
plunged / into our personal weather /
they were headed somewhere else but
their beaks and pinions drove / along
the shore, through the rags of fog /
where we stood, saying


8

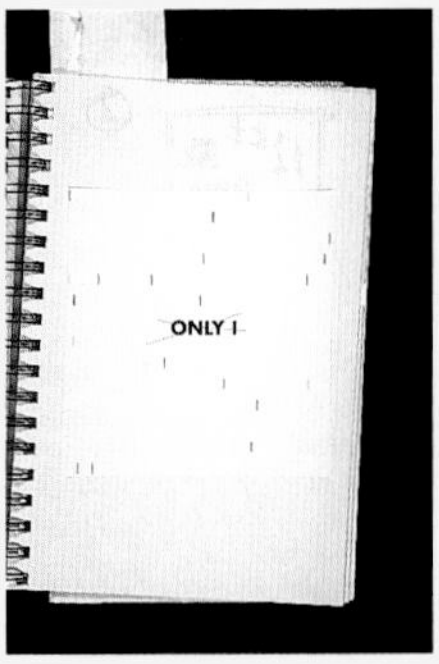


9

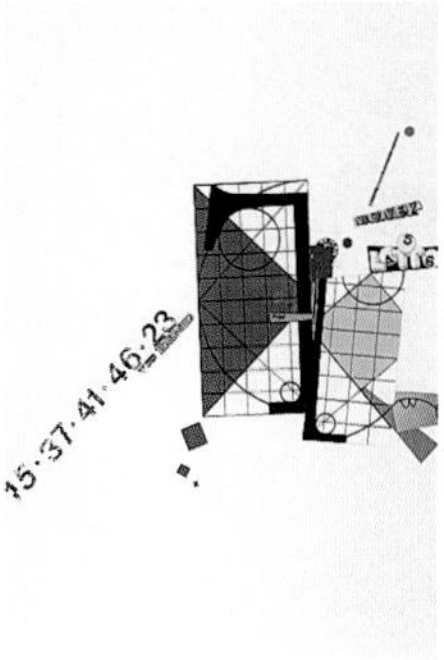

10

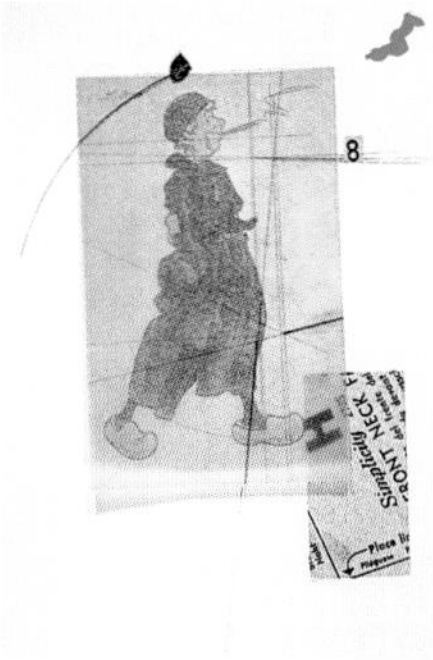

11

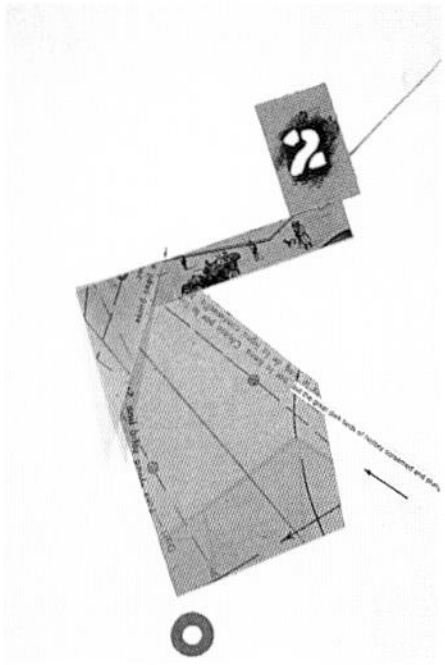

12

wemempty
in those years, people will say, we lost
track of the meaning of we, of you
we found ourselves reduced to i and
the whole thing became silly, ironic,
terrible: we were trying to live a
personal life and yes, that was the only life
we could bear witness to but the great
dark birds history of screamed and
plunged into our personal weather they
were headed somewhere else but their
beaks and pinions drove along the
shore, through the rags of fog where
we stood, saying i

13

"'More' seems to be an environmental statement. If it is an environmental statement, then the statement should be based on a fact. It should mean something. It should be this or that. I mean you can't stand outside of that. In your idea something is wrong because it doesn't do this or that. You can't stand on the side with this kind of subject. . .you **must express an opinion one way or another, but you don't do that." V.L.**

10-12

**Free compositions constructed with old postcards and found typographic objects that reference Dutch and American cultures.**

13

**By combining three words, *we, me,* and *empty,* a new word signifying the essence of the poem is created. The *m's* substituted with upside-down *w's* create a rhythmic pattern.**

**10-13: Kristin Hughes**

14

**Letter specimens mounted with pins inside a glass frame metaphorically represent a butterfly collection.**

15

**A list of words containing the word, *self,* provides a possible theme for further typographic investigation.**

16-17

**Pages from a sketchbook reveal an active ideation process.**

**14-17: Margaret Pharr**

14

15

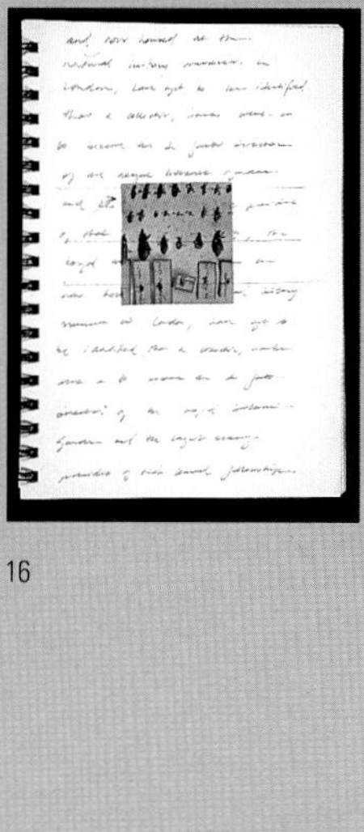

16

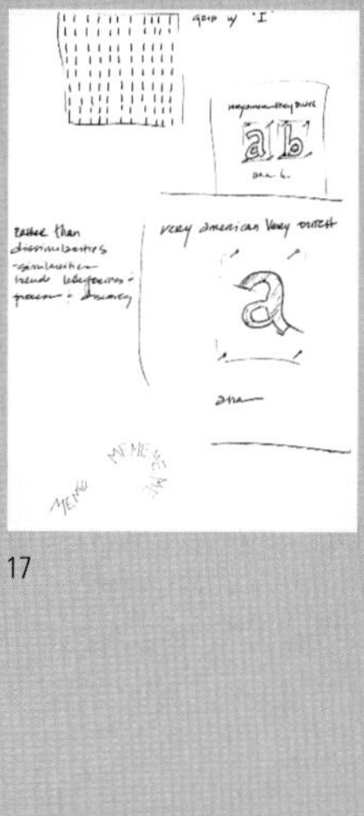

17

18
**The handprint is often found in primitive cultures as a sign for personal identity. Here it is used as a symbol in combination with the letter *i* to say "i am here; i am important."**

19
**In this permutation, selected lines from the poem appear on torn strips of paper running along the fingers of the hand.**

20
**The hand and the letter *i* joined into a single sign.**

21
**Page from a sketchbook showing further interpretive possibilities.**

22
**American price stickers attached to the notebook. Ordinary typographical objects found in the environment can provide impetus for investigation.**

23
**The poem written alternately in English and Dutch suggests a blending of two different cultures.**

24
**Type is extracted from its original context and presented in a new context to form a mirror image.**

**18-24: Barbara van Ruyven**

20

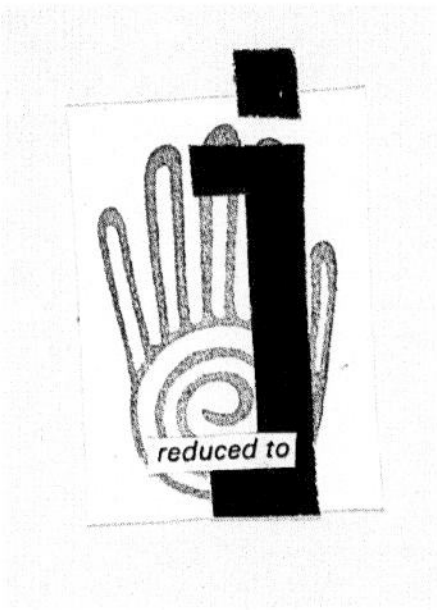
reduced to

21

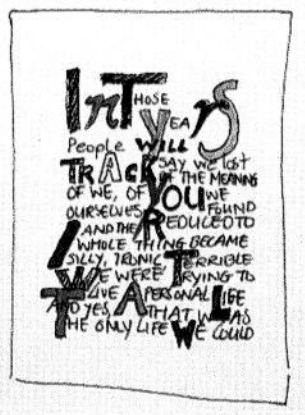

18

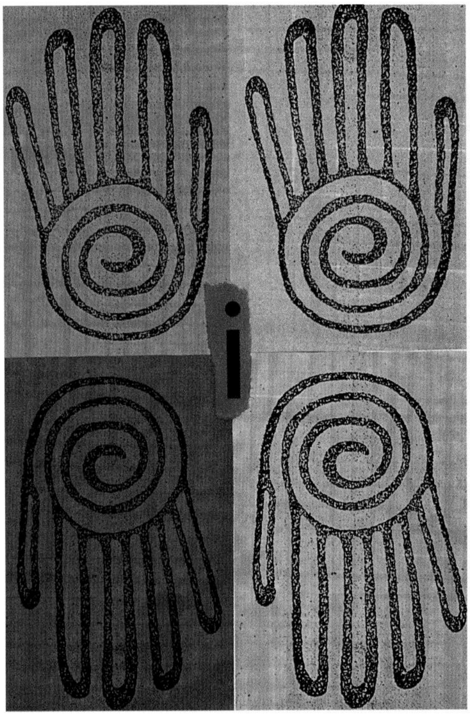

19

24

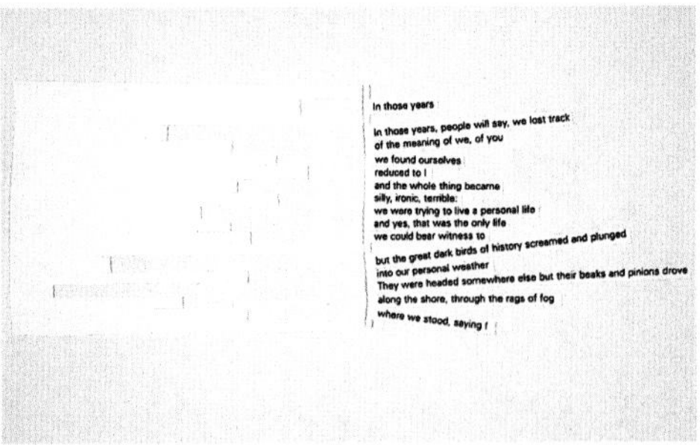
In those years
In those years, people will say, we lost track
of the meaning of we, of you
we found ourselves
reduced to I
and the whole thing became
silly, ironic, terrible:
we were trying to live a personal life
and yes, that was the only life
we could bear witness to
but the great dark birds of history screamed and plunged
into our personal weather
They were headed somewhere else but their beaks and pinions drove
along the shore, through the rags of fog
where we stood, saying I

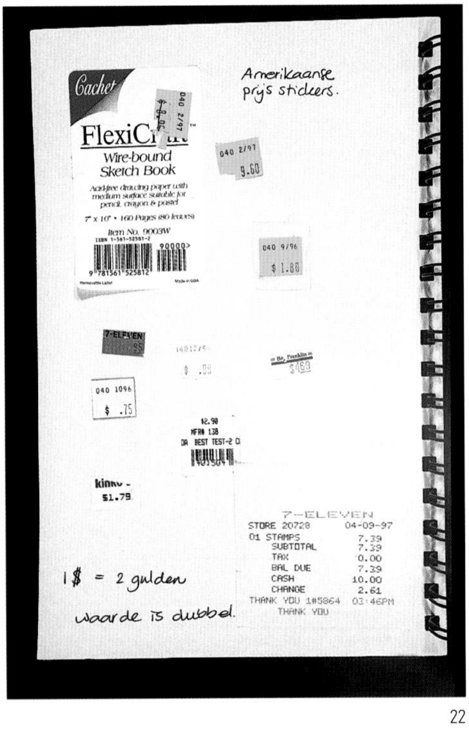
Amerikaanse
prijs stickers.
Cachet
FlexiCraft
Wire-bound
Sketch Book
7-ELEVEN
STORE 20728 04-09-97
01 STAMPS 7.39
SUBTOTAL 7.39
TAX 0.00
BAL DUE 7.39
CASH 10.00
CHANGE 2.61
THANK YOU
1$ = 2 gulden
waarde is dubbel.

22

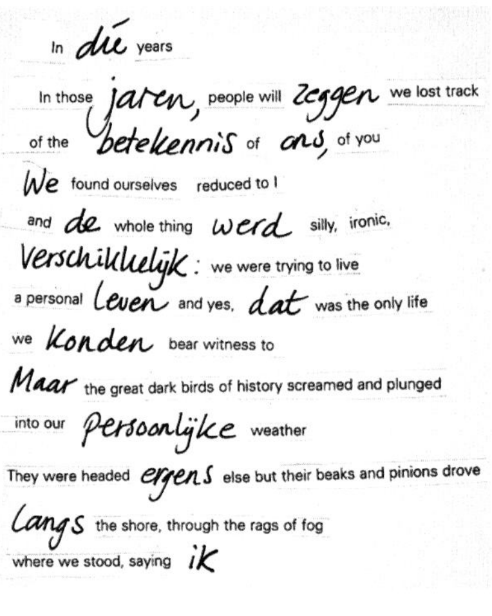
In die years
In those jaren, people will zeggen we lost track
of the betekennis of ons, of you
We found ourselves reduced to I
and de whole thing werd silly, ironic,
verschikkelijk: we were trying to live
a personal leven and yes, dat was the only life
we konden bear witness to
Maar the great dark birds of history screamed and plunged
into our persoonlijke weather
They were headed ergens else but their beaks and pinions drove
langs the shore, through the rags of fog
where we stood, saying ik

23

e g i n s v

e g i n s v

e g i n s v

e g i n s v

e g i n s v

e g i n s v

scheveningen

25

26

*A personal track*

*I drove somewhere, along the shore*
*we headed into rags of people*
*they were silly, reduced to beaks*
*great, their life was history*

*but then, in the fog*
*stood that whole terrible dark thing*
*we screamed to the birds:*
*we found a bear*

*and so we were trying*
*to witness the only meaning of life*
*for years and years and years and yes*

*the weather plunged*
*I became ironic*
*we lost the pinions*

**"It is true that with a flip book, you can add something to make a transformation. I think there is some confusion between more and a lot. You must take care that you don't deal with the meaning of a lot instead of more. More is growing. It is something active."**

H.G.

27

25

**An experimental interactive program enables the user to click various letters with the computer mouse. This activates an equivalent sound in the voice of the person seen on the screen. Potentially, any word or phrase can be generated. In the last frame, the word *scheveningen,* a Dutch beach resort, is heard.**

26

**The poem is rearticulated into a new poem with a new meaning.**

**25, 26: Persijn Broersen**

27

**A computer is used to swell the type of the poem beyond recognition. Only the poem's title is readable. The new image represents the failure of the poem's idealism.**

**27: Dima Stefanova**

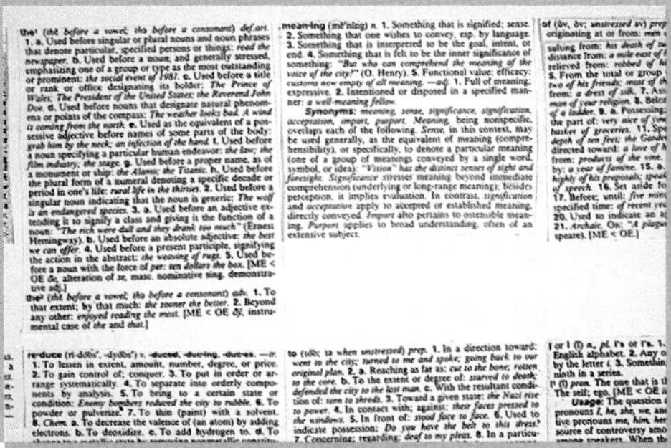

29

28

"One of the things I want to say about the format and the type size is that unlike Michel's piece, where he brought things that are very public and very large to a small space, you brought something very very small to a large space. What you have done in a very different way is to encourage people in a public setting to get close to something, to get intimate with it." S.W.

28

For this poster, which is perhaps more like a book due to the degree of text, dictionary definitions of the poem's words are presented. Whereas in most graphic design something large is introduced into a small space, this poster presents something small in a large space.

29

Detail of poster

28, 29: Esther de Vries

30

This experimental poster obliquely references the separateness of *I* and *WE*, as indicated in the poster's title, *Film sans me.*

31-34

A series of experimental postcards based upon the social and cultural words and images of workshop participants.

30-34: Jason Smith

30

31

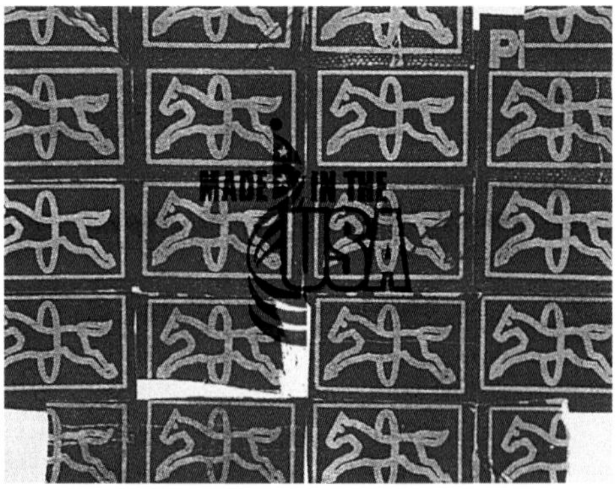

32

33

34

36

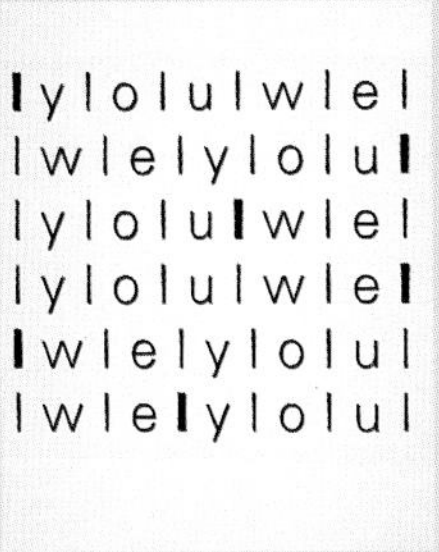

37

38

39

35

**The Dutch words *IK* (I), *JIJ* (YOU), and *WIJ* (WE) simultaneously form a rhythmic typographic pattern and a representation of human interaction. Red letters *I* suggest individuality within a social group.**

36

**The *I* forms in this experiment separate letters of the words *you* and *we* to suggest compartmentalization, alienation, and privacy.**

37

**A further investigation physically links the words *I*, *YOU*, and *WE* into a single new word, a statement of cooperation and community.**

38-39

**Environmental typography (billboard), and kinetic poster (t-shirt).**

**35-39: Christine Alberts**

"There was a study that preceded this, I think it was last night I saw you working on it. And I guess again I am not trying to find solutions for you, but if your goal is to find a purity of this form and idea, it seemed that what I saw was going in the right direction. It's kind of interesting, too, to think about the polemic of something being both pure and heroic. But that's a topic for another day. . .but then you know we do have examples of heroic sculpture on Monument Avenue, and there are days when it is more heroic than others. If you're looking for conditions that emphasize that sort of emotion, consider the sky, the way the monuments are lit from below, the effect of sunny and rainy days, how a specific group of people is interacting with them. All of this decreases or increases the heroicism of these objects."

J.M.

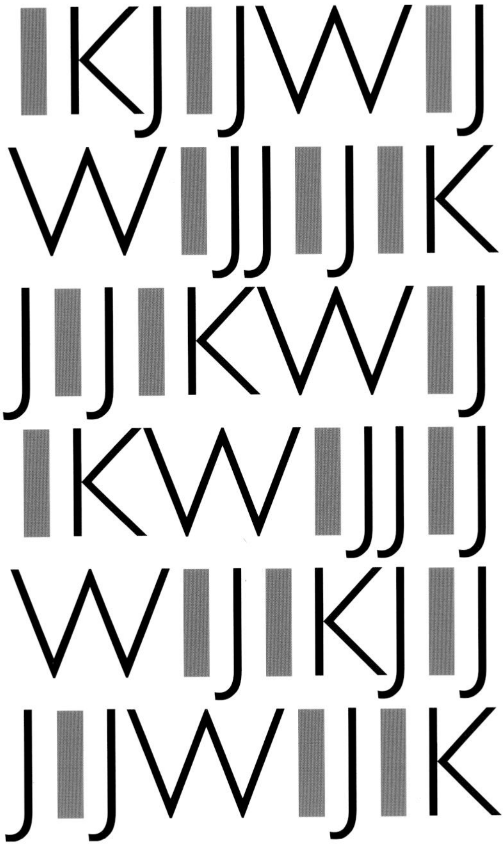


35

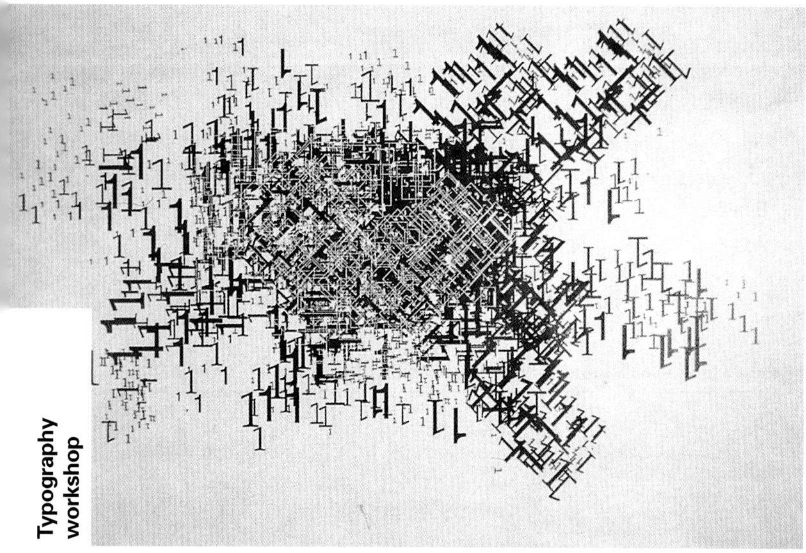

40

"That is a valid function for a poem on a poster. But in the end, a poem is more at home in a book. Very few poems are suitable for a poster, particularly if it is complex poetry. As poetry becomes a little more complex, as it becomes necessary to read a piece four or five times before it makes sense, the book is the most appropriate form.

**W.B.**

43

42

i sometimes wish to fly
quietly
impossibly          on air

but when i see you
i smile
wave hello
and want          to stay

41

+ex.ist
–ex.ist

44

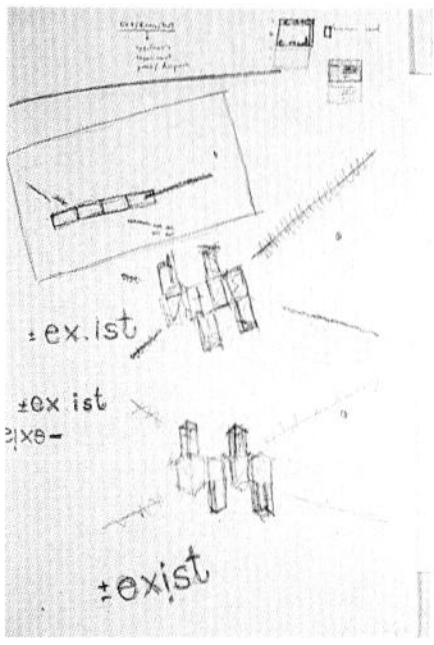

40
**A portrait of the city. Within crowded cities live both the rich and the poor, the famous and the obscure. The reality of the city is that it is a conglomerate of individuals.**

41
**The student's initial reaction to the poem was to write another poem, which focuses on an I/We theme in the context of his relationship to his wife.**

42
**The wing is part of a typographic performance wherein actual wings are worn as the poem is read aloud. The wings represent the student's wish to fly alone, though the bond to his wife beckons him to stay.**

43
**A sketchbook investigation of words and phrases about the student's life, which led to the design of a typographic time line.**

44
**By modifying the word *exist* with plus and minus signs, a statement about existence and nonexistence is made. The period separating the two parts of the word evokes a decimal point, and its role in denoting the whole and the fraction.**

**40-44: Erik Brandt**

4★4
★★★★
DONT WALK
LIVE FAST
TOGO AWAY
GULP FUEL
PUSH THRU
FEEL SURE
FLOW INTO
YOUR MYTH
TaKE CARe!

45

45

Shown here are spreads from a small, experimental book based on the designer's three obsessions: 1) cars, speed, and horses; 2) vernacular American type; 3) four-letter words. The word pairings, which express the obsession themes, consist entirely of four-letter words and are set in Venus Bold Extended. The title, 4★4 refers to the 16 words used in the book.

45: Harmen Liemburg

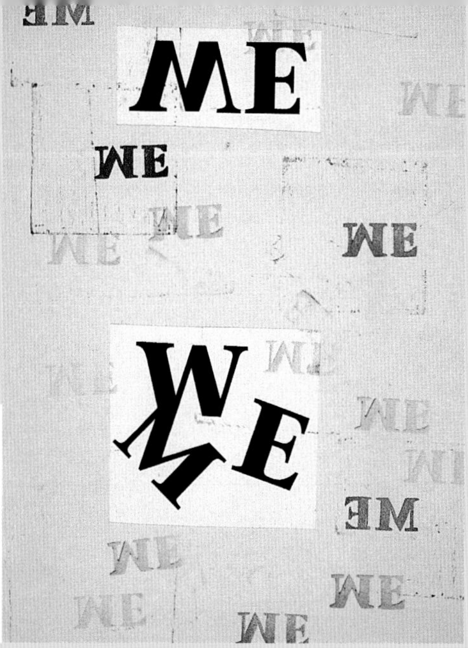


46

47

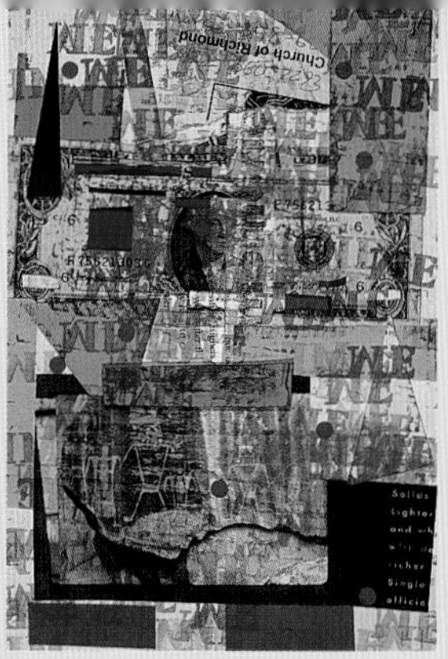

49

48

we lost track
of the meaning of WE , of you


46, 47
**Sketchbook investigations showing a rubber stamp design that reads *me* before it is stamped, *we* after it is stamped, and *me* after it is stamped and turned upside down.**

48
**The double reading of the stamp is used as an effective element in a poster design.**

49
**In an exploratory page from the sketchbook, the rubber stamp is used in combination with a multitude of cultural artifacts.**

50
**The American dollar bill, a global economic symbol, is deconstructed into typographic units and reconstructed into a thought-provoking visual poem related to wealth, greed, and selfishness.**

**46-50: Michel van Duyvenbode**

50

53

54

55

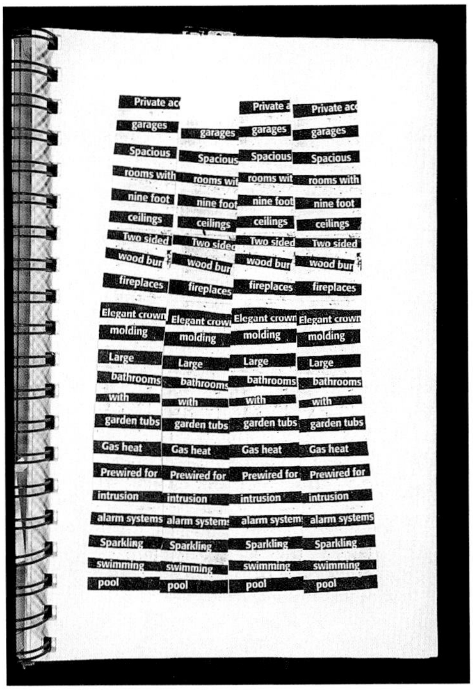


51

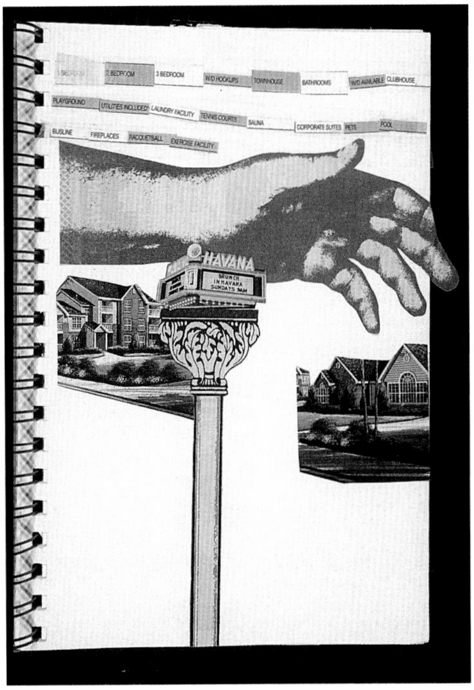


52

51, 52

**Fascinated by American suburbia, this Dutch student created collages that make statements about things people buy but really don't need. Amenities for purchasers of new homes are extracted from home listings magazines and presented as a dizzying repetitive pattern. Another collage combines this typographic information with suburban images.**

53-55

**Expressive sketches by a Dutch student visiting America for the first time, reveal impressions of social and economic conditions.**

**51-55: Margit Lukacs**

56

**Interpretive poster.**

57

**Type and image combine to express the you/I duality. An outstretched finger is substituted for the *I*.**

**56, 57: Jennifer McMaster**

**"It was towards the end of the book that you established the idea of the meshing and cluttering of everything. I don't feel that this device is as effective. At some point it becomes too muddy." B.R.**

56

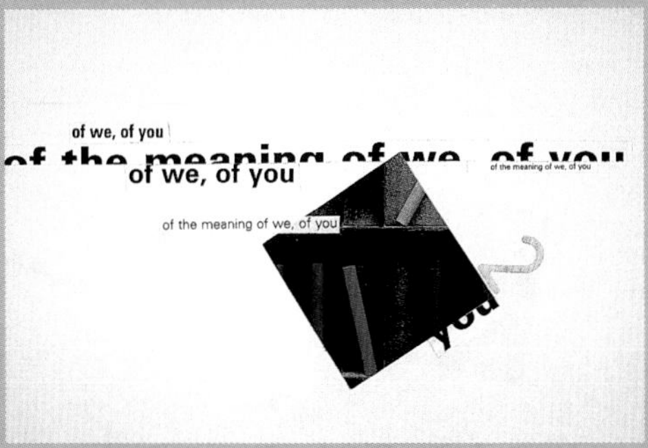


57

# COMMUNITYSM

58

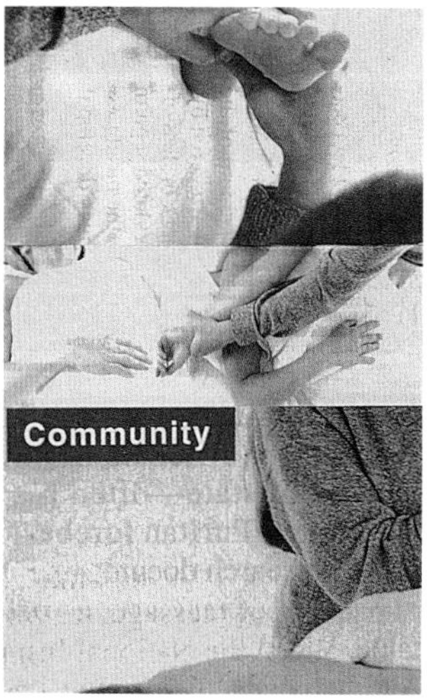
Community

59

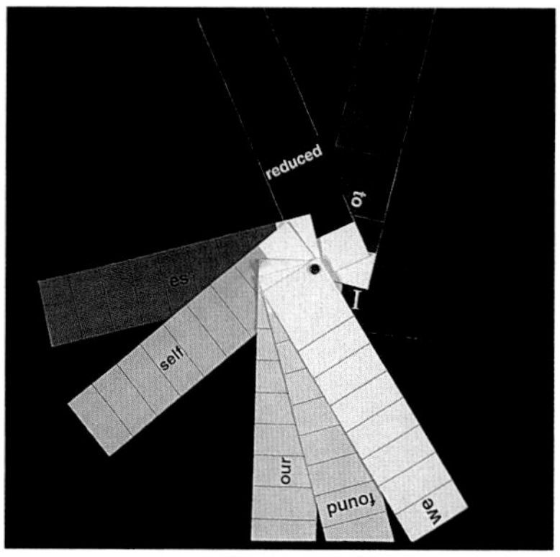
reduced
to
I
es
self
our
found
we

60

58
**COMMUNITY and ISM are combined into COMMUNITYSM to reveal an active, ideal word for community.**

59
**In a poster, the concept of an ideal community is illustrated through a combination of type and image.**

60
**Pronouns extracted from the poem are placed upon pages of a swatch book for an interactive book that is each time read differently.**

**58-60: Monika Wiechowska**

61
**The question of how a poem might be used in a poster is answered by enlarging the provocative typographic phrase, *we lost.* The comma suggests that the phrase is but a part of the poem.**

62
**In a preliminary study, the theme "we lost" is referenced by that which is missing. Words of the poem encircle a torn hole in the paper.**

63
**The poem forms *we* to reveal its essence.**

64
***WE* as a typographic expression of many *I*s**

65
**Studied analysis of the poem's content.**

**61-65: Yael Seggev**

61

, we lost
In Those Years - a poem by Adrienne Rich

62

63

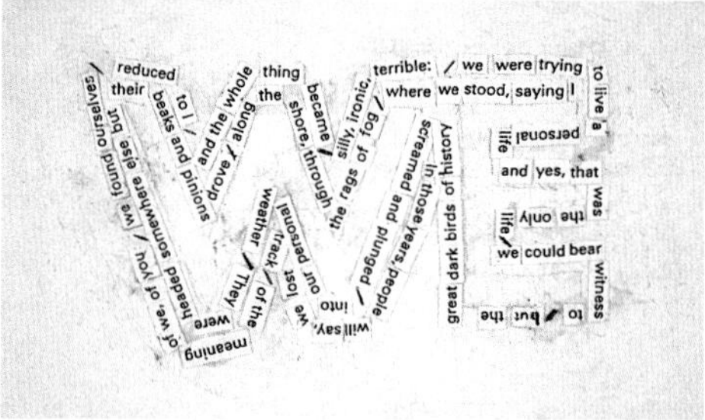

WE
I
WE

64

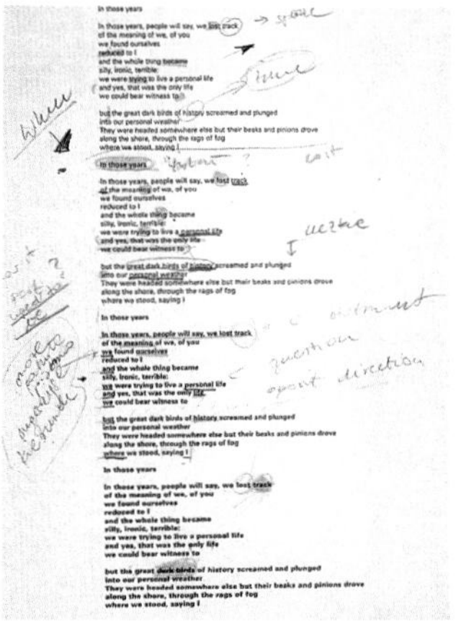

65

66

67

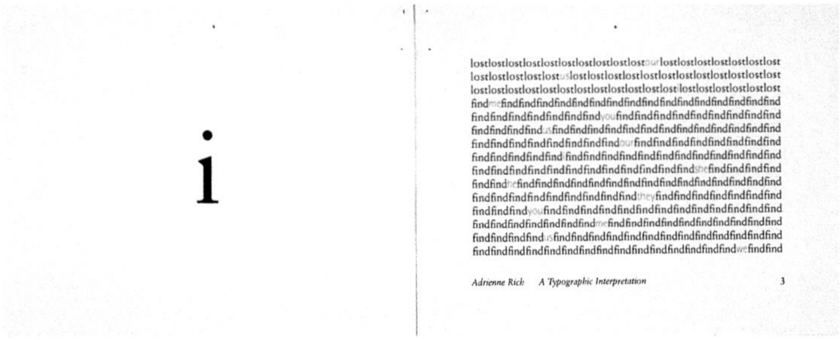


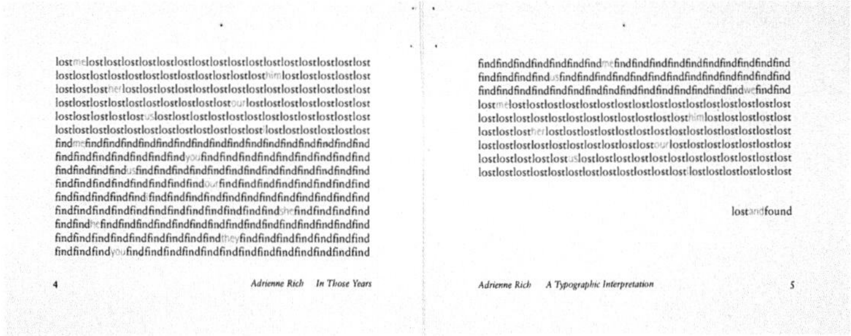


68

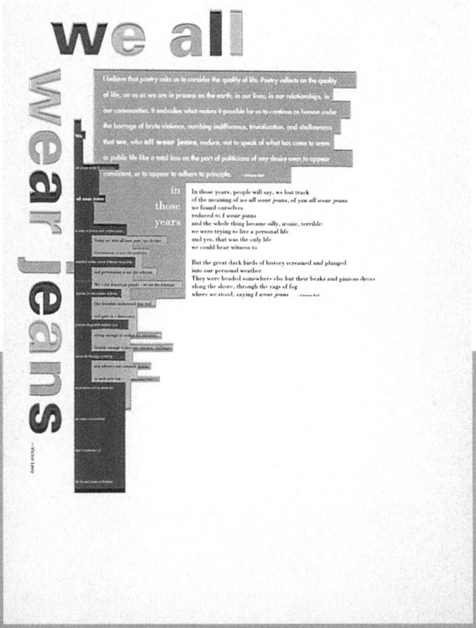


69

66

A typographic experiment exploring the relationship between numbers and words: 1 is for me, 2 is for we, 3 is for community.

67, 68

Pages of an experimental book with the theme of being lost and then found.

66-68: Sheila Barrett

69

The statement "we all wear jeans" references human equality, and the fact that many people share similar needs and desires.

69: Libby Hiller

70

The letters of the word *CAUCUS*, which refers to a group of people seeking agreement on an issue, are formed by plucking kernels from ears of corn. The kernels provide an apt metaphor for people cooperating with other people, and of parts creating a whole.

70: Barbara Spies

"Going back to your stamp, I think there is potential here that you haven't tapped in terms of the technology or the process of making a stamp. . . that by making it into a stamp there is an opportunity to make many of them very easily. Yet there has remained a singular, one-of-a-kind juxtaposition of me/we. I think that the ease with which you can now make a hundred of these gives you the opportunity to expand on the opposition between the two things. As you have it now, 'me' is one object; 'we' is another object. They are related in their reflection. I think you have the opportunity through the technology you have used to very easily make multiples of them. In what I see, this potential is untapped." C.W.

70

# P

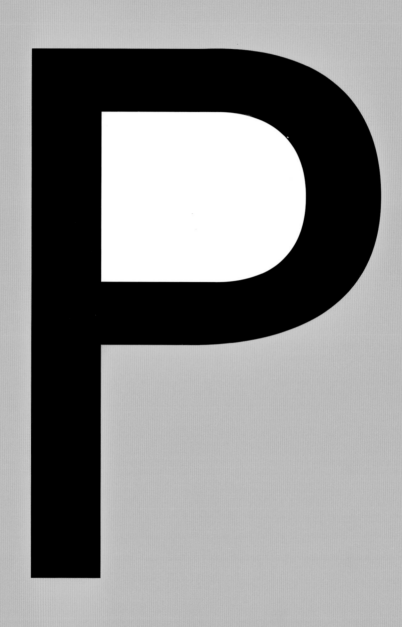

# Designer profiles

5

This chapter presents profiles of four professional graphic designers, each with a distinct and innovative typographic voice. Each profile features a designer's statement, a portfolio of work, and typographic experiments conducted specifically for this book.

# Elliott Peter Earls

For Elliott Peter Earls, experimentation is not a luxury for which he must scratch time out of his day. Since his student days at Cranbrook Academy of Art, where he received an MFA in design, it has been integral to his creative process, something wired into his psyche, a driving force in his life and work.

Earls is founder of The Apollo Program, a design firm, type foundry, and multimedia studio. As well as his involvements in print-based graphic design and type design, he freely crosses interdisciplinary boundaries to create highly sensory, interactive, multimedia environments that combine images, sound, type, poetry, and movies.

His work is driven by a personal philosophy shaped in large part by an amalgamation of thought. Based on the writings of futurists, literary figures, and filmmakers, including Alvin Toffler, Hal Foster, and Italo Calvino, he has defined the "prosumptive" designer. The prosumptive designer is totally immersed in culture, a relentless consumer of new technology and a producer of "info-tainment" products – products ranging from basic broadsides to interactive CD-ROMs. The prosumptive designer is uncompromisingly self-reliant, passionate, committed, and true to self. The prosumptive designer is a lateral thinker who subverts and deconstructs convention, intentionally misreads and misinterprets, rejects his or her own conclusions, and shifts comfortably between related disciplines.

A series of posters designed by Earls for the Apollo Program have over the years gained wide notoriety. They function simultaneously to promote The Apollo Program's fonts, among which are *Dysphasia, Blue Eye Shadow, Hernia,* and *Subluxation.* They also provide a canvas for exploring poetry and thought. The viewer is jerked about in a curious discourse of form, and if typographic conventions are adhered to at all, they are intentionally masked.

*Throwing Apples at the Sun,* a pioneering interactive CD-ROM by Earls, is a richly layered and highly unpredictable experience. Without actually experiencing it firsthand, any attempt at describing it in words falls far short. But here is a vain attempt: by passing the cursor or clicking the mouse over a dense backdrop of images and type elements, additional layers are revealed. These layers are not only visual; they are also audible and kinetic. Clicking on a text block, for example, activates another image, a movie, or a spoken phrase. Upon interacting with this CD, one soon finds that it bears no resemblance to the predictable structures of most other multimedia projects. This one is totally unpredictable, and it is this attribute that makes it so enjoyable. This interactive feast reveals Earls' unconventional visual sensitivity, and his uncanny ability to remove the viewer from cultural expectations by making the familiar strange.

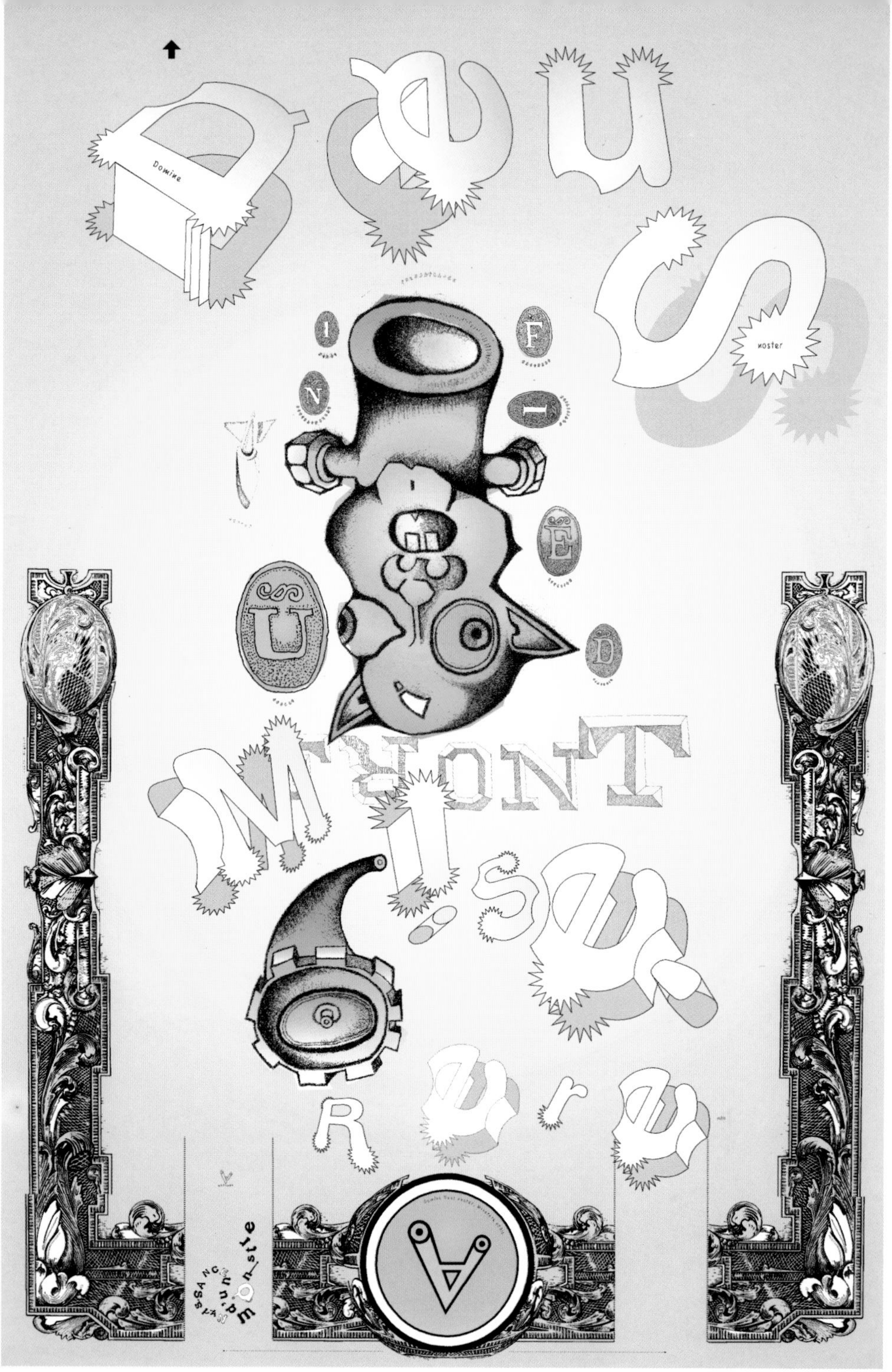

1
**The Apollo Program experimental poster**

1

Designer's statement

**1997, situated like a human head on the shoulders of the millennium, forces us into solitary dialog with his-story. Think of this as my Vision Induced by a String Found on my Table or my Pietà, or Revolution by Night. The grotesque caricature of the post world war one avant-garde, the ennui of the venetian-poser-skate-punk, all tools at our disposal. Like the half-wit Karl Appel, flung cannonballish at circus clown canvas, I too paint grunt "like a barbarian in a barbaric age." I'm thoroughly disinterested in the eloquence and simulated profundity that lies between quotation marks, but for the sake of ritualized discourse, let me take a stab at it:**

**"A painter is lost if he finds himself." –Max Ernst**

**The fact that he has succeeded in not finding himself is regarded by Max Ernst as his only 'achievement'.**

**Well played. . . I too cherish the suppression of logic and midnight games of linguistic Chinese checkers. But to what end? This question sweeps across my cerebellum like some medieval bubonic plague. Leaving in its foul wake the stench of value relativism and post-utopian thought. I'm the sad child of a tribe of ebola monkeys. Intellectually, environmentally and financially disenfranchised.**

2-4
**The Apollo Program experimental posters**

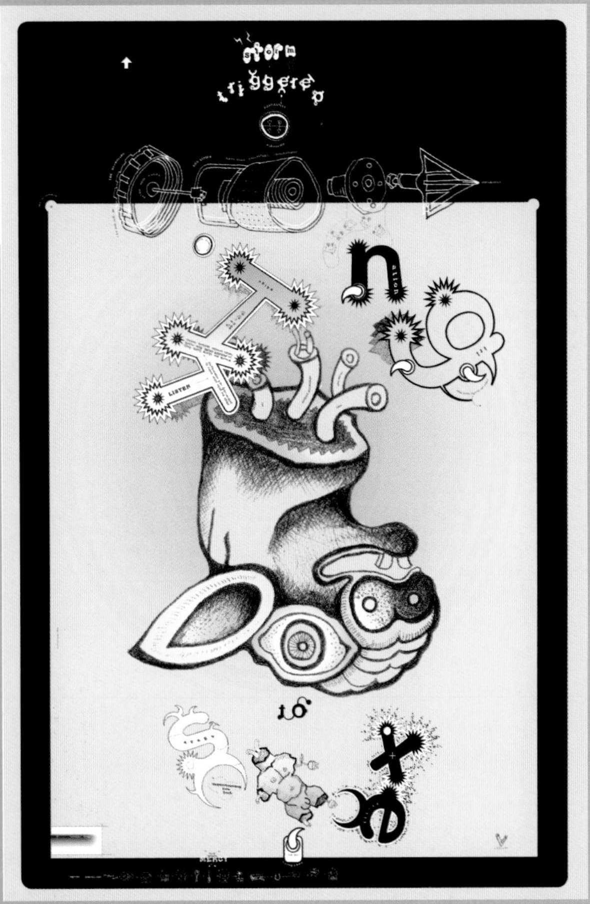

2

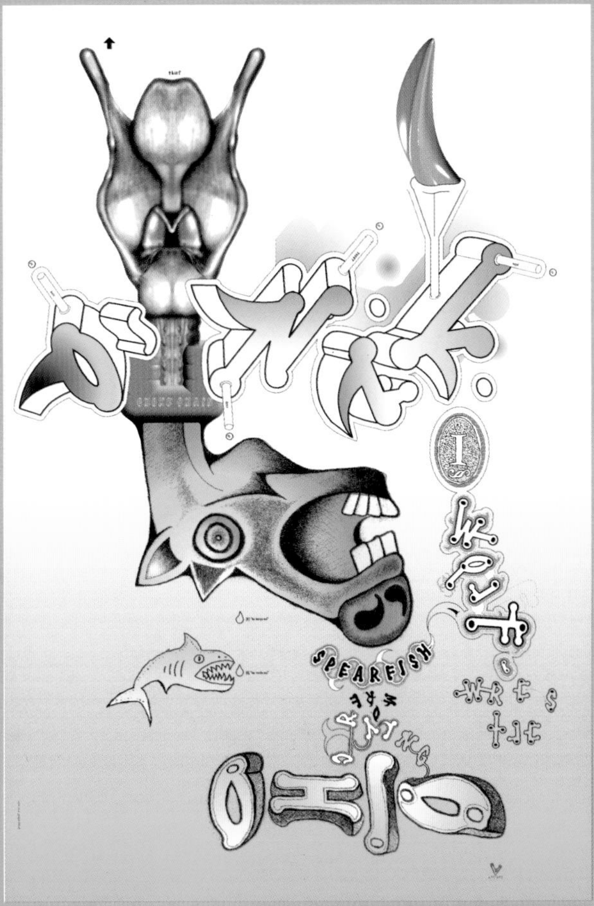


3

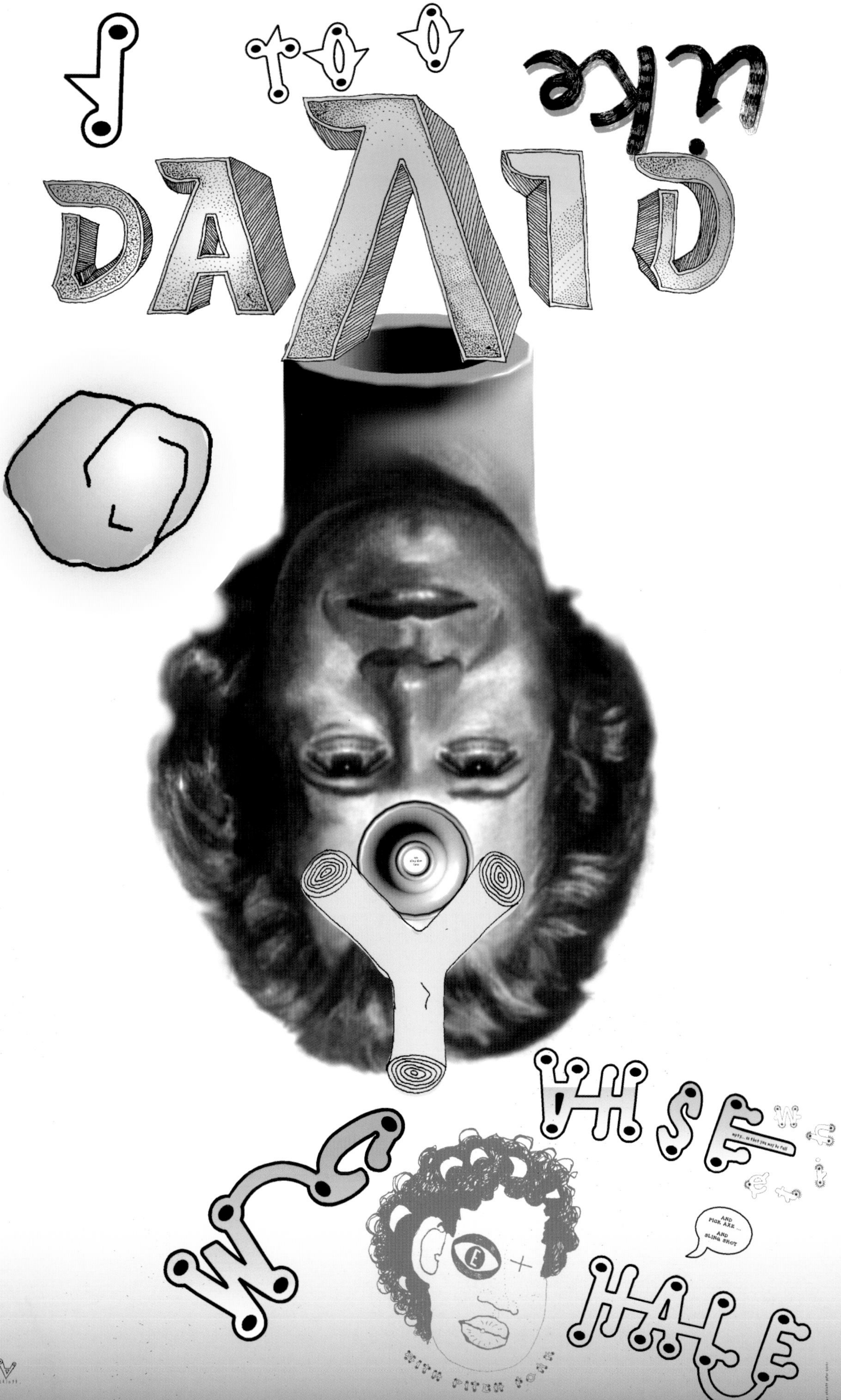
DAVID
like
WAY
WISE
AND PICK AXE ... AND SLING SHOT
HALE
WITH PITCH FORK

5, 6
**Screen samples from interactive CD-ROM, *Throwing Apples at the Sun***

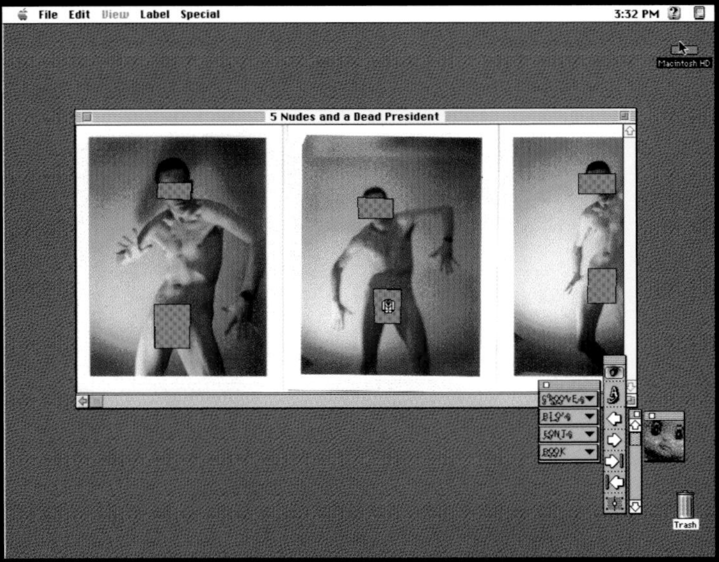


5

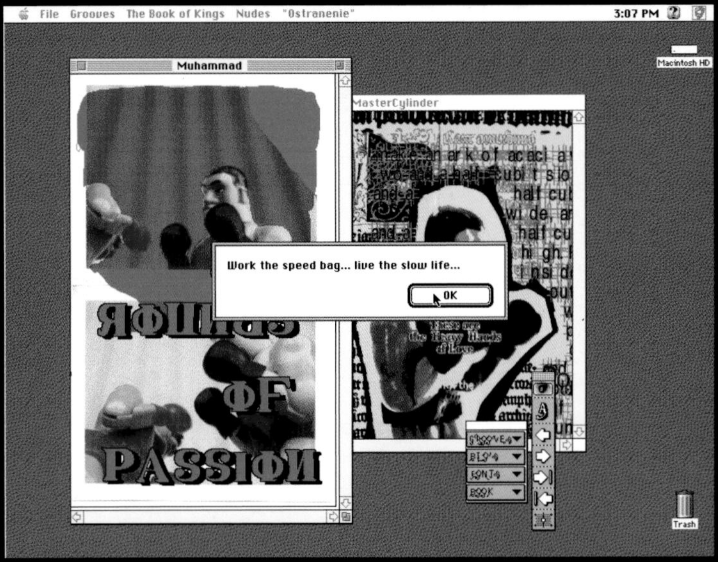


6

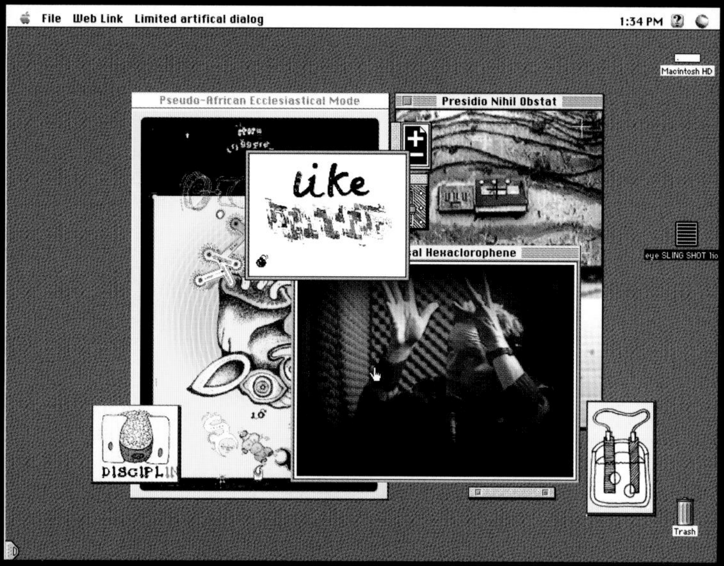


7

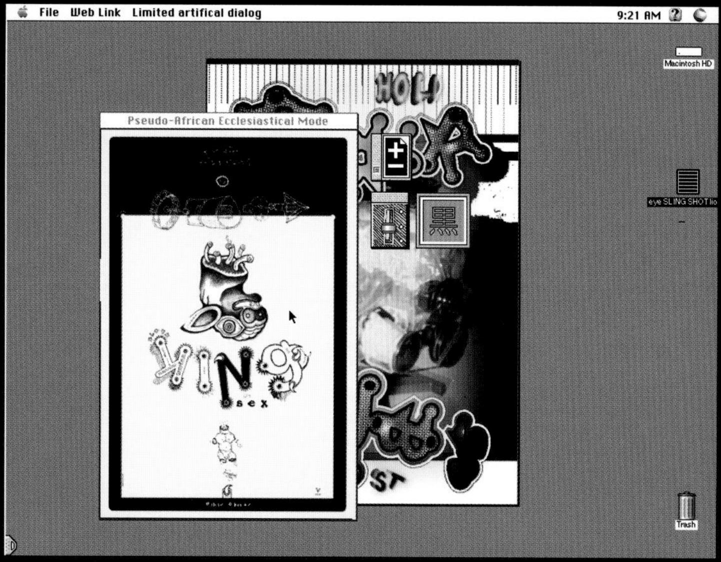


8

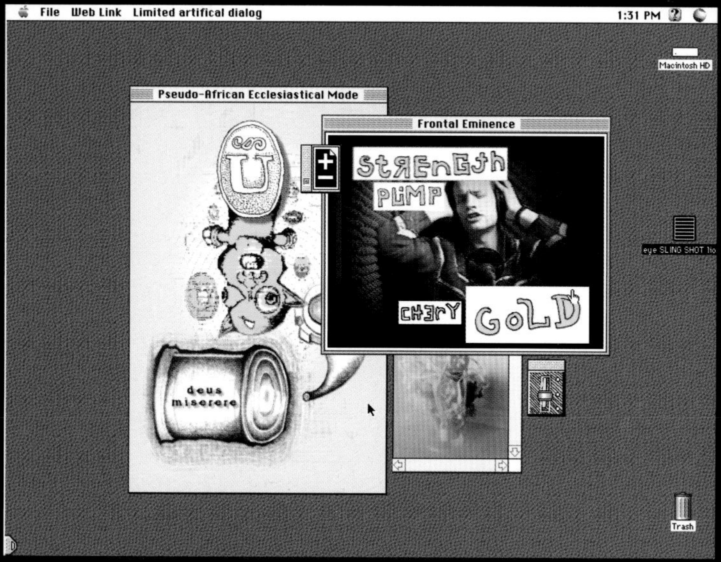


9

7-9
**Screen samples from interactive CD-ROM, *Eye Slingshot Lions***

sometimes
s e l f
or trait or
I'M STRONG

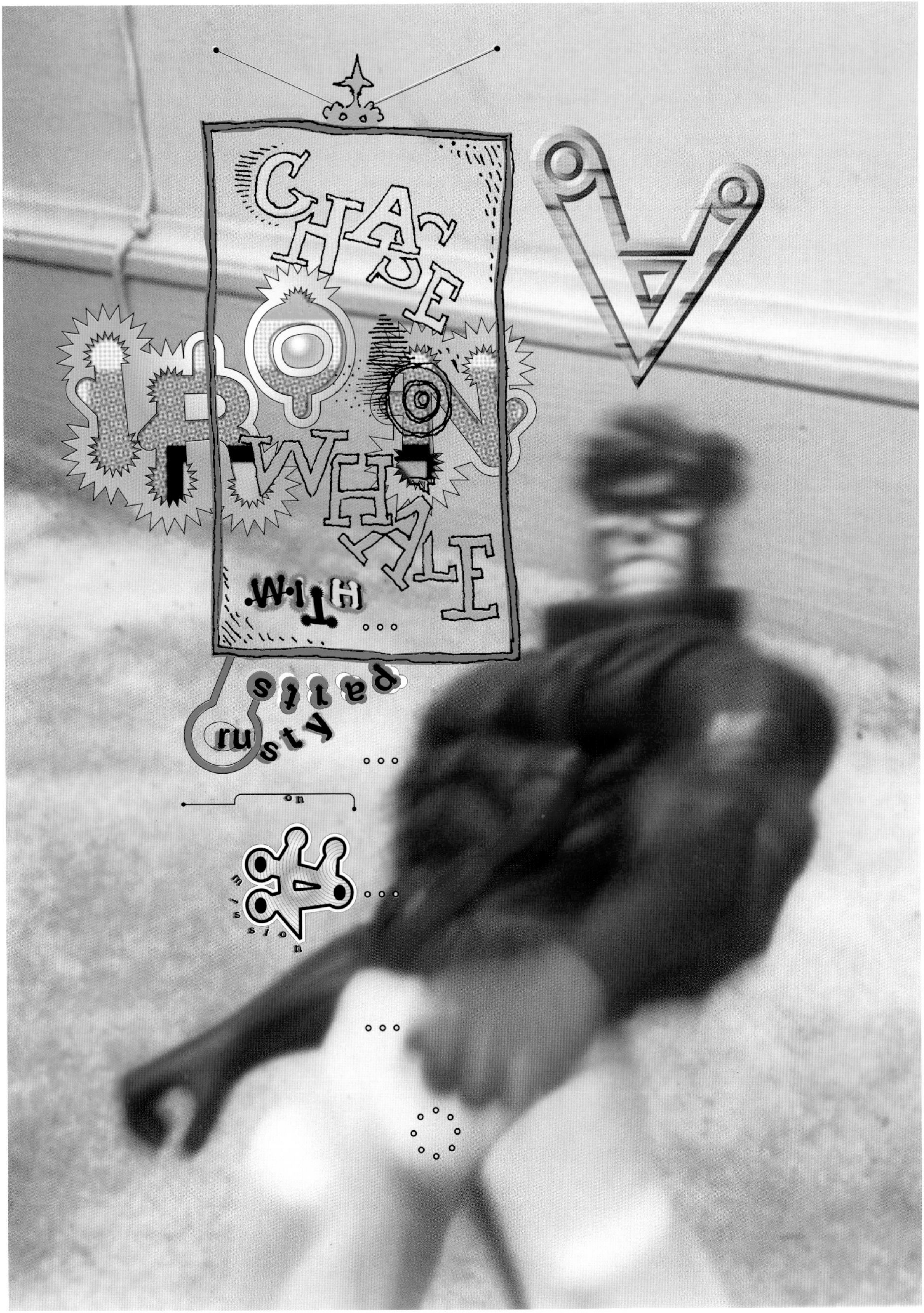
CHASE
IRON
WHALE
WITH
rusty
pants
on
mission

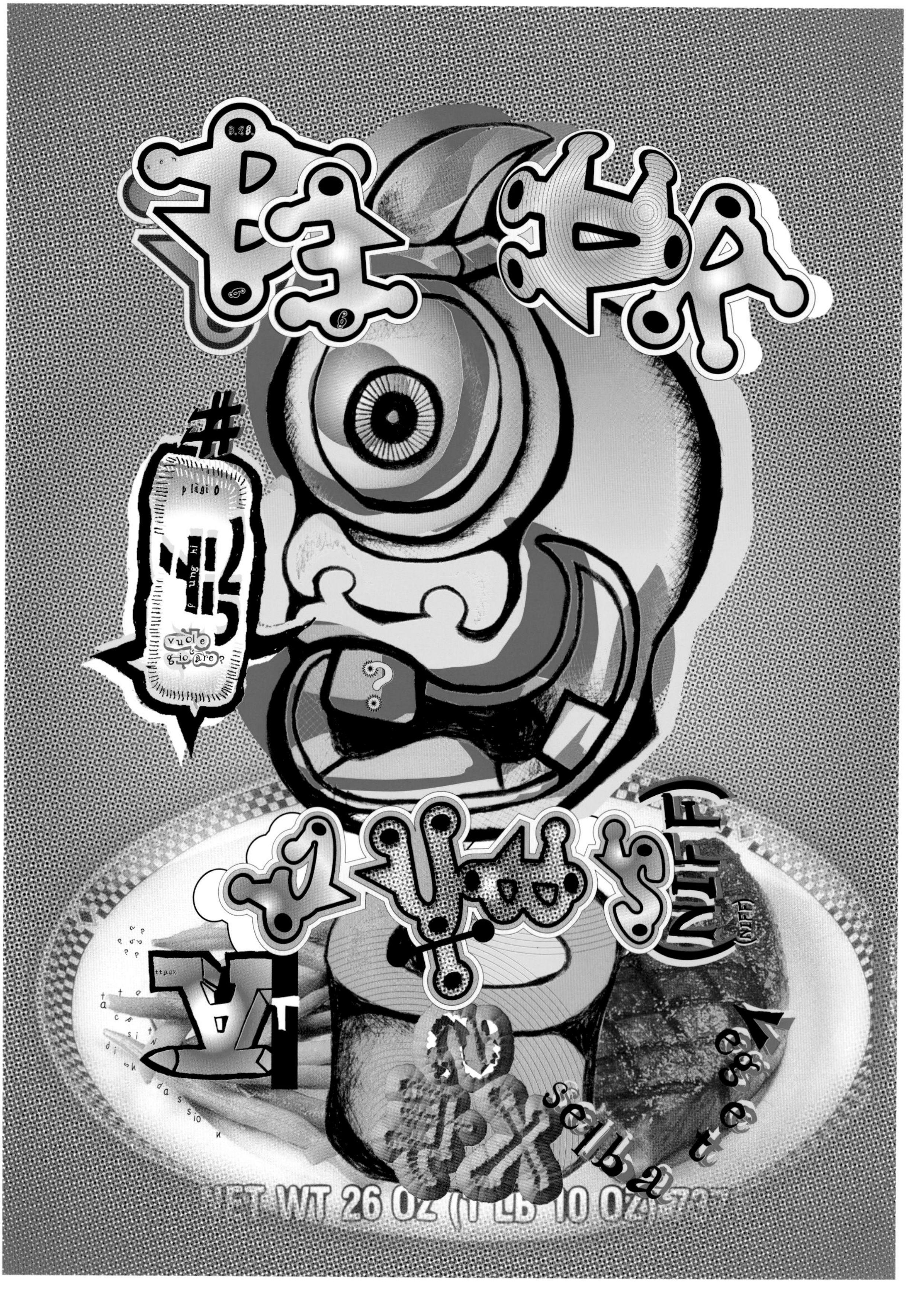

3.28.
plagio
vuole giocare?
(NUFF)
ET WT 26 OZ (1 LB 10 OZ)

Wood
POW
FLY

Jean-Benoît Lévy was born in a small village in the vineyards overlooking Lake Geneva, Switzerland. He now lives and works in Basel. His studio, which he founded in 1988, is named AND (Trafic Grafic). "AND" because without clients, designers are nothing; (Trafic Grafic) because once graphic design is produced, it travels, and because Lévy himself loves travel.

Without knowing the city's reputation for design, Lévy went to Basel to study graphic design. In 1978, he entered the graduate program at the Allgemeine Kunstgewerbeschule (School of Design), where he studied with Armin Hoffman, Wolfgang Weingart, and Max Schmidt. Since then, he has lived and worked in San Francisco, and taught at various design schools, including the Art Center College of Design, Europe, and the Rhode Island School of Design. Having a passionate need to be aware of current design developments, he stays in close contact with designers throughout Europe and America.

Lévy finds ample opportunity to experiment with typography while designing street posters, large-scale broadsides that evocatively and dramatically inform pedestrian traffic. These posters visually suggest moments frozen in time through various graphic processes. Lévy uses the street poster as a platform for typographical exploration, for he finds this medium provides opportunities for free and lively expression.

A pivotal characteristic of Lévy's posters is a magnetic synergy between type and image. He often art directs or relies upon talented photographers to create evocative images and contribute to visual solutions. These images, often montages of photographs, are characteristically processes, he then applies typography that visually optimizes and energizes the images and thus the message.

The street posters on pages 126 and 127 reveal Lévy as a visual poet who rather than persuading his audience, creates mood pictures that evoke positive responses in viewers. "I want to create posters that have the impact of modern poems or rock songs," he says. Lévy does not ascribe to a specific visual style or formula; rather, he explores many different possibilities, attempting to find solutions that through some twist, transcend the ordinary and the mundane.

The theater posters shown on pages 128 and 129 evolved from preliminary sketches, made after reading the plays. Lévy then art directed the photography, using the actors for models. The experiment for these posters was to push the limits of his design and typography, while also preserving the spirit of the theater company's advertising.

A point of fact about street posters in general is their impressive scale and dominant presence in the environment. Though their life is usually very short, they can potentially remain in the mind of the viewer long after they weather and decay. Lévy's posters achieve this with an articulate blend of type and image. He states, "My work is really good to me when I feel I can view my own posters without becoming bored. I am able to observe what they give to the public and to me, as if someone else had designed them."

The secret to Lévy's experimentation lies not only in his playful typographic processes, but also in his creative involvement with clients and

**My life is an experiment**

Being experimental with typography is a complex exercise, because it requires time. In my life I have met only a few people who have decided to use some of their precious time for typographic experiment. Wolfgang Weingart and Helmut Schmidt are among those that appear to have this desire. Weingart's Basel School program remains one of the rare places in the world where it is still possible for the willing student to try and try again, and to reserve time for this process.

It is rare to provide yourself with an opportunity to make what you want, particularly in graphic design. I am an independent graphic designer, and beyond the "real" works that I do for my clients, I find much less time to be really experimental in my work. Posters are one of the only chances for me to play as I wish. If I'm lucky, I can make between 3 to 5 posters in a year's time.

Personally, I don't see myself as an experimental graphic designer. For me, "experimental" is more related to how the public reacts to my work. I then use this feedback as a guide for my global work. When designing a poster or a special page as in this book, I feel more involved in a process of expression than of experiment. Personally, I'm not really sure if I am just reproducing what I know graphically or if I am experimenting with emotions.

Experimenting involves real creation. Maybe it is about making typographical accidents, recognizing them, and then finding the courage to use them in applied projects. That's why I'm always pushing young students to take the opportunity – when they are in school – to be experimental, and not just to try to imitate what they see in books in order to develop a style. Style may or may not come later.

For the four experimental pages in this book, I chose 20 postcards – messages written to me by women over a period of about 20 years. Half of them are relatives or good friends; others are more a part of my sentimental life. From each postcard I chose a sentence that is important to me. From each sentence I selected an expression. Combining all the statements together results in a new message, something that is like a resumé of my past life, a record of my relationships with women over the years. The experiment here aims to extract written statements and to reorganize them into a typographical composition.

Where I go from here in typography or in my life, remains to be seen. But I think of this open future as an opportunity. With a little bit of luck, this fragile state of things could lead me to a few moments of real experiment.

1
Poster
Photography: Alan Humerose

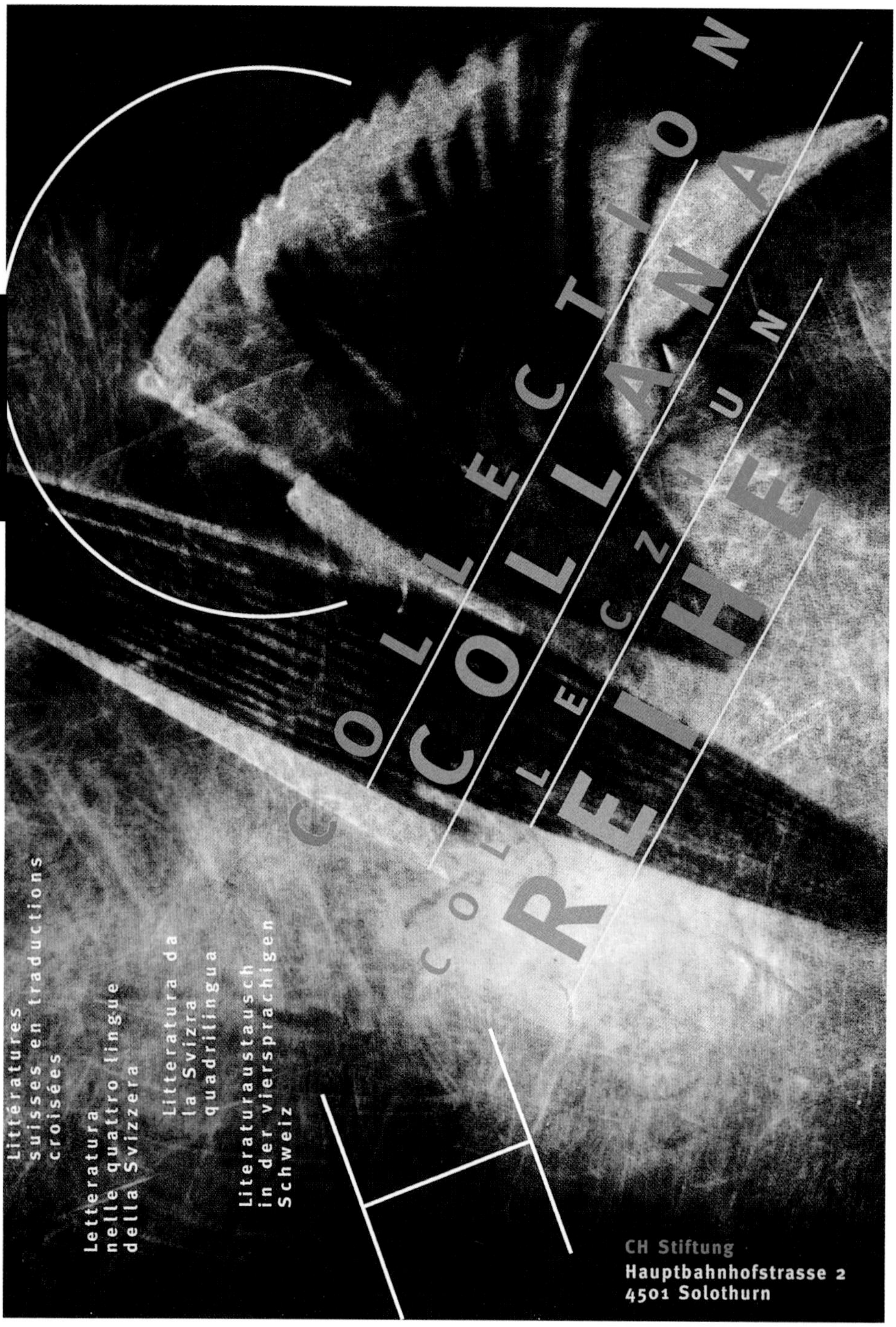


1

2
Exhibition poster
3
Poster for the Watch & Jewelry Store
Photography: Franz Werner
4
Concert poster
Photography: Jean-Pascal Imsand
5
Poster for a hairdresser
Photography: Leah Demchick

1993
du 13 mars
au 18 avril
Exposition
Galerie de Ballens
1144 Ballens/Morges
(021) 809 54 35
Jean Claude Vieillefond
Galerie de Ballens
2

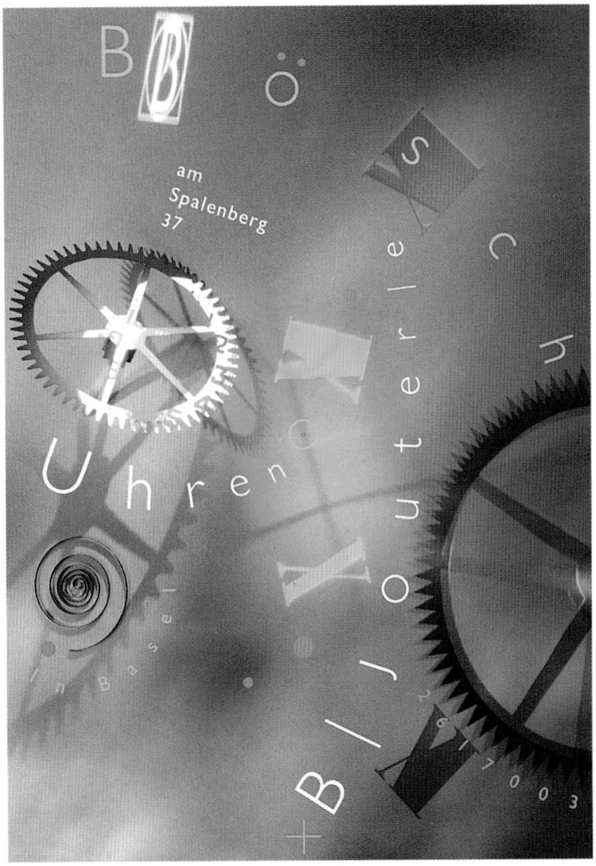
am
Spalenberg
37
Uhren
in Basel
+Bijouterie
3

Société des Concerts
de la Cathédrale de Lausanne
4

LEONHARDSSTRASSE 3 BASEL
ADRESSE
5

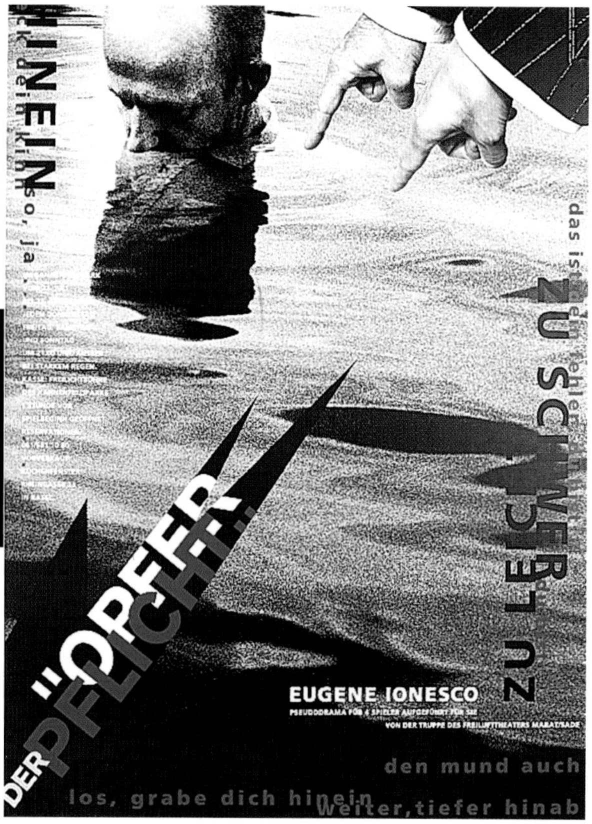
HINEIN
so, ja...
das ist ein fehler
ZU SCHWER
ZU LEICHT
DER
"OPFER
PFLICHT
EUGENE IONESCO
PSEUDODRAMA FÜR 4 SPIELER AUFGEFÜHRT FÜR SIE
VON DER TRUPPE DES FREILUFTTHEATERS MARAT/SADE
den mund auch
los, grabe dich hinein
weiter, tiefer hinab

6

DIE
VOM
BALLADE
GROSSEN
MAKABREN
Das Spiel beginnt
MICHEL DE GHELDERODE
MARAT / SADE
LARM

7

SURABAYA
warum bist du so roh ?
mein Gott, ich liebe dich so.
JOHNNY
HAPPY
END
DOROTHY LANE
MARAT / SADE
BRECHT WEILL
HAUPTMANN

8

Prix de Lausanne
1994
Lausanne
22e concours international pour jeunes danseurs
Théâtre de Beaulieu
Location Billetel
Demi-finale: 29 janvier, 14.00 h.
Finale: 30 janvier, 17.00 h.
Classe sur scène: dès 16.30 h.

11

9

10

6-10
**Theatre posters**
**Photography:**
**Stefan Meichtry** (6-9)
**Martin Klotz** (10)

11-13
**Dance theatre posters**
**Photography: Philippe Pache**

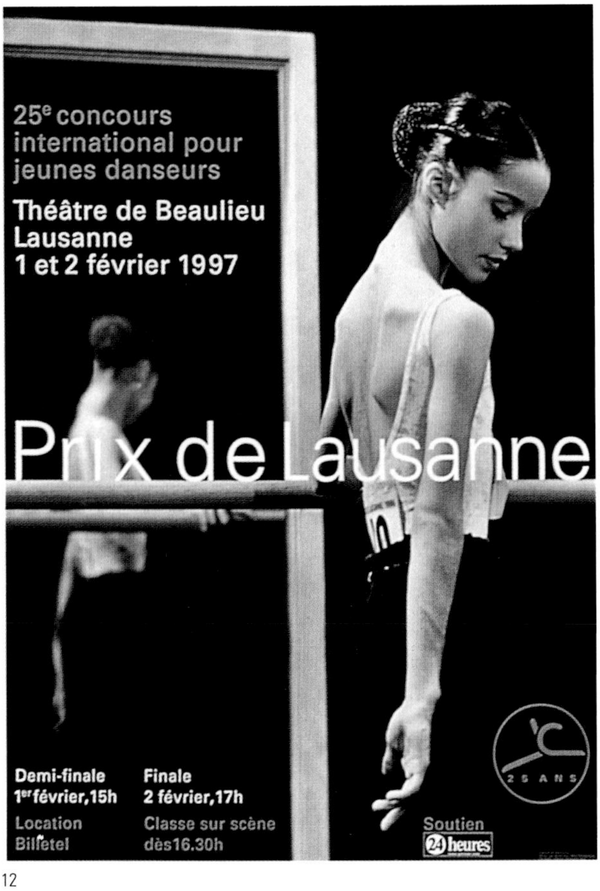


12

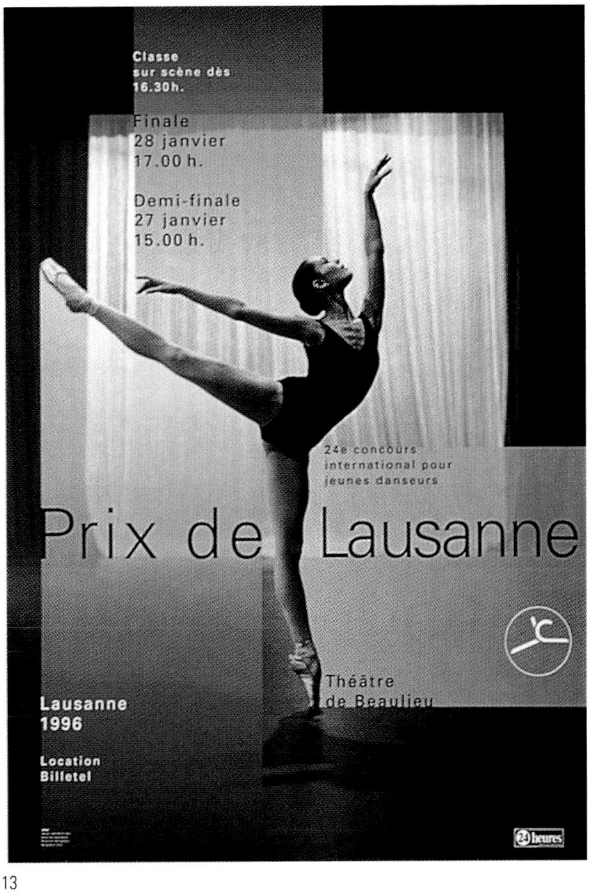


13

C'est vraiment parfait ici

Merveilleux endroit pour les amoureux: Hôtel de charme, vue sur la mer, patisseries magiques

Birte

I know you thought that you would never hear from me - but here I am

E

Ton téléphone m'a fait plaisir, je suis heureuse pour l'affiche

Sabine

Nathalie

Je m'y prends un peu tard pour les nouvelles, mais mieux vaut tard

F

Comment vas-tu? Que fais-tu? Où es-tu? Combien es-tu? Un, un 1/2, deux, deux 1/2, trois?

Leah

I hope that you are enjoying this snowey winter. One of the whitest that I can remember.

I

Je suis contente que tu aies chaud avec ce pull. J'ai reçu ce pain de fruit, je te l'envoie car j'en ai deux

Mirella

Le silence existe-t-il ? Qu'il y a-t'il de plus bruyant que le silence ? Il est minuit

L

Nous espérons que le beau temps va continuer à nous gâter, avec le soleil il fait bon vivre

Catherine Z

Leurs souffrances sont terminées – la vie continue, c'est triste, c'est bien, c'est ainsi

Myriam

Je serais bien venue, mais je redoute fort que ma conférence ne s'éternise au-delà de 18 heures

Sophie A

Je conservais très précieusement ce petit texte, convaincue qu'il plaîrait à quelqu'un sans savoir qui

Bobby

Je t'écris dans la jolie brume de Marin. On aura le soleil pour midi. Je suis très contente ici

Ruth

Je ne voulais pas te fâcher. C'est encore un malentendu. Je t'expliquerai. Je t'embrasse

Monique

À quand une heure de discussion sans téléphone ou intéruption?

Marie-Claude S

Il fait un beau primptemps, il y a des odeurs de terre et d'herbe nouvelle, je pense à vous

Anita

Tombés sur la lune – il n'y a pas de paroles pour ces paysages ici – que des larmes de je ne sais quoi

Katy I

Life bounces along – up and down – I'll fill you in more with the exiting stuff in my next letter

Comme l'Amérique est grande et belle | Je comprends que tu t'y plaises. Nous faisons un voyage formidable

Stéphane magiques

Birte but here I am

Sabina plaisir

Nathalie un peu tard

Cecilia Combien es-tu?

Leah remember

Alice chaud

Mirella Le silence

Suzi vivre

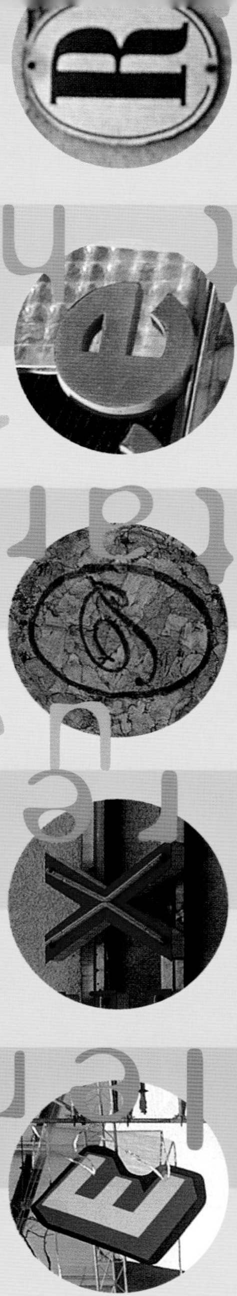

Kathy

up and down

Anita

que des larmes

Marie-Claude

je pense a vous

Monique

interruption

Ruth

encore un malentendu

Boby

le soleil

Sophie

sans savoir qui

Myriam

ne s'éternise

Catherine

la vie continue

# John Malinoski

Through his work, John Malinoski attempts to reconcile the complexity and contradictions of society, which he observes with intense curiosity and amusement. His typographic design and related work are simultaneously ordered and chaotic, logical and intuitive, crude and refined. These and other dual themes are the means by which he structures his life and makes sense of it all.

Malinoski was born and raised in a tiny rural town in west upstate New York. He enjoyed a Tom Sawyeresque boyhood which fed his curiosity of the world and fueled his imagination. He studied graphic design at SUNY College at Fredonia and the Rochester Institute of Technology. At RIT he was mentored by Heinz Klinkon and most significantly by R. Roger Remington. Here, he was thrown into the headwaters of graphic design history, most particularly the avant-garde period. He empathized with the work and theories of El Lissitzky, Alexander Rodchenko, Herbert Bayer, Moholy-Nagy, and Piet Zwart. Malinoski's formal vocabulary is clearly reminiscent of these and other individuals of the avant-garde. His desire to is to delve into complexity at times, and at other times to express ideas and form with great economy, a commitment intensified by his close association with the Dutch architect, Han Schroeder.

Malinoski's typographic work is informed by playful explorations that challenge his intellect and provide an escape from purely applied projects. Since his childhood, he has had an affinity for making things, for recycling material from old objects into new objects. Malinoski appropriates found and discarded materials to create three-dimensional, architectonic constructions that reflect a passion for form and space, line and shape, texture and tone. They are meant to serve no practical purpose other than to provide fuel for thought and a model for the design process. In these fantasy objects, one sees evidence of flying machines, of sailboats; they are the embodiment of his passion for straight-ahead jazz, the strains of John Coltrane, Miles Davis, Keith Jarrett. This music provides a backdrop for his studio activities.

Referred to as the last Gepetto, Malinoski also makes unconventional hand puppets consisting of fabric, cardboard, papier maché, wood, metal, buttons, cork, and type fragments. Through the use of abstract, geometric forms, these puppets express a plethora of human emotions, recalling the costume designs of Oscar Schlemmer of the Bauhaus. Malinoski's typographic designs are consistent with this visual vocabulary.

In a very real sense, Malinoski is a typographic archeologist, a practitioner who digs and rummages through the past in an attempt to revitalize and give new form to the present.

In addition to his addiction to typography and design issues in general, Malinoski heads the graduate program in Communication Design at Virginia Commonwealth University. His focus is to provide a program that encourages independent thinking and a global outlook in design.

## Designer's statement

i am asked to write something about my work for this book
this is a difficult thing to do for two reasons:
1. it is hard to write about design (matters of my heart).
2. it is hard to write about typographic experimentation. (what is/isn't it now)
but i will try.
someone told me lately that design was something a lot more than pushing
two squares around on a piece of paper to make them look good.
for a while i got absorbed by this thought --- the formalist in me was
ridiculed into a minor, insignificant position.
then i started thinking true to myself.
i respect the good concept.
i laugh, i choke, i think when involved with the very good narrative.
but can i make people do this?
can i make things that result in evocative responses?
does printed ephemera ever succeed in doing these things?
i present here what i think i do best.
critics may call it fun with form.
(the last formalist?)
i am activator of relationships.
each piece is placed with a consideration for an architectonic whole.
i am thinking in three dimensional space.
it is a nice space and my thought actions fluctuate between extreme scale
changes
sometimes i am standing between two forms, other times i am looking down on
them from a very distant vantage point.
i am touching and feeling form --- senses are activated and acute.
when i am this deep in the composition it is a very private, romantic,
insular and unique place to be.
a fellow creator and i were talking about the uniqueness of this experience,
we agreed it's like being in a movie.
that was the first half of my statement.
here is the second. . .it is my admission, my response to experimentation
and its dovetailing with computer type.

i don't like the premise of computer type for this book because i see
typography as being so much more.
in my mind, the computer is only a small part of things.
however it has evolved into too big a part.
this isn't probably going to change but shouldn't individuals monitor it?
everything is computer type now.
this is my point.
i find a shard of a letter in a rain gutter.
i glue it.
it gets scanned.
it becomes digital.
chances are this is its second time through the binary process.
we live in a day when typographic and human anatomy are increasingly
digitally governed
sometimes this frightens me and threatens and even debilitates my process.
what of the senses?
the act can still be digital free.
i am not saying it should be, only that it could be.
maybe experimentation is computer free,
flush left, rag right.
objective,
formal prowess, and restraint
two points of lead,
if this is the case then we have effectively turned things upside down.

1
**Faculty/staff directory**
**State University of New York**
**College at Cortland**

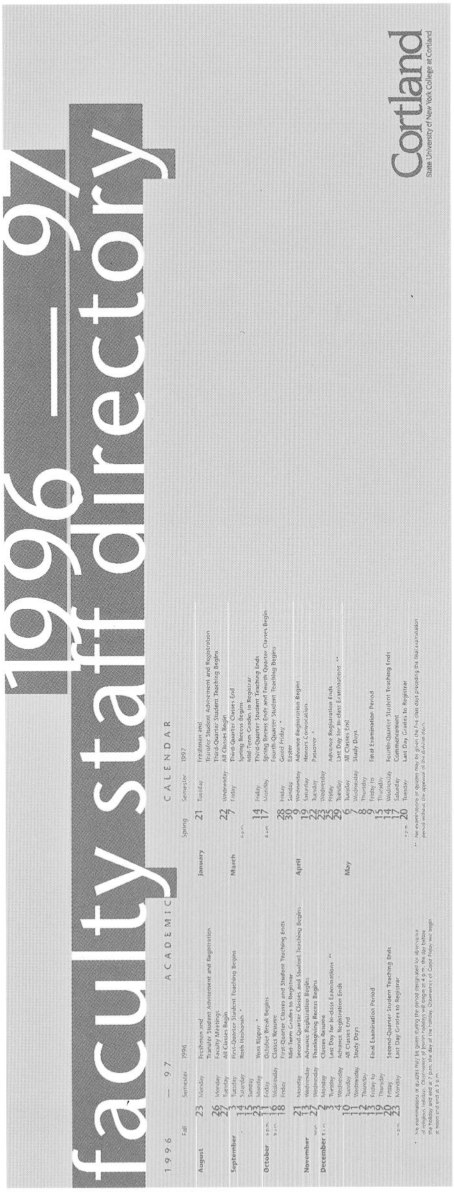

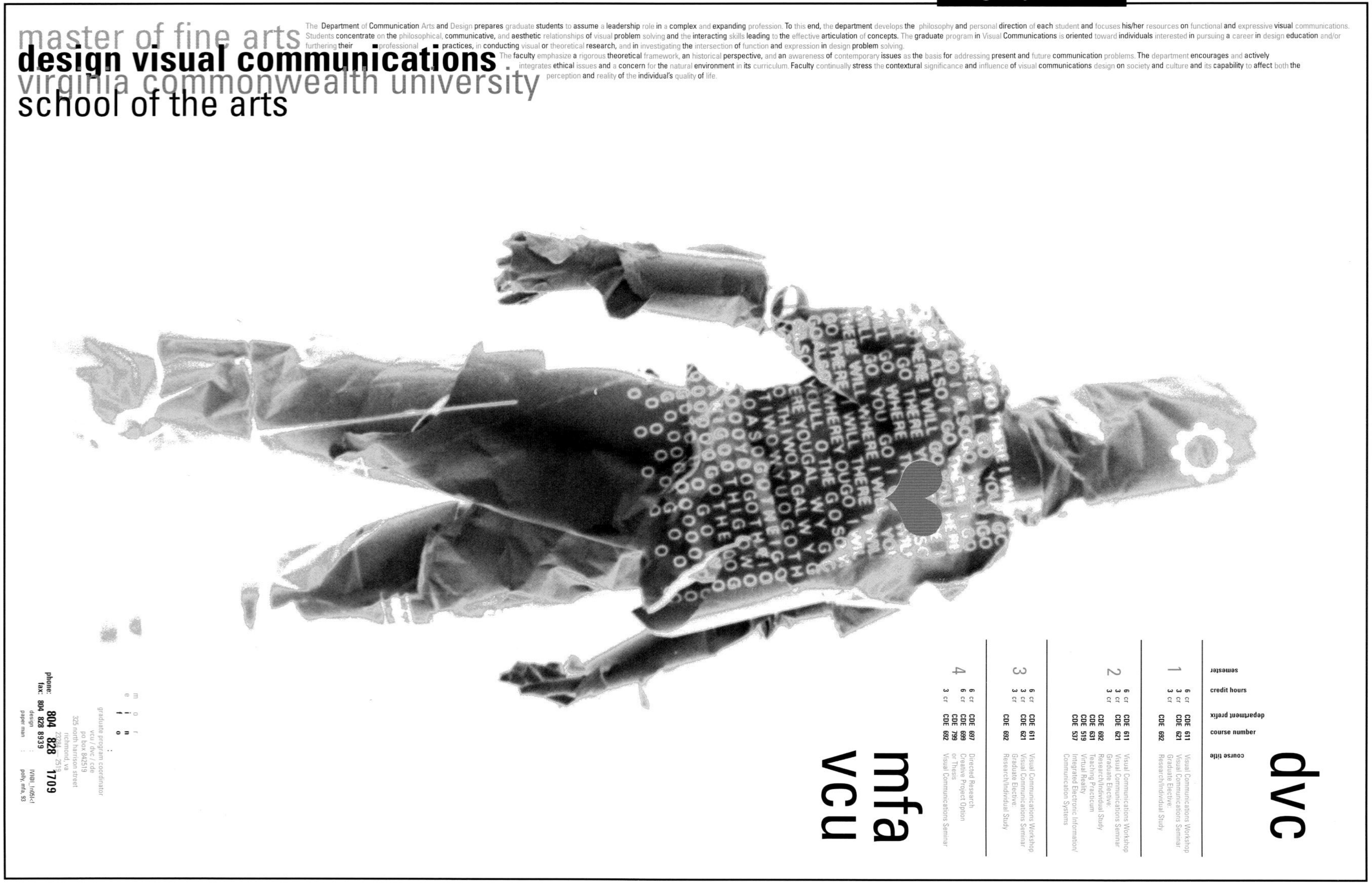
master of fine arts
design visual communications
virginia commonwealth university
school of the arts
The Department of Communication Arts and Design prepares graduate students to assume a leadership role in a complex and expanding profession. To this end, the department develops the philosophy and personal direction of each student and focuses his/her resources on functional and expressive visual communications. Students concentrate on the philosophical, communicative, and aesthetic relationships of visual problem solving and the interacting skills leading to the effective articulation of concepts. The graduate program in Visual Communications is oriented toward individuals interested in pursuing a career in design education and/or furthering their professional practices, in conducting visual or theoretical research, and in investigating the intersection of function and expression in design problem solving.
The faculty emphasize a rigorous theoretical framework, an historical perspective, and an awareness of contemporary issues as the basis for addressing present and future communication problems. The department encourages and actively integrates ethical issues and a concern for the natural environment in its curriculum. Faculty continually stress the contextual significance and influence of visual communications design on society and culture and its capability to affect both the perception and reality of the individual's quality of life.
dvc
semester
credit hours
department prefix
course number
course title
1
6 cr CDE 611 Visual Communications Workshop
3 cr CDE 621 Visual Communications Seminar
3 cr Graduate Elective:
CDE 692 Research/Individual Study
2
6 cr CDE 611 Visual Communications Workshop
3 cr CDE 621 Visual Communications Seminar
3 cr Graduate Elective:
CDE 692 Research/Individual Study
CDE 631 Teaching Practicum
CDE 519 Virtual Reality
CDE 537 Integrated Electronic Information/ Communication Systems
3
6 cr CDE 611 Visual Communications Workshop
3 cr CDE 621 Visual Communications Seminar
3 cr Graduate Elective:
CDE 692 Research/Individual Study
4
6 cr CDE 697 Directed Research
6 cr CDE 699 Creative Project Option
CDE 799 or Thesis
3 cr CDE 692 Visual Communications Seminar
mfa
vcu
m o r
e i n
f o
:
graduate program coordinator
vcu / dvc / cde
po box 842519
325 north harrison street
richmond, va
23284 – 2519
phone: 804 828 1709
fax: 804 828 8939
design : IVI@I_!n05I<!
paper man : polly, mfa, 93

2

2
**Promotional poster**
**MFA Program in Visual Communication**
**Virginia Commonwealth University**
**Photography: Polly Johnson**
3
**Experimental hand puppets**

3

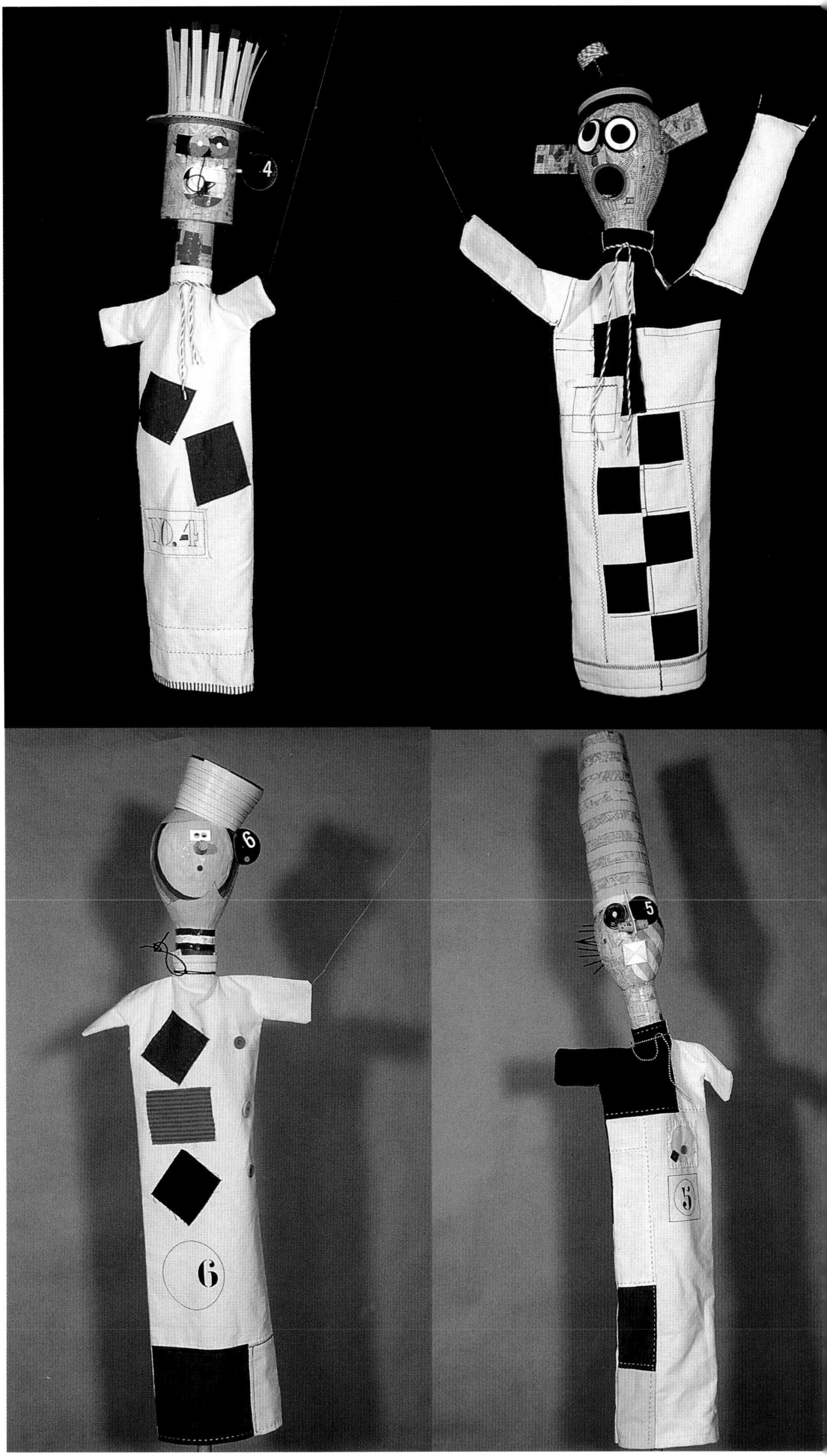

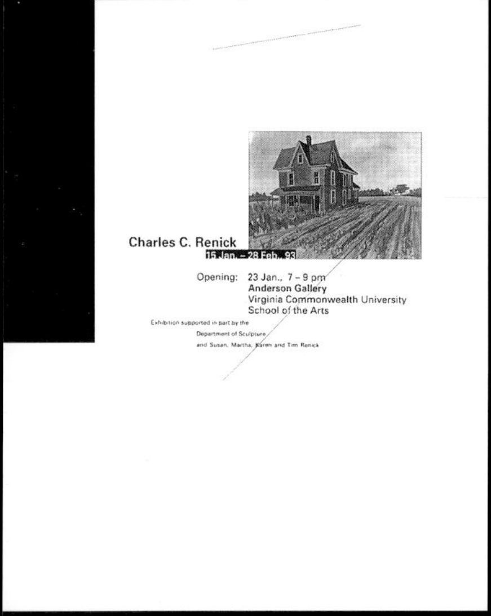


4

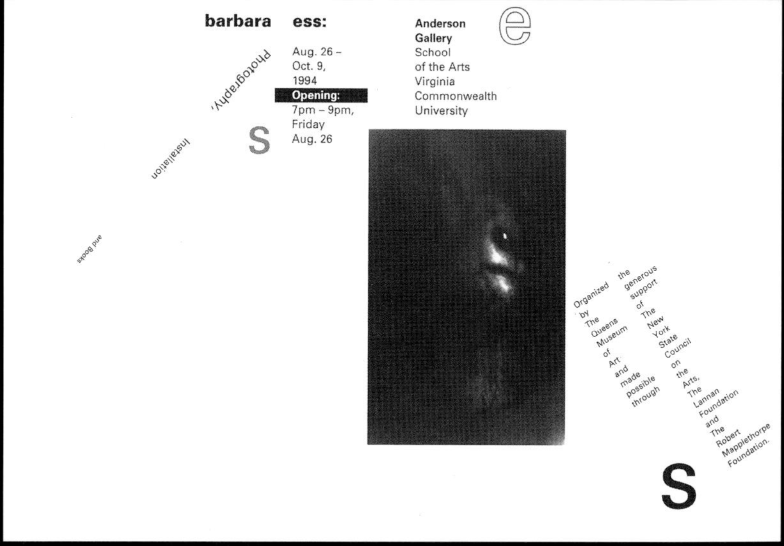

barbara ess:
Aug. 26 – Oct. 9, 1994
Opening: 7pm – 9pm, Friday Aug. 26
Anderson Gallery
School of the Arts
Virginia Commonwealth University
Photography,
Installation
and Books
Organized by The Queens Museum of Art and made possible through the generous support of The New York State Council on the Arts, The Lannan Foundation and The Robert Mapplethorpe Foundation.


5

4, 5
**Exhibition postcards**
**Anderson Gallery**
**Virginia Commonwealth University**
6
**Faculty Biennial Announcement**
**Anderson Gallery**
**Virginia Commonwealth University**

7
**Visual identity program**
**Tom McLaughlin, Architect**

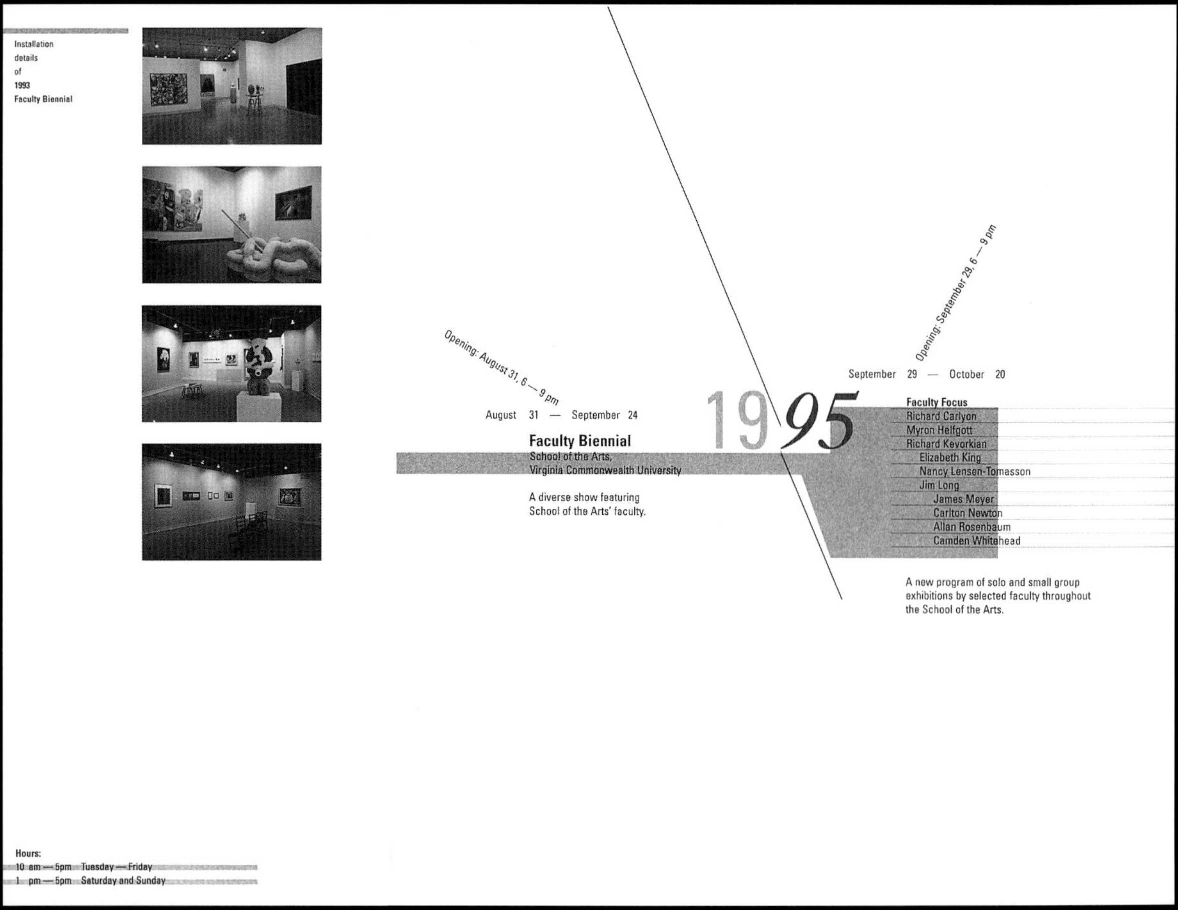

Installation details of 1993 Faculty Biennial
Opening: August 31, 6 — 9 pm
August 31 — September 24
Faculty Biennial
School of the Arts,
Virginia Commonwealth University
A diverse show featuring School of the Arts' faculty.
1995
Opening: September 29, 6 — 9 pm
September 29 — October 20
Faculty Focus
Richard Carlyon
Myron Helfgott
Richard Kevorkian
Elizabeth King
Nancy Lensen-Tomasson
Jim Long
James Meyer
Carlton Newton
Allan Rosenbaum
Camden Whitehead
A new program of solo and small group exhibitions by selected faculty throughout the School of the Arts.
Hours:
10 am — 5pm Tuesday — Friday
1 pm — 5pm Saturday and Sunday


6

portfolio

**Tom McLaughlin**

In recent years, I have made an attempt to focus my Design and Typographic sensibility into a distinct and personalized vision. In this endeavour, my curiosity, suspicion and trepidation with regard to design have become the driving force behind the manifestation of my emotions on paper - in a truly honest and sincere way. As a jazz musician, my musical peers have been a unique inspiration to me and I have striven to isolate the spirit in which their self-expression is employed and to understand the methods by which they create their own artistic voice. I have listened not for the outward musical devices that make up who they are, but rather for those that define who they have become. These are the principles that guide my work and which nurture my typographic sensibility.

It has been a difficult process for me to bridge these parallels between the musical and visual arts, but at the same time it has represented an exciting challenge for me. Through an ongoing visual experimentation I have come to understand who I have become and where I am going. This period of evolution has been met, like anything new or different, with criticism and rejection; but these criticisms have only helped nurture and develop my current work and have helped me to regain a trust in myself and what I have to say visually.

I feel especially fortunate that Rob Carter has invited me to participate in this book and, through these typographic experiments, it has enabled me to contribute a body of work that is entirely personal and unbridled by rules or commercial considerations. I hope that these works are received favourably more as a reflection of my own personal vision and not simply as a demonstration of technical and creative artifice.

a r c h i t e c t

ph + fax
804 231 6686

1110
West 42nd Street
Richmond, Virginia
2 3 2 2 5

**Tom McLaughlin**

architect

ph + fax
804 231 6686

1110
West 42nd Street
Richmond, Virginia
2 3 2 2 5

1-3
**Promotional posters for Annan and Sons Trade Lithography**

4
**Self-promotional postcard: *faith***

1

4

a r c h i t e c t

**Tom McLaughlin**

ph + fax
804 231 6686

2

1110
West 42nd Street
Richmond, Virginia
23225

**Tom McLaughlin**

architect

1110
West 42nd Street
Richmond, Virginia
2 3 2 2 5

3

7

ph + fax
804 231 6686

Ei,
RED
BAND
SÃO PAULO-S
ONE
U
can
C
V
concepts

expressed
19/08/96
22723/6442 15
14
be
P
DANK
SAYS

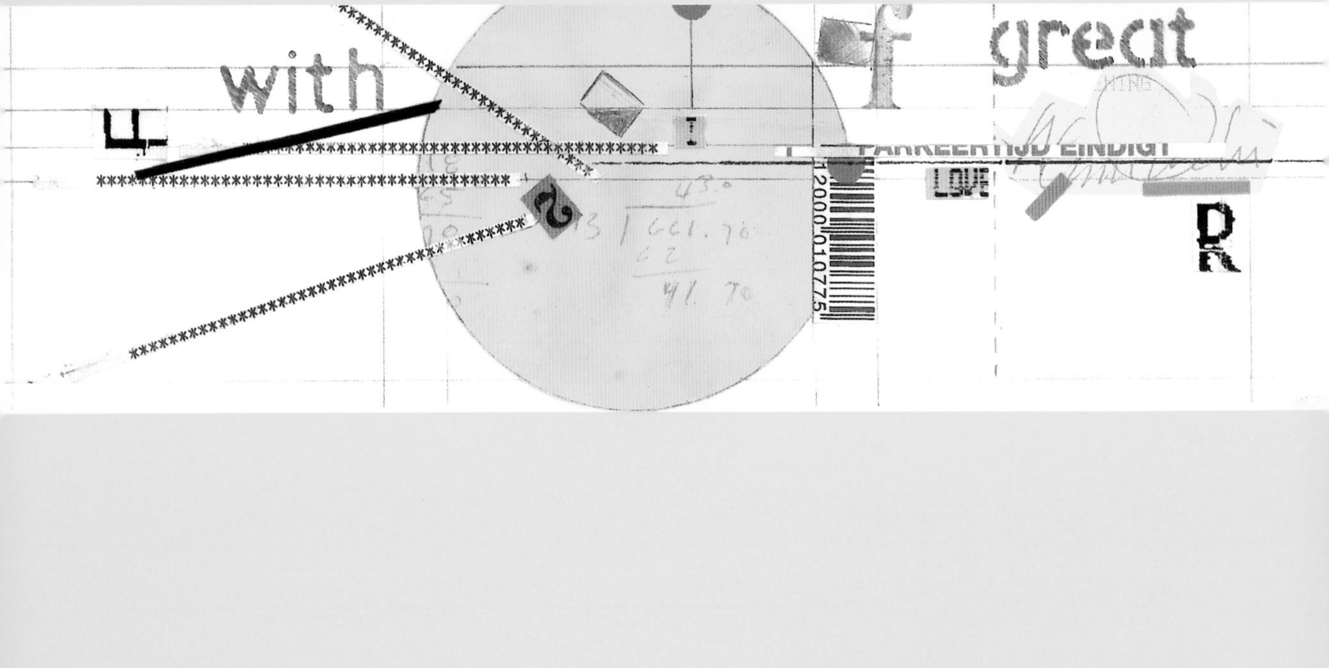
with
great
LOVE

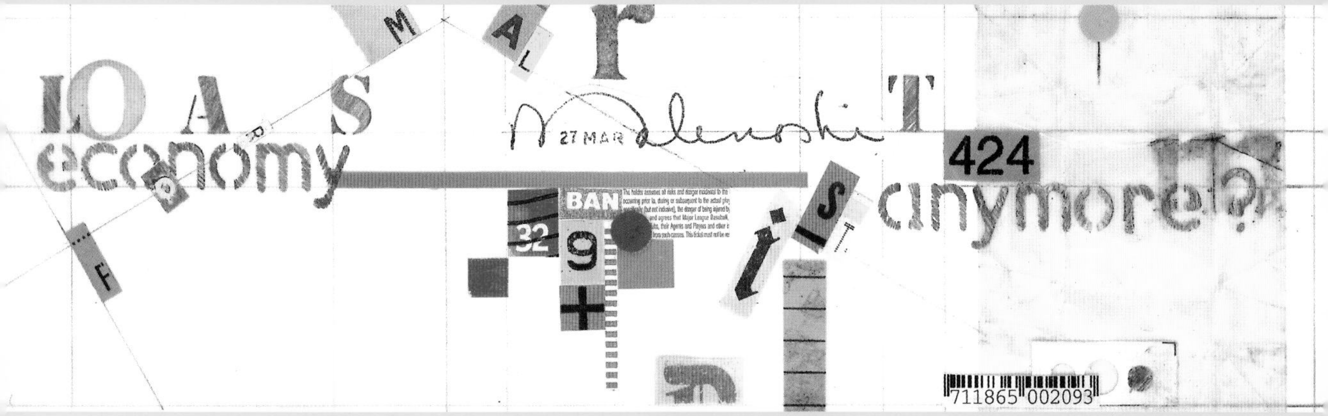
economy
27 MAR
424
BAN
32
9
anymore?

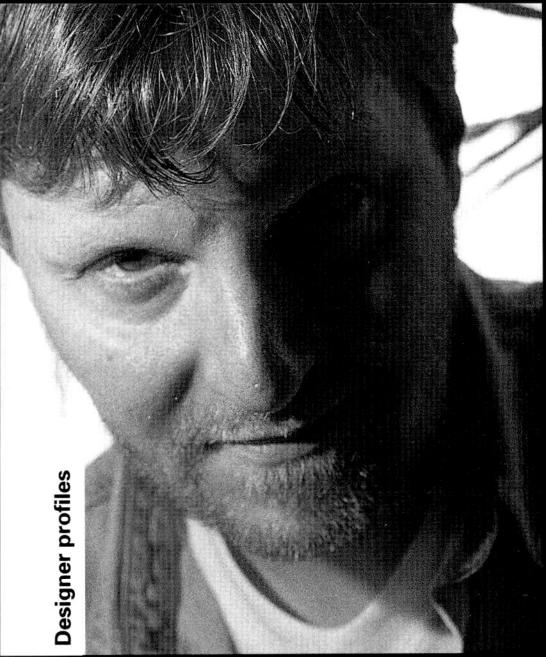



# Paul Sych

Paul Sych is a stalwart individualist who has invented an approach to typography based on the synthesis of two passions: design and music. Concurrently, Sych studied design at the Ontario College of Art, and jazz at York University. Upon leaving school, and after deciding he could not make it as a graphic designer, he made his living as a jazz musician. Seven years passed before he decided to re-enter the design field. Performing in the smoke-filled night clubs of Toronto proved a pivotal experience that undoubtedly nurtured his unique vision of graphic design practice.

Sych integrates that which he both sees and hears into a highly sensory and evocative typographic style, a rare blend of form and rhythm. His design process parallels musical improvisation in that it is highly intuitive spontaneous, and emotional. Sych describes structure in music as the number of bars in a piece of music. Within this structure is form consisting of melody, harmony, and rhythm, which may be freely interpreted. In design, structure is a problem's parameters, and the formal elements of color, shape, and texture may be freely explored in the course of solving a problem.

Sych is continuously influenced by what is happening in the world around him, but he ignores the trappings of conventions and trends. Looking at problems from the inside out rather than from the outside in, he attempts to take his audience (and himself) to where they have never been before. Because he is a visual adventurer who takes many risks, he relies entirely on the power of faith.

Sych's studio, appropriately named Faith, is located in Toronto, Canada. Studio involvement design/advertising/ typographic projects for established international clients. Sych's clients have also learned to exercise faith as they hand projects over to him, but rarely do they impose restrictions, for they have gained confidence in the power of the visual messages that he creates through his experimental processes. The primary studio activity is typography, including typeface design. Among the fonts he has designed are *Dig, Dog,* and *Hip*, available from FontShop, and the *P.S. Faith* collection for ThirstType, which includes four fonts: *Wit, Toy, Fix, and U.S.*

Despite the fact that technology is inextricably linked to Sych's creative process, he believes that the computer is no substitute for good ideas and that it is not the most important tool for graphic designers. Often, Sych makes rough, hand-drawn sketches that are scanned and then placed into the computer to be used as a template for further development. Then, as in a good jam session, he experiments with the arrangement of line, shape, color, and type, constructing, deconstructing, and synthesizing these elements until an image emerges, a blend of harmony and emotion.

Sych's typographic designs are charged with emotion, a quality that lures viewers into them, providing exotic experiences far beyond expectation. His goal is always to excite his audience in some way, to stretch the imagination, to provoke. His work is either loved or hated; but regardless of opinion, it continues to make a profound impact on the international typographic scene.

## Designer's statement

In recent years, I have made an attempt to focus my Design and Typographic sensibility into a distinct and personalized vision. In this endeavour, my curiosity, suspicion and trepidation with regard to design have become the driving forces behind the manifestation of my emotions on paper - in a truly honest and sincere way. As a jazz musician, my musical peers have been a unique inspiration to me and I have striven to isolate the spirit in which their self-expression is employed and to understand the methods by which they create their own artistic voice. I have listened not for the outward musical devices that make up who they are, but rather for those that define who they have become. These are the principles that guide my work and which nurture my typographic sensibility. It has been a difficult process for me to bridge these parallels between the musical and visual arts, but at the same time it has represented an exciting challenge for me. Through an ongoing visual experimentation I have come to understand who I have become and where I am going. This period of evolution has been met, like anything new or different, with criticism and rejection; but these criticisms have only helped nurture and develop my current work and have helped me to regain a trust in myself and what I have to say visually.

I feel especially fortunate that Rob Carter has invited me to participate in this book and, through these typographic experiments, it has enabled me to contribute a body of work that is entirely personal and unbridled by rules or commercial considerations. I hope that these works are received favourably more as a reflection of my own personal vision and not simply as a demonstration of technical and creative artifice.

1-3
**Promotional posters for Annan and Sons Trade Lithography**
4
**Self-promotional postcard: *faith***

1

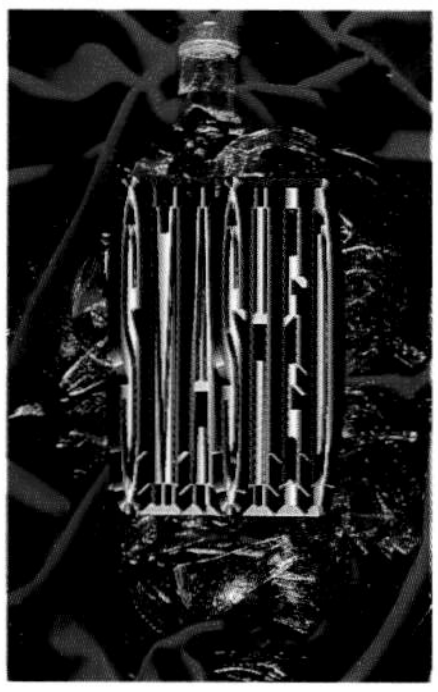
2

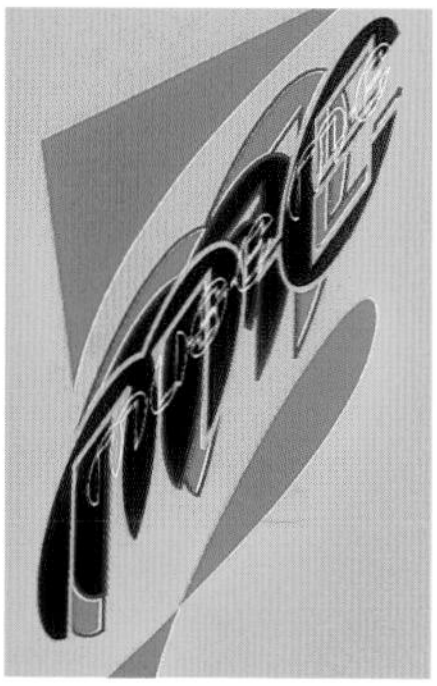
3

4

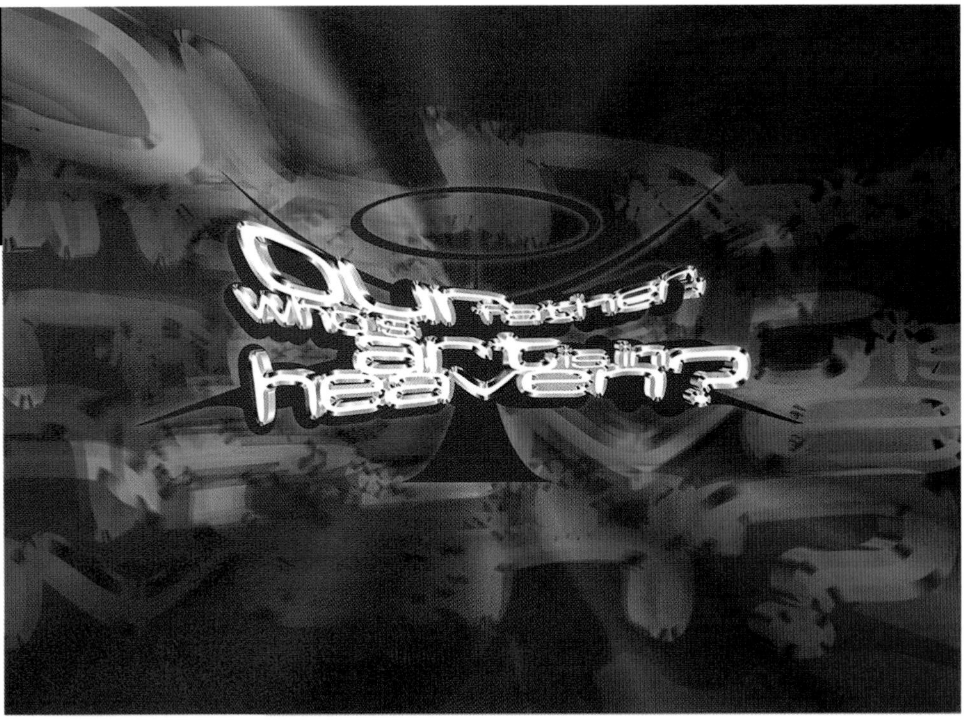


5

6

5-7
**Self-promotional postcards:**
***Our Father***
***Rip Off***
***Flower Power***

*Either Or:*
**Which way to go, good or bad, happy or sad.**

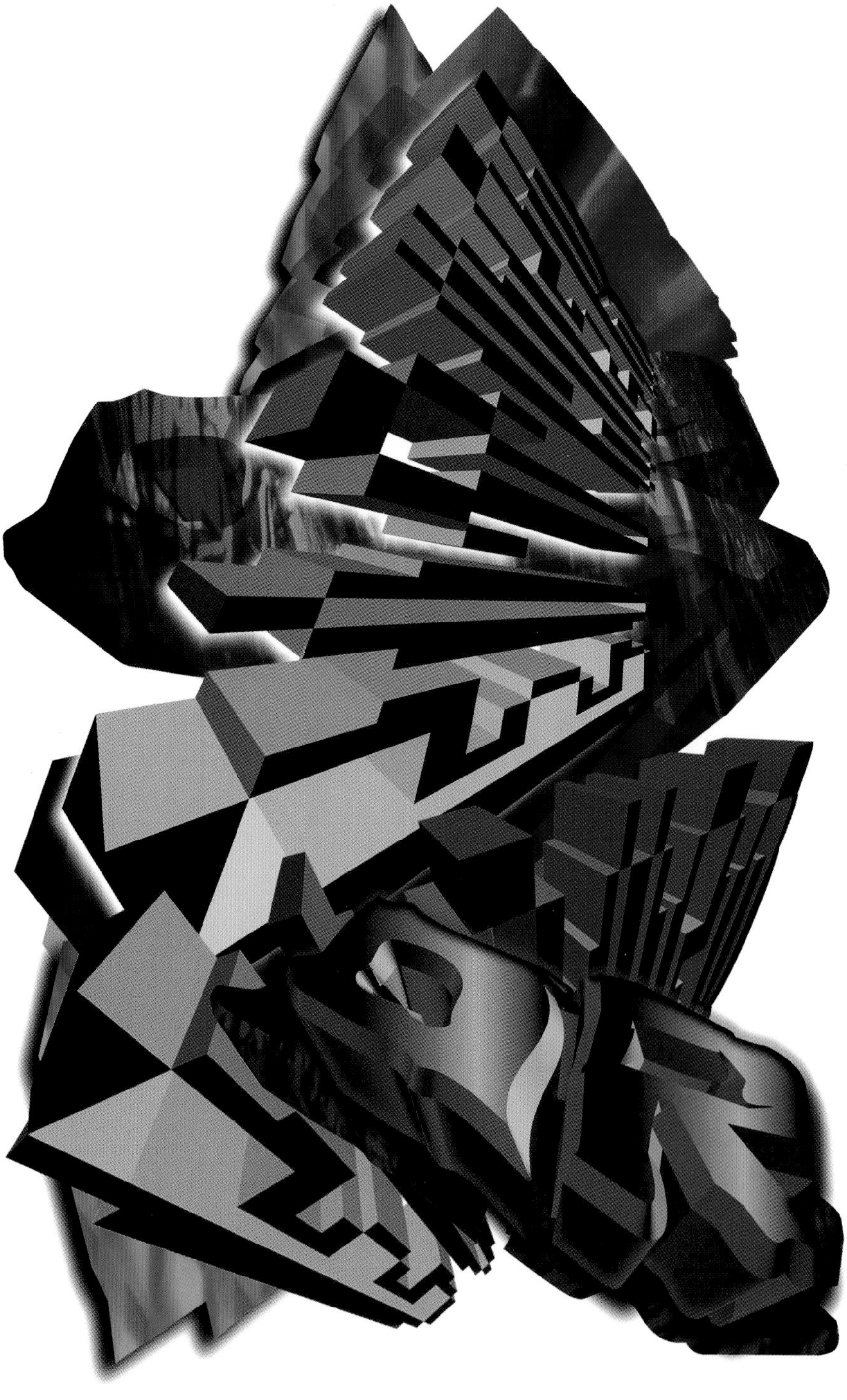

*Be Thy Name:*

**To believe in oneself – no matter who we are, and the uniqueness of us as individuals.**

*Popeye:*
**A tribute to Popeye who was my idol when I was 10, and how I visualize his persona today.**

*What If:*

**The question of questions.**

*War of Words:*
**A sort of war of words with myself – call and response.**

*Power:*

**The power to be anything you want to be.**

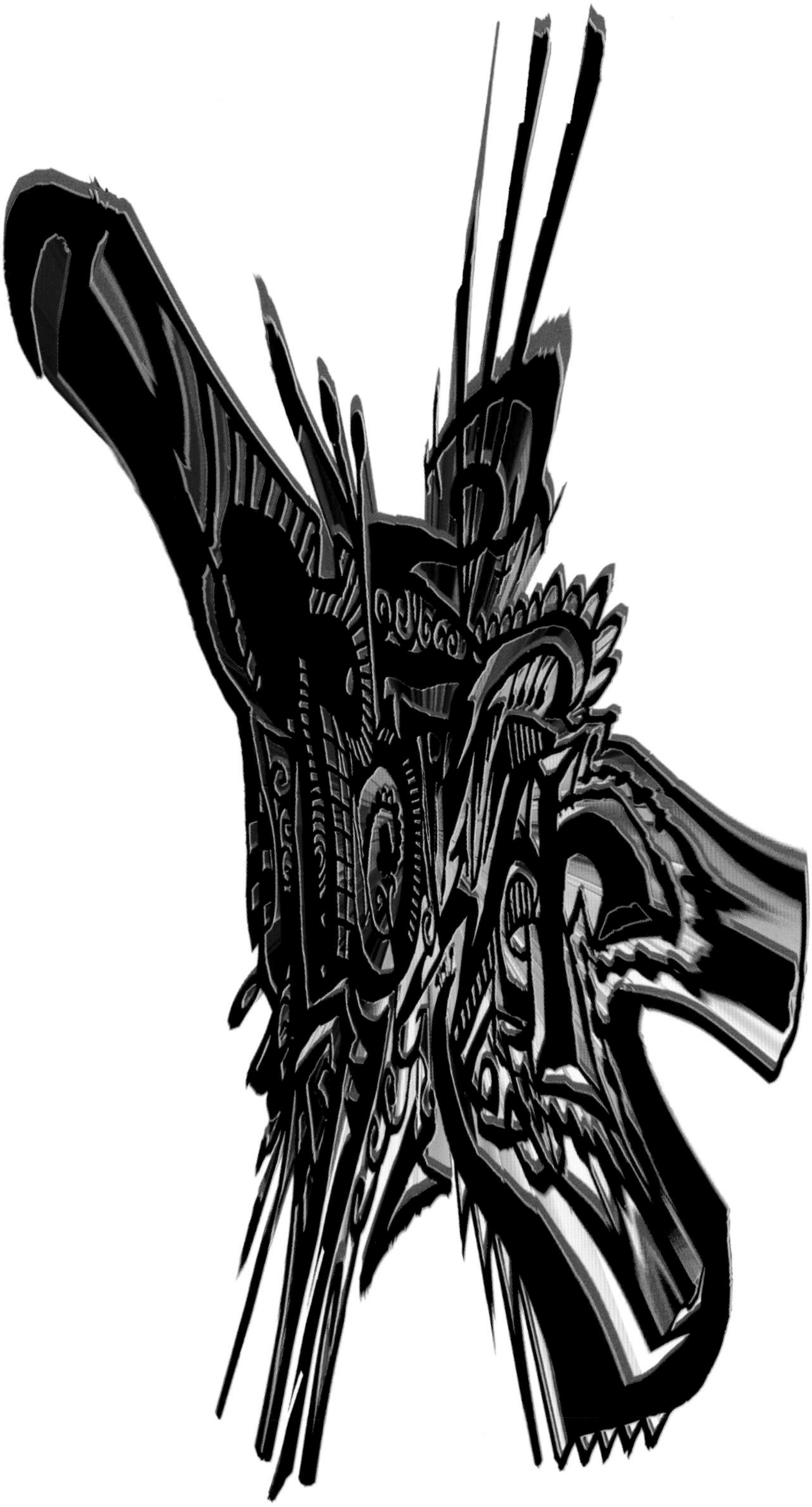

**Elliott Peter Earls**
82 East Elm Street
Greenwich, Connecticut 06830

**Jean-Benoît Lévy**
Spalenvorstadt 11
4051 Basel
Switzerland

**John Malinoski**
2508 East Franklin Street
Richmond, Virginia 23223

**Paul Sych**
1179a King Street West #202
Toronto, Ontario
M6K 3C5
Canada

Students from Rob Carter's class in Experimental Typography whose work appears in Chapter 3:

Timea Adrian
Ginger Cho
Ann Ford
Krysta Higham
Veronica Ledford
Jesus Palacios
Kelly Perkins
Priya Rama
Chris Raymond
Rosemary Sabatino
Joshua Sandage
Minh Ta
San Van

Typography workshop participants from the Graduate Program, Communication Arts and Design at Virginia Commonwealth University (CDE) and the Gerrit Rietveld Academy (GRA):

**Faculty:**

Wigger Bierma (GRA)
Rob Carter (CDE)
David Colley (CDE)
Ben Day (CDE)
John DeMao (CDE)
Leo Divendal (GRA)
Aaf van Essen (GRA)
Henk Groenendijk (GRA)
Victor Levie (GRA)
John Malinoski (CDE)
Roy McKelvey (CDE)
Mary McLaughlin (CDE)
Philip Meggs (CDE)
Akira Ouchi (CDE)

**Students:**

Christine Alberts (GRA)
Sheila Barrett (CDE)
Erik Brandt (CDE)
Persijn Broersen (GRA)
Esther de Vries (GRA)
Libby Hiller (CDE)
Kristin Hughes (CDE)
Harmen Liemburg (GRA)
Margit Lukacs (GRA)
Jennifer McMaster (CDE)
Margaret Pharr (CDE)
Nicolet Schouten (GRA)
Yael Seggev (GRA)
Jason Smith (CDE)
Barbara Spies (CDE)
Dima Stefanova (GRA)
Monika Wiechowska (GRA)
Judith van der Aar (GRA)
Michel van Duyvenbode (GRA)
Sonja van Hamel (GRA)
Barbara van Ruyven (GRA)

**Guest critics:**

Ned Drew, New York City
Brad Rhodes, Boston
Sandy Wheeler, Boston
Camden Whitehead, Richmond

# Acknowledgments

The realization of this fourth book in the *Working with Computer Type* series would not have been possible were it not for the generosity, support, and commitment of several people. My warmest thanks go to the four profiled designers, Elliott Peter Earls, Jean-Benoît Lévy, John Malinoski, and Paul Sych. Each of these designers contributed many hours of precious time, providing information and samples of their work, preparing statements, and making typographic experiments specifically for this book. John Malinoski also designed the book's cover. My very talented student, Minh Ta, shared his typographic journey by designing and writing part one of Chapter 3. Kristin Hughes provided the experiments for the book's front and back pages. Erik Brandt designed the chapter division pages. Profound thanks go to Simon den Hartog, Victor Levie, and the students and faculty of the Gerrit Rietveld Academy in Amsterdam. The exchanges have yielded significant experiences, ideas, and lifelong friendships. I am indebted to poet Adrienne Rich whose poem inspired and informed the experimental typography workshop. As always, my regarded colleagues Philip Meggs, John Malinoski, and Sandy Wheeler shared gentle but cogent criticism. As copy editor, Diana Lively brought precision and refinement to the book. My daughters Molly and Mindy Carter read the manuscript and provided excellent feedback; Mindy also prepared the index. At Virginia Commonwealth University, Richard Toscan and John DeMao provided support and encouragement. I am deeply indebted to Brian Morris and Barbara Mercer at Rotovision for their continuing support and confidence in this series of books. Once again, Alice Goh, Eloyse Tan, and Larry Lee of Provision Pte. Ltd., Singapore, expertly and lovingly took the book through production stages. My climbing partner, Jamie McGrath, energized me with his spirit and friendship. My wife, Sally Carter, continued to smile and prod on even the darkest days of the book's preparation.

*Working with Computer Type 4: Experimental Typography* was typeset and designed on a PowerComputing PowerWave 604/132. Software used includes QuarkXPress, FreeHand, Illustrator, and PhotoShop. The primary text of the book is set in the Univers family.

BLUE

123